Contextualizing the Renaissance

Returns to History

Contextualizing the Renaissance
Returns to History

Selected Proceedings from the
28th Annual CEMERS Conference

Edited by

ALBERT H. TRICOMI

Center for Medieval and Early Renaissance Studies
Binghamton, New York

BREPOLS

© – BREPOLS

The article by Keith Moxey (pp. 119-140) appeared first in *Art Bulletin* 77 (1995),
© College Art Association Inc. All rights reserved. Reprinted here by permission.

Portions of the article by Louis Montrose (pp. 171-201) appeared first in
*The Purpose of Playing: Shakespeare and the Cultural Politics
of the Elizabethan Theatre* (Chicago, 1996), chapters 5-6,
©University of Chicago Press. All rights reserved. Reprinted here by permission.

Portions of the article by Jean A. Howard (pp. 21-40) appeared first in
*Engendering a Nation: A Feminist Account
of Shakespeare's English Histories* (London, 1997),
© Routledge. All rights reserved. Reprinted here by permission.

Printed in the E.U. on acid-free paper
D/1999/0095/109
ISBN 2-503-50849-9

All rights reserved.
No part of this publication may be reproduced, stored in a retrieval system or
transmitted, in any form or by any means, electronic, mechanical, photocopying,
recording or otherwise, without the prior permission of the publisher.

Table of Contents

Introduction: Trends in Historicizing Early Modern
Literature, History, and the Visual Arts   1
ALBERT H. TRICOMI

PART ONE

Literature and History as Critical Practices

Writing the History of the Present: Contextualizing
Early Modern Literature   21
JEAN E. HOWARD

Mapping Theory in History: Conceptual Cites and Social
Sites in the French Monarchic State   41
SARAH HANLEY

Dueling and Civility in Sixteenth-Century Italy   67
DAVID QUINT

The Place of Vives's *Instruction of a Christen Woman* in
Early Modern English Domestic Book Literature   105
MARGARET MIKESELL

PART TWO

Rehistoricizing Through the Visual Arts

Motivating History   119
KEITH MOXEY

Tainted Image/Sacred Image: The Wandering Madonna
of S. Maria in Vallicella   141
LAURA MACCASKEY

Viewing Foucault Viewing Velásquez's *Las Meniñas*   157
JAMES BYRNES

PART THREE

New Historicism and Representation

Form and Pressure: Shakespearean Drama and the
    Elizabethan State   171
    LOUIS MONTROSE
Embodying Origins: An Anatomy of a Yeoman's Daughter,
    Spenser's Argante, and Elizabeth I   203
    DAVID KINAHAN
Reading History, Reading Power, Reading Plays:
    Graham Holderness on Shakespeare's History Plays   221
    WILLIAM O. SCOTT

Acknowledgements

The twenty-eighth annual conference of the Center for Medieval and Early Renaissance Studies was an intellectually vibrant event. I hope much of that will live on in the pages that follow. Steady supporters and fellow planners, including CEMERS' director, Robin Oggins, and CEMERS' administrative secretary, Anna Di Stefano, assisted me at every stage as I carried out my duties as conference director and volume editor. I am also pleased to recognize the advice and encouragement of my colleague and friend, Alvin Vos, a previous volume editor, as well as the talented, albeit unnamed, scholars who reviewed the submissions.

Deserving of special recognition is the present CEMERS' Director, Associate Professor of Art History Charles Burroughs, who, working through a period of transition at CEMERS and the Medieval-Renaissance Text Society at Binghamton, provided the leadership that ensured publication of this and future CEMERS volumes. During this period Lori Ann Vandermark, production editor for the volume, worked hard and expeditiously to bring the volume to the final stages of production.

I feel especially indebted to the distinguished publishing house of Brepols for seeing the virtues of this and future CEMERS volumes. Finally, I am grateful to the contributors for the depth and range of thought that characterizes the essays comprising this volume.

ALBERT H. TRICOMI

Introduction

Trends in Historicizing Early Modern Literature, History, and the Visual Arts

THE TWENTY-EIGHTH ANNUAL CONFERENCE of the Center for Medieval and Renaissance Studies, held October 21–22, 1994 at Binghamton University, featured thirty-three panel sessions and approximately 150 essay readers, responders, and session chairs. The ten essays in this volume consist of the addresses of the five plenary speakers—leaders in their field—and five panel essays, each of which was reviewed for this volume.

As the title indicates, the volume comprises a body of work organized around a governing theme—modes of historicization. Each of the following essays demonstrates the practice of or a commentary upon a distinctive historicized criticism. By "historicized" as contrasted with "historical" criticism, I mean that these essays problematize, stretch, or reconceive traditional historiographical practices. Challenging the notion that the production of paintings, dramatic texts, or even conduct books can be read against a stable historical ground, they show that paintings, works of literature, and treatises not only participate in history but are exemplars of textual instability. The very content of these texts can be shown, in various editions, to change over time—and yet each bears a single, determinate title. In such ways the contributions gathered here all show that they have been affected by "the new history."

This is not to say that the essays offered here under the banner of "Returns to History" exhibit a paradigmatic methodology. On the contrary, no one practice of historicized study prevails. In fact, several of the essays offer contrasting assessments of common or overlapping subject matter and are methodologically at odds. For me the sustaining interest in organizing the 28th Annual CEMERS Conference was to invite methodologically informed submissions from the several major disciplines of early-modern study and then to assess the results. To determine what the new history can or has yet to achieve, I believe it is first necessary to determine what current practices are. Perhaps the best way to state this purpose is to invoke the Conference Announcement:

> Over the last twenty years Renaissance studies have undergone a stunning reconfiguration. Once traditional and highly stable in their methods and subject matter, academic disciplines have been energized by strategies that contextualize and recontextualize the objects of study. Interdisciplinary fertilization has provided new contexts for scholarship, and the theoretical movements of our generation have all insisted on the importance of contexts in producing understanding.
>
> Few doubt any longer the vitality generated by these approaches; the need now is to produce a set of critical practices that shows an awareness of its commitments and of what it can achieve. This is a time to assess our methods, while extending our knowledge of the period and of ourselves by continuing to contextualize our practice.

The format and organization of this volume reflects my interest in comparative assessments. All three parts of the volume begin with one (or more) of the addresses delivered by a plenary speaker. These essays are "leading" in several ways. Characteristically, they are self-conscious explications of method and are given to generalizations about how a field of Renaissance studies functions. At the same time, each plenary essay exhibits a concrete critical practice that invites review and assessment. In Part One I have presented a succession of three plenary essays since each exhibits a distinctive conception of the relationship between literature, including literary tropes, and history. This sequence encourages the kind of comparative assessments that provide a foundation for the volume. In all three parts there follow essays from panelists whose method deviates from or challenges that of a previous plenary essay in some surprising or distinctive way. Almost half these essays are by younger scholars whose work raises a special issue or exhibits a potential new direction. The final essay in each part offers an assessment or review of one of more critical practices under discussion in that part.

For these reasons, I observe that the volume format is intended to offer readers a reflection upon as well as a practice of the new history. In most edited volumes with multiple contributors, readers tend to seek out the essay or essays whose subject matter speaks directly to their particular interests. In this case there is, I believe, much more to be had. The three broad areas of study on which I have fixed, with significant overlapping, are Literature and History, the Visual Arts, and the New Historicism. The section on the visual arts, for example, exhibits principles of historiography that offer both the literary critic and the historian useful ways of apprehending artistic representation as an ideological act. This kind of cross-fertilization, from literature to history to art history, appears throughout the volume. Then too, half the essays in this volume are seriously concerned with philosophical questions, particularly in the field of epistemology.

1

In assessing the essays that follow, I am struck by their emphasis on "presentist" issues—that is the self-conscious practice of a historicized criticism that aims to engender political or ideological awareness and social change. Jean Howard's "Writing the History of the Present: Contextualizing Early Modern Literature" champions this goal explicitly. The study of early modern literature, she says, teaches us the excesses of nationalism, reveals the submerged voices of women and other marginalized or excluded groups, and keeps the past constantly before us through the criterion of usefulness today. By the questions asked of that literature we affirm both our values and our concerns. In this way we are all writing histories of the present.

To illustrate her method, Howard takes as her subject the confluence of gender and work in the second Henriad. In celebrating the emergence of an English national identity, Howard argues that Shakespeare's histories, unlike Heywood's, obscure the participation of a major constituency—women. Working in the Boar's Head alehouse, the tavernkeeper Mistress Quickly and the whore Doll Tearsheet represent England's vibrant commercial urban class. But instead of celebrating this busy world, Howard contends that Shakespeare scapegoats it, making Doll's profession of prostitute symbolize the play's core anxiety—the erasure of class and the possibility of a radical social leveling.

Analogously, Quickly's malapropisms—her promiscuous substitution of the wrong word for the proper word—bespeak at the linguistic level this same social disorder. Taken together, Doll and Quickly are "public women" representing, respectively, the sexually independent and the economically independent woman. As such, they are ruthlessly criminalized and excluded from the emergent (male) national identity.

As a reader, what is most intriguing to me about Howard's method is its relationship to historical knowledge. That is to say, Howard's analysis of Shakespeare's histories produces historical insights about Elizabethan England as well as historical generalizations. For example, to clinch her argument, Howard writes, "There seems, finally, no way for the entrepreneurial urban woman to exist in the nation forged within Shakespeare's history play except on terms of criminality." The sentence maintains a careful distinction between the world of Shakespeare's historical drama and the "forged" nation itself. But the tension between the play-world and the historical past itself is not easily broken. Do these plays "forge" the nation, or is the nation "forged" only in the imaginative text, or something in between? And how important is such evidence? Through questions such as these, the domain of new- historicizing literary criticism and the epistemological challenges it faces may be mapped.

When Howard argues that Shakespeare's dramatic narrative "suggests something of the intolerance haunting the early moment of English national identity formation," she clearly asserts a sort of palpable but indeterminate nexus between play and world. Shakespeare's narrative is part of the world; it literally represents it. So it is a constituent part of England's national identity formation. But to what extent? Are history plays somehow more central to the questions Howard raises than others? That we don't know, and one wonders on what ground we could know. For example, are Shakespeare's Henry plays—or any other early modern English history—*more* about England's emergent identity formation than, let us say, *As You Like It* or *Mucedorus* or *The Witch of Edmonton*? I would say we can "read" England's national identity in most every early modern play, not merely in its histories. There may be something special and distinctive about a play that reenacts its idea of history, but how such a narrative would distinctively contribute to our understanding is an unresolved question.

The methodological issue historian Sarah Hanley treats is the problem of historical knowledge as seen from the perspective of the historian. In "Mapping Theory in History: Conceptual Cites and Social Sites in the French Monarchic State," Hanley takes concrete events as her basic unit of analysis, but finds their meaning and logic in the discourse that constitutes them. In this way she makes a *concordia discours* out of the relationship between event and structure or, to put the issue in disciplinary terms, between a traditional historical unit of study (events or sites) and sociological and anthropological units of study in which structure (variously construed as institutional and cultural) is the fundamental object of study. Her work is exciting because it treats *cultural metaphor* as a fundamental unit of thought. Cultural metaphor winds up driving events, providing the impetus for new social structures. By reading history in this way, Hanley's methodology offers a promising approach to one of the historical issues embedded in Howard's reading of Shakespeare's history plays, the problem of defining—and then measuring—the role of what literary critics might call "imaginative thought" in the structuring of historical sites.

Taking as her starting point Olympe de Gouges' *Declaration of the Rights of Woman and Citizeness* (1791), with its demand that the deputies of the French Revolution repeal laws that victimized the nation's women, Hanley sets out to explain why her argument ran up against what she calls powerful "relations of practice." Explicitly rejecting the notion that her interpretation can be explained by recourse to the "immediate context of events," Hanley urges that the static separation between structures and events be broken by attending to interactive, long-term processes of structuration. With recourse to a rich archive of law briefs extending over three centuries, Hanley identifies a pattern in French canon law that she calls "a *marital regime* system of male governance empowering husband and kings as rulers in household and state." The word "regime" is not a rhetorical flourish. This regime validated male authority over women by invoking the image of male "generative" capacity. Emphasizing that systems of knowledge appear incontrovertible in their own time (cf. Foucault's concept of the episteme), Hanley points out that national, public, civil, and moral law all legitimated males' rights over women. By analogic application this male "generative" capacity was extended to kings, husbands, and all the contractual relations between men and women embodied in the laws of civil marriage.

The metaphoric maxim embodying this suffusive truth reads, "*The King is the husband and political spouse of the kingdom.*" Because women were seen to be disconnected from the generative act of reproduction, they were excluded, as if by Nature's warrant, from the generative activities of the body politic. From such generative metaphoric truths proceeded the French project of both family formation and state building. Tellingly, women remained crucial to these projects, but in negative terms. The French canon law that defamed women misogynistically was part of that structurating process by which women's misdeeds were seen as wrecking families and, in particular, the social position and aspirations of male heirs and heads of households. Hanley's accounts of the late seventeenth-century marital suits and counter-suits of Marie Anne Rainssant and Marguerite Aurillon vividly demonstrate the social practices that made these women's suits so difficult to prosecute successfully.

But the past Hanley construes is not merely oppressive. The affected women hawked broadsides in the streets to defend their honor, and they challenged the structure of law that subordinated their suits to that of their spouses. In this way Hanley shows that "the harbingers of change" were present all along. Early modern history was being forged in the multitude of actions that both sustained and challenged the dominant patterns of law and thought. For "strong" historians such as Hanley, the successful reversal of entrenched habits of thought emerges out of struggle, whose dynamic structuration the historian can discern. Thus, different as Hanley's disciplinary methodology is from Howard's, the two share as a common goal the resuscitation of a dynamic if submerged past that challenged mainstream authority. Especially remarkable is the attention Hanley pays as a historian to the power of language—here the simile of political rule embodied in male generativity—as it works its structurating way through culture to *make* history.

Examining literary texts in the context of contemporary Renaissance discourses about dueling, David Quint's essay—"Dueling and Civility in Sixteenth-Century Italy"—appears to, and in some ways does, fall well within traditional scholarly methodologies. Nevertheless, the informing spirit is anthropological and sociological. Displaying a characteristic erudition that traverses Italian, French, and English literatures, Quint reads the Renaissance duel in terms of its functionality in early modern Western culture. The very representation of the duel in literature, Quint shows, has social consequences that affect the conduct of dueling itself. Instead of setting his literary texts against a static historical ground, Quint treats them dynamically, reading such texts as *Orlando Furioso* and *The Faerie Queene* recursively alongside treatises on dueling so as to adduce emergent patterns in the development of early-modern Western culture.

The romance, Quint emphasizes, is not about love alone, but just as equally about honor, each of which supported the aristocratic values of individualism. Since honor was construed as the personal property of an individual, it could be lost to another person unless defended. As a cultural practice then, the duel provided a means of sustaining aristocratic culture as independent of, and in some sense outside of (if not above), civil law. For that reason, the dueling code, almost by definition, is full of prescriptions: It not only demands but shapes attitudes of civility and courtesy.

Just as important, the duel was a socially designed mechanism to direct and limit indulgence in anger and violence. As Quint memorably puts it, the duel is a ritualization of violence which is also violent. But its key function, Quint contends, is conserving. By limiting violence and prescribing an ever-lengthening list of requirements that must be observed before a bloody confrontation, the duel provided an important means of conflict resolution. Its prescriptions also provided a socially acknowledged peacemaking process through which the honor of each of the principals could be preserved intact.

This essentially anthropological interpretation of the Renaissance duel leads Quint to one his most important cultural insights. Since the duel was intrinsically dramatic and consequently an inexhaustible storehouse of materials for novelists, poets, and playwrights, there followed both the dissemination and the magnification of the dueling code in European culture. This literary outpouring had its own result.

So full of regulations did the duel become that it actually took on a singular bookishness. In this, Quint observes, life began to imitate literature. Even as the aristocratic values of the duel were being disseminated, that very success exposed the dueling code—itself dramatized and promoted in romantic narratives—to the kind of mockery we see exhibited in Jacquis's speech on the degrees of affront in *As You Like It* (5.4).

An important measure of the utility of Quint's essentially anthropological analysis is the degree to which it makes sense of texts not treated in his paper. For example, I find Quint's methods helpful in explicating the complex functions of the dueling scenes in George Chapman's *The Tragedy of Bussy D'Ambois* (1604). Bussy's great duel with Barrisor and his retainers can no longer be read simply as an unpardonable act of "willful murder"—King Henry's first pronouncement about it—but as a dramatization of a contemporary issue that demands to know what place aristocratic values are to have in a national culture. Even apart from producing fresh insights into Renaissance texts, Quint's contribution, like those of Hanley and Howard, is that he maps out an interdisciplinary, preeminently cultural space for literary studies. In Quint's handling, the duel as imaginatively represented in literary romances, is effectively shown to be a recursive part of the historical development of the duel itself.

The concluding essay in Part One, that of Margaret Mikesell on Vives's *Instruction of a Christen Woman*, reveals, like Quint's, the increasing importance of the treatise and the conduct book in literary studies. In an era when criticism has turned to identifying cultural forms of subjectification, the conduct book, with its avowed goal of shaping behavior, assumes special significance. "The Place of Vives's *Instruction of a Christen Woman* in Early-Modern English Conduct Book Literature," which examines the proscriptions set forth for women, also adduces something more interesting and subtle when it focuses on the series of distinctive editions in which Vives's *Instruction* appeared. These editions show conclusively that Vives's text cannot be viewed statically. Different groups used the *Instruction* to serve distinctive ideological ends, for which reason, Mikesell deduces, it appeared in several languages in new editions, some given to careful abridgment. Considered in this light as a cultural phenomenon, it is impossible to identify any one *Instruction* book, or any one fixed point of stability, that stands outside historical circumstance.

On the contrary, by investigating the content of these editions and placing the *Instruction* within the tradition of conduct book literature, Mikesell shows the extent of the discontinuity between Vives's Catholic treatise and English Protestant domestic conduct literature, which was able to absorb Vives by deft adaptation and abridgment. A second important feature of Mikesell's inquiry is her identification of the continuity and difference between patristic and post-Reformation domestic treatises. And since the persisting subject is "a Christen Woman," Mikesell is able to locate a varied field of ideological forces to which such women were subjected. Her work thus avoids the pitfalls of appeals to reductive abstractions such as *the* patriarchy. Instead, Mikesell's examination of editions of the *Instruction* that crossed national as well as religious frontiers shows textuality itself as inescapably, and diversely, ideological. And it also permits us to see the building of a place—in fact, a number of places—for women within early modern European culture, but always within strict, ever-changing boundaries.

2

Keith Moxey's plenary essay, "Motivating History," takes the signal step of recommending a fundamental change in the way art history is taught in institutions of higher learning. Canon formation is his theme. However, he is concerned not with how truth is created, but with how a particular history is transmitted to create canonical masterpieces.

Using the aestheticism of Irwin Panofsky to illustrate his conviction that a theory of aesthetics inherently supports the notion of timeless universalism in art, Moxey shows how the adoption of such values leads to an unwitting engagement "in the unthinking reproduction of culture," with the consequence that "the discipline as a whole becomes a powerful conservative force in a rapidly changing society." In opposition to this view, Moxey cites the evidence of recent scholars showing that the value one places on cultural circumstances in one's own time determines the values by which one assesses works of art.

To demonstrate the operation of this dynamic, Moxey turns to the history of Northern Renaissance art and its uncertain attempts to achieve parity with Italian Renaissance art. Panofsky's influential opinions are pivotal. While he argued that the artistic accomplishments of Albrecht Dürer merited comparison with the great artists of the Italian Renaissance, he did so on problematic grounds. As Moxey explains it, this elevation rested partly on Panofsky's view that the Dürer of *Melencolia I* represented "the German national spirit," a view that Moxey associates with Panofsky's forced exile from Nazi Germany. But in the main, Panofsky, falling back on his universalist aesthetics, presented Dürer's achievements on "disinterested," objectivist grounds. In opposition to this view, Moxey highlights the relativist histories of the Northern Renaissance presented during the Napoleonic era by Friedrich Schlegel and Wilhelm Wackenroder. These thinkers, on whom Panofsky himself drew, articulated an unabashed artistic relativism that insisted on "the singularity of the historical moment." By this standard, Dürer was hailed as the equal of Raphael because he was so powerfully effective in transmitting what we now describe as the Romantic values of spirituality and religious emotion. At the same time, Wackenroder's and Schlegel's relativism enabled them to enlist Dürer's art in the service of a burgeoning German nationalism.

This inability to escape from a time-bound aesthetic colors Panofsky's own not altogether forthcoming assessment of the Northern Renaissance, and it leads Moxey to his most important contribution. Instead of continuing to teach the canonical masterpieces of art history as if there were a universalist standard, instructors can do something more productive and exciting. They can teach the multiple canons of our time—a Marxist, a feminist, a gay and lesbian, and a post-colonial canon. In this way, students can be introduced to and examine the concepts of artistic merit that respond to the diverse political and cultural beliefs of our own changing society. Such an educational program will not reclaim "objectivist" art; rather it will show students the process of canon formation and the diverse values that sustain them.

Laura MacCaskey's, "Tainted Image/Sacred Image: The Wandering Madonna of S. Maria in Vallicella" is an important, concrete demonstration of the principle that canonical masterpieces in art history (and not just critical accounts of them) are inescapably fashioned by political and religious, not just aesthetic, considerations. MacCaskey's stellar examples are the high altarpieces Rubens was commissioned to paint for Vallicella's old church of Santa Maria. The first altarpiece was a scene depicting the bath-washing of the Virgin Mary, and the second, a hieratic representation of Madonna and Child. The latter was placed in front of the Nativity of the Virgin, concealing it from the congregation and making it accessible only by the priest.

Of this displacement, MacCaskey observes that the washing of a newborn is "a more demotic image relating to women." However, the appeal of this painting gave way to an anxiety aired at the Council of Trent—the issue of clerical celibacy. One implication of the first painting was that the Virgin, traditionally associated with Mother Church, was tainted, because born of a human mother through the stain of birth, and thus in need of purification. Such representation, MacCaskey maintains, revealed the need for religious authorities to exercise control over the presentation of sacred images. Answering this concern, the Council of Trent moved in 1563 to promote miraculous representations of the Madonna. Rubens's second painting conforms with these directives and appears to solve the problem by merely alluding to the Virgin's human birth while foregrounding her triumph as the immaculate Mother. By thus shifting the emphasis from Mary as human mother like other mothers to Madonna, the unstained, transcendentally pure Mother of God, Rubens's second altarpiece reveals itself as the product of a disputatious Counter-Reformation ideology. Behind the seemingly innocuousness of its present placement are revealed a series of political and religious considerations that, one might say, "transcend" aesthetics.

Just as important, MacCaskey's essay might encourage us to make cultural rather than aesthetic explanations for the dominance of one genre over another. Far more than still-life painting, for example, narratives (both literary and art-historical) have assumed a dominant place as a form of representation in Western culture and in assessments of what constitutes "great art." Narratives, especially grand narratives, as we see from Moxey's account of Wackenroder's veneration of Dürer's art, are a means of making histories. They are the stuff out of which myths and epics are created and through which national and religious identities are shaped. In aesthetic evaluations of great paintings or in great literature (as in Aristotle's *Poetics*), epic narratives are accorded a dominant place. All too unnoticed, however, is that such narratives are aptly suited to grand ideological pronouncements. As MacCaskey's account of Rubens's second altarpiece shows, epic narratives painted on canvas can, like literary epics, enshrine the values of a people and a way of life. MacCaskie's history of the central altarpiece in Santa Maria in Vallicella permits us to see the struggle beneath the enshrinement.

The third essay in this group, James Byrnes's "Viewing Foucault Viewing Velàsquez's *Las Meniñas*" takes us one step beyond these perspectives. Building on Foucault's critique in *Les mots et les choses* of Velàsquez's painting *Las Meniñas*, it shows how our very categories of art history description are conventional and epistemic rather than objective. Foucault's formalist treatment, it occurs to me, is like Eric Auerbach's *Mimesis* in the last generation, with its penetrating, typological distinction between the Greek and the Hebraic manner of representing reality. But more radically than Auerbach, Foucault is interested not in narrative history nor styles of representation, nor even the socio-political functions of genre discussed in the previous paragraph; rather, Foucault concerns himself with the external, surface aspects of the painting as representation. Alternatively put, his sole concern is the way reality is represented to ourselves.

Las Meniñas attracts Foucault's analytic eye because it is a painting of a painting. It depicts the artist in the act of painting as he faces the spectator. The result is that the spectator occupies a position outside the painting where the unseen model would be, with the image of the model reflected in a mirror situated behind the artist. In Byrnes's telling, the self-consciousness of Velàsquez's portrayal of the act of representation signals for Foucault "the death of Renaissance representation" and allows us to hold up to analysis the Classical manner of representation, with the images, eyes, and gestures "that call it into being." In this manner the structure and coherence of classical knowledge become provisional. As spectators occupying the same privileged site as both the model and the sovereign, we ourselves become sovereigns.

Ironically, as Byrnes explains it, the spectator is at once in the position of autocrat, who may interpret as he sees, and the democrat, who occupies a site open to anyone. The interpretive authority of the painting is thus impugned. But however this struggle for interpretive authority is read, Foucault's project of reading "surfaces" instead of historical narratives radically alters both the subject matter and the manner of conducting art-historical criticism.

3

Another major area where Foucault's influence has been profound is in the critical practice now referred to as "the New Historicism," a term ascribed to a diverse group of mostly American, mostly literary, practitioners whose work may be characterized by a desire to read the power of representation, especially in dramatic texts and in memorabilia where visual images are present. In Louis Montrose's plenary essay, "Form and Pressure: Shakespearean Drama and the Elizabethan State," the author—the leading new-historicist theorist along with Stephen Greenblatt—treats one of the most intractable new-historicist issues, the relationship between the power of theatrical representation and the political power of state.

Returning to a *locus classicus* of Shakespeare studies, the performance of *Richard II* on the eve of the Essex rebellion, Montrose peruses the source materials pertaining to that event. He does so to articulate his own distinctive view of the political and cultural functions of theater. Montrose's avowed interest is the now decade-long debate initiated by Stephen Greenblatt on whether theatrical representation subverts the dominant order only to be contained by that order in the end. Montrose's guiding point of view emerges from a June 22, 1600 document of the Privy Council stating that the problems of behavior caused by the public theaters are best treated by regulation, not suppression. For Montrose this means that the relationship of government to theater is uneasy, but it is not reducible to a formula that can determine the outcome on theoretical grounds alone.

Montrose argues for the same indeterminate complexity in treating the inquiry into the players' part in performing *Richard II*. Taking the view that the performance was intended not for general consumption but as a means of rousing the conspirators to action, Montrose makes the point that any play that rouses to action in this way—like drum and fife in battle—is *prime facie* a powerful instrument. Nonetheless, the exoneration of the players argues that a competing set of considerations was also operative. These Montrose identifies in the class relations between the players and the noble patrons who solicited the performance. As both inferiors and clients of nobility, the players were acknowledging their place in the social order by acceding to the performance. This complex situation reveals a tension between marketplace motives and the older principle embodied in relationships of *noblesse oblige*. Considered from these two vantage points, the theater reveals itself as powerful in its own right, but tied to the social order by an intricate web of relations that can tug in several directions.

Focusing on Greenblatt's formulation that "Elizabethan power ... depends upon its privileged visibility," Montrose takes issue with this argument and its corollaries—that the practices of state are bound to the practices of the professional Elizabethan theater and, reciprocally, that Elizabethan theatricality is bound to political absolutism. In particular, Montrose maintains that the theater's power to represent Richard II as a sovereign analogous to Elizabeth reveals the vulnerability to which sovereigns are made subject by theater. In short, sovereigns do not entirely control their own representation. These circumstances lead Montrose to the comprehensive, carefully expressed conclusion that Elizabethan theater brought together two competing world views—one orthodox, providentialist, and hierarchical, the other secular, pragmatic, and relativist. Shakespeare's histories, in Montrose's understanding, decenter the orthodox, hieratic view by the very act of representing an alternative to it. So too, by embodying these points of view in the lives of competing figures on the stage, Shakespeare invites reflection on these models of history. Coming full circle back to Greenblatt, Montrose acknowledges that the histories may arrive at various sorts of closure, but "it was wholly beyond the capacity of the Elizabethan state," he asserts, "to achieve the uniform and absolute containment of alternative and oppositional discourses. Indeed, it could be argued that such total control is (as yet) beyond the power of any state."

Montrose's argument is one of many making headway against theoretical discourses that would predetermine the character of the Elizabethan state and the relationship of theater (or any other discourse) to it. This circumstance discloses an ironic condition. The powerful theoretical arguments of the last generation—Foucaultian, neo-Marxist, Derridean, and feminist—have generated new paradigms for reading literature, history, and culture, yet they also stimulate analyses in which evidence (now adduced reflectively in thoughtful rather than self-evident ways) continues to exert its force *in relation to* those theoretical arguments. This is a situation I take to be altogether salutary.

David Kinahan's "Embodying Origins: An Anatomy of Spenser's Argante, a Yeoman's Daughter, Elizabeth I" employs several techniques associated with new-historicist inquiry. Chief among them is the use of a literary and a generally obscure non-literary parallel text to illuminate a pervasive cultural condition—here, the meaning of monstrous female sexuality in Elizabethan culture. Beginning with an inquiry into Richard Jones's 1600 pamphlet, "A Monstrous, Deformed Infant," Kinahan expresses a view of cultural processes apposite to those articulated by Louis Montrose. One of Montrose's central points about Elizabeth I is that representation exposed her vulnerability as well as her power. Kinahan's essay may be viewed as corroborating this hypothesis, but from an unexpectedly new direction.

Jones's little-known pamphlet describes as "wonderfull *iudgement of God*" a monstrous, deformed birth "begotten by incestuous *copulation*" by a young maiden who is denounced both for having had sexual relations with her cousin and for having hitherto refused proper offers of marriage. The monstrosity which Jones denounces, follows, as Kinahan points out, a pervasive Elizabethan cultural logic. The crime of lust leads to and becomes promiscuously associated with many others, including onanism, whoredom, adultery, sodomy, and fornication. Using the pamphlet as a cultural ground, Kinahan explains that Elizabeth's own birth was surrounded by questions of illegitimacy and incest inasmuch as her mother, Ann Boylen, was accused of committing incest with her brother. These accusations were rife and appeared in incest narratives in French and Latin. Because Ann Boylen's execution for her criminal sexuality threatened to define her daughter in much the same way that the pamphlet does the monstrous birth, Elizabeth, in a compensating gesture, reasserted her claims to authority by fetishizing herself as England's Virgin Queen.

These circumstances provide a cultural as well as a political or literary explanation for the Cult of Diana around which Elizabeth's chastity was celebrated. For Elizabeth, establishing the cult was a politic act of self-protection. Ironically, Kinahan observes, this solution carried its own dangers, for chastity in its extreme begets nothing; it is "self-consuming," and in a queen it precludes dynastic succession. From this perspective, the sexual body of Elizabeth is dynastic as well as personal, and it explains why Spenser's famous *Faerie Queene* can allegorize the female body both as monstrous and as fecund with its own future. The particular allegorical kinship between Elizabeth and such monstrous females as Gerines in Book 5 shows not that Elizabeth or her birth could be viewed as monstrous, but that her reign could be read in relationship to a cultural discourse on monstrosity as incest. The discourses of monstrosity as incest and of virginity as divinity thus reveal themselves as two extremes of the same complex discourse. In this way Kinahan, like Montrose, discerns a pattern of culture in which a vulnerable sovereign queen both creates and is created by discourse. In Elizabeth's case, the discourse of the monstrous female birth threatened to define her rule as much as she defined herself through her own Cult of Chastity.

The final essay in this volume, "Reading History, Reading Power, Reading Plays: Graham Holderness on Shakespeare's History Plays," by William O. Scott is an evaluative review of Holderness's materialist readings in Shakespeare's history plays. Taking Holderness as a representative point of focus, Scott seeks to assess modernist reading practices in relationship to the production of cultural change. In particular, Scott examines what he describes as an increasingly prevalent, modernist manner of reading—call it "presentist"—that makes Shakespeare the promulgator of avant garde ideas. Characterizing Holderness and others as "agents of rereading," Scott appraises the arguments for a Shakespeare ahead of his time and therefore a Shakespeare who is an agent for reform (as seen from a modern materialist perspective). The issue, as Scott frames it, is whether Shakespeare is enmeshed in the Tudor ideology he presents or whether by some special power to operate outside it he merely represents it.

A close, analytic reader, Scott is good at assessing the underpinnings of a given reading. Taking up Holderness's claim that John of Gaunt's strictures about Divine Right in *Richard II* should be read not chorally but locally and restrictively as expressing only the claims of the feudal barons, Scott explains that the argument relies heavily on the chivalric language of the early scenes. But he then points out the play's ceremonial language "may not necessarily imply endorsement of a feudal code"; it may "show Richard's insistence on pageantry and the barons' manipulation of it." Similarly, in response to Holderness's argument that the prophecies about England's travail after Richard's fall are to be read as ideological mystifications, not providential admonitions, Scott points out that since the prophecies continue to come true they must be reckoned with as more than mystifications. Similarly, when Holderness treats the garden scene, along with numerous allusions about parks and forests in *Richard II* as elements of "pastoral" (thus urging a view of the histories as proffering heterogeneous values), Scott asks whether "pastoral" is really the appropriate term since the frame of reference in *Richard II* remains so thoroughly aristocratic and the play is neither idyllic, romantic, nor innocent.

At stake in these arguments is not so much the preferability of one reading over another as the necessity of evaluating the reading practices that generate interpretation. What we see in Scott's assessments is an implicit series of criteria for valuing competing readings. These involve the adequacy of basic terminology, evaluated in terms of commonly shared understanding, the extent of the evidence provided, and the reader's ability to generate plausible counter-readings within the assumptions offered by the critic at hand. In assessing Scott's own arguments, we may or may not be convinced that Shakespeare was not an avant garde dramatist. To me what seems more important in the long run is that arguments for such claims are in practice (de facto) amenable to the kind of scrutiny—call it testing—that Scott furnishes. The fact that such assessments are possible and that reading them may evince in us responses such as "This is good counter-evidence" or "This argument is based on a persuasive definition of terms," shows that the struggle for meaning is in practice not as indeterminate or remote as may appear from essays grounded in the radical indeterminacy of interpretation.

Certainly, when Scott's review of Holderness on Shakespeare's histories is set beside Howard's essay on Shakespeare's histories, marked differences in perspective and interpretation appear. Holderness's idea that the carnival-like elements in the Henry plays undercut the sober authority of state is at some distance from Howard's contention that Doll Tearsheet and Mistress Quickly are "infantilized" and thus devalued. Scott's own view adds a third perspective, for he holds that the most vivid characters in the histories are flatly unhistorical. Their presence he calls "a poetic supplement to history." They offer the audience "a corrective filling-in of values." Against those materialist readings that locate the history plays in Tudor history, Scott calls for a reversal of figure and ground. He argues for a new model of interpretation, one in which the plays are a context for history and express a larger sense of life. As against the new-historicist notion that theater reproduces the drama of state power and actually makes that power possible, Scott urges a model of theater that has the power to reconfigure or reconstruct the structures of power on which political authority is predicated.

The impression we are left with, or certainly that I am left with after perusing these essays, is that no settled epistemology undergirds literary, historical, and artistic-historical studies in our time. Nonetheless, if we step back a bit to view these essays as a group, it becomes clear that we are witnessing the ascendancy of a historicized mode of criticism, one that takes meaning to be contingent and that therefore finds no significant meaning outside a contextualized history. Beyond this quite generic accord, it must be acknowledged that these essays show neither the emergence nor the prospect of a single methodology. What they do show—and this is a significant shift from some of the more assertively agnostic modes of deconstructive criticism prominent in the eighties—is a rejection of the kind of epistemological relativism that questions the very idea that there is a world with a history "out there" to know. All of the essays in this volume appear predicated, implicitly or otherwise, on the view that criticism is made possible by a trifold interaction among sign, object, and interpreter. Yet for all that these essays are unrelievedly and self-consciously constructionist. In them we see the protean character of historicized interpretation in our time and an oppressive consciousness of our indeterminate relationship to the early modern world and to the very idea of history. For us there is no prospect of a historical knowledge separable from the double mediation of the historical record, a mediation brought about by the generation of the historical traces themselves as well as by our own necessarily constructionist modes of representing those traces to ourselves.

State University of New York at Binghamton

JEAN E. HOWARD

Writing the History of the Present: Contextualizing Early Modern Literature

IN BOSNIA, IN THE UKRAINE, IN THE WESTERN SAHARA, even next door in Quebec, Canada, the present moment sees the emergence of powerful ethnic nationalisms. They challenge many of us who, in other contexts, celebrate difference and critique the way traditional nation states have often suppressed the cultural traditions and elided the political rights of minority groups. However, the hypernationalism of the postmodern moment has brought with it much that liberals and radicals in the West find repellant: ethnic cleansing, fundamentalism, and disregard for Western ideas of individual human rights. Even among progressive voices in the West, one response has been to find renewed comfort in the supposed cosmopolitanism of post-Enlightenment European and American thought: its celebration of secularism, tolerance, and human equality. Left unsaid, but surely implied, is that those peripheral to this cosmopolitan tradition—the Slavs, the Arabs, the Rwandans—are fanatics: anti-rational and brutal. It is hard at such moments to keep the critique going in many directions: to protest the genocidal slaughter and rape of Muslims *and* the *fatweh* against Salmud Rushdie, while also exposing the role of the West in helping to create the conditions in which such practices can occur *and* pointing to the ways the "cosmopolitan" West engages in its own practices of brutality and exclusion.

When academics write about medieval and early modern England, none of us ever does so in isolation from the intellectual and political contexts in which we live. Modern feminism, for example, has generated considerable scholarship dealing with gender and sexuality in early modern texts. It has not dictated what scholars discover about these topics, but it has made them *imaginable* topics for scholarly investigation. In less direct ways, the multiculturalism of the last decade has encouraged a pluralization of the literary canon, bringing in more writers of color and women writers, but also causing critics to *attend* to canonized texts in different ways, reading them, for example, for their production of racial difference or their implication in colonial discourse. What results is as much a *refiguring* of the potential significance of the present canon by placing it in a new context for inquiry as a modification of what is *included* in that canon.

I think one need no longer argue for the inevitable interconnections between the present moment and scholarship on the past. In strong and weak senses of the term, we are all writing histories of the present; weak histories simply find the present in the past, strong ones chart the difference of the past and the historical conditions of possibility within which prior social formations changed. But the question that interests me, given that we are all working within the horizons of the present, is whether it makes a difference what quadrant of past culture we light upon and how reflexive we are about the consequences of our admittedly circumscribed "choices." When I look at the field of Renaissance studies today, for example, I see that while few are writing the history of work, many are writing the history of sexuality. The history of sexuality for this period certainly needs to be written, and much of the best political scholarship of the last five years has emerged from that project. But I have to ask what configuration of current cultural factors make sexuality a "hot" topic and work a subject almost below the threshold of visibility in early modern studies?

Nationalism is another of the topics made "hot" by the events of the last half decade. To take up its early modern manifestations seems almost inevitable in the contemporary moment. Yet it is a topic that invites caution, including the historicist caution that we not proceed anachronistically, assuming we will find Renaissance discourses of nationalism that look just like modern ones. It is, for example, not possible fully to engage the topic of early modern English nationalism without talking about the vital role religion played in its construction.[1] The nation of England was forged in a Protestant crucible that would appall some of those who delight in the cosmopolitan and secular traditions of the West. The topic also invites the political caution that one not inadvertently slip into either an unreflexively celebratory or condemnatory mode of framing a discussion of this early modern phenomenon.

My focus is Shakespeare's history plays and the role they played in the formation of ideas of the nation in the 1590's, and I am aware of the need to take seriously my own injunctions. In their own time, as well as in the present, these plays have often been celebrated as patriotic masterpieces, creating a shared memory of the national past and of its heroes. In Thomas Nashe's words, the subject matter of these plays "is borrowed out of our English Chronicles, wherein our forefathers' valiant acts (that have line long buried in rustie brasse and worme-eaten books) are revived, and they themselves raised from the Grave of Oblivion, and brought to pleade their aged honours in open presence...."[2] The stage, in short, makes the glorious dead revive and replay their historical deeds before the eyes of theater goers. Yet feminist critics have demonstrated the androcentrism of these plays and, consequently, the partial nature of their accounts of the nation. There are more forefathers than foremothers on offer. As Phyllis Rackin writes; "No woman is the protagonist in a Shakespearean history play."[3] Moreover, a look at other histories written contemporarily with Shakespeare's, such as Heywood's *Edward IV*, reveals from a different angle what is distinctive and partial about Shakespeare's presentation of the nation. For Heywood it is apprentices and guildsmen and their wives who fill the dramatic foreground, but these social types hardly make an appearance in Shakespeare's histories. In what follows I will be looking at some figures in the later histories who fit only uneasily within the framework of the Shakespearean history play—figures such as the women in the Boar's Head Tavern in *Henry IV, Parts I and II* and *Henry V*—in order to understand where these plays were situated in the cultural landscape in which they were produced and how we might use them today in thinking about the contradictions of contemporary nationalism.

Shakespeare's histories were written almost exclusively in the 1590's and deal primarily with English monarchical history from the late fourteenth, fifteenth, and early sixteenth centuries. Collectively, these plays formed part of the cultural materials through which late Tudor England forged a sense of national identity. They were sites, for example, where national differences were elaborated, as in the repeated juxtaposition of the English and French in the first tetralogy, and where exemplary national heroes were depicted such as Talbot in *I Henry VI* and Henry V in the play of the same name. While national history flourished in many places in the sixteenth century, it was embraced on the stage with remarkable enthusiasm. In fact, defenses of the stage often became entwined, in the writings of Heywood, for example, with celebrations of the history play as a particularly edifying genre.[4] In the theater these dramatic versions of national history were seen by people who could not have read the prose chronicles popular at the same time, and while many of these chronicles were multivocal in their incorporation of diverse materials, the stage took its own liberties with these source materials, inserting clowns into stories of statecraft, giving speaking parts to commoners, and making up out of whole cloth scenes involving women.[5]

For some time, feminist critics had very little to say about the Shakespearean history play in comparison with the amount of feminist work done on comedy and tragedy. In focusing on the events of battlefield and council chamber these plays depicted domains where men were in control. Moreover, many of the women characters who actually do appear on stage in Shakespeare's histories are demonized (Joan of Arc, Margaret d'Anjou, and Elinor Cobham, for example) or given decidedly minor or subsidiary roles (Isabell, Mortimer's wife, and Doll Tearsheet). However, in the larger book of which this paper is a part, Phyllis Rackin and I argue that gender is everywhere crucial to the genre's formulation and reformulation of what constitutes proper kingship and membership within the nation. Even when roles assigned to women are demonized ones, or when women are rendered invisible or marginal, those facts are themselves important in understanding how the masculine subject in the foreground is being constructed, and how certain social groups and their work are being excluded from view in the narratives of nationhood.[6]

Shakespeare's history plays are especially interesting in this regard, in part because there are such marked differences between the first and second tetralogies. In terms of subject matter, of course, while the second tetralogy was composed after the first, it deals with historical material that occurred prior to the events Shakespeare examined in his first spate of history plays. Paradoxically, though they dramatize what preceded the War of the Roses, the plays from *Richard II* to *Henry V* bear the imprint of modernity in ways the earlier histories do not. Nowhere is this more apparent than in their treatment of kingship, of the nation, and of gender.[7] In the early plays, genealogy authorizes social position and title. Claims to the throne are repeatedly asserted by recitation of male lineage beginning, typically, with Edward III, moving to an enumeration of his seven sons, and then to an elaboration of the claims to the throne of the offspring of one of those sons. These set pieces are crucial to an imagined world in which legitimacy descends through a blood line; women figure most often in these early plays as threats to the purity of those blood lines.[8] Insinuations of sexual promiscuity cling to the majority of the women in these early plays. Their power to undermine patriarchal power (here meaning the power of the father) is indirectly registered in the degree of demonization attending the representations of many of these women such as the witch, Joan; the sorcerer, Elinor; the madwoman, Margaret. In these plays, marriages are dynastic and the state is organized around and is conceived as inseparable from the body of the monarch.

The second group of history plays seems to emanate from a different world. In the second tetralogy, England is a bounded geographical space with borders, landmarks, cities, and local histories. No longer confined to the elevated domain of court and battlefield, the world of Henry IV includes a variety of vividly detailed contemporary settings, ranging, like a disordered choreographic "perambulation," from Shallow's bucolic Gloucestershire to the yard of an inn on the road to London, to Falstaff's bustling, urban Eastcheap.[9] Less defined by reference to the monarch than before, the nation becomes a geographical and cultural entity. Simultaneously, kingship is secured less by genealogy than by performance, and women cease to be presented primarily as monstrous adulteresses disrupting, or threatening to disrupt, the purity of blood lines. The question I am addressing in this paper, in fact, is how this more recognizably modern vision of the nation puts the figure of woman to new uses.

A striking thing about these plays is the sudden "peripheralization" of the women. Instead of warrior queens and spectacular adulteresses who play major roles on the battlefield and in the court, the women of the later histories reside, often literally, in the subplots of the narrative and in the borderlands of the plays' geographical economy whence they attempt to seduce the virile English to take up foreign, "effeminate" ways. They thus perform the familiar role of defining what is not English as being foreign and dangerous. Mortimer's Welsh wife is the prototype of such a figure, never speaking English and functioning to draw her husband away from his public duties.

But the group of women who interest me most do not inhabit a borderland, but a London tavern, a sort of anti-nation or kingdom of rogues tucked *inside* the larger entity called England. In the rest of this paper I will explain why I think these "ahistorical" tavern women are in Shakespeare's later history plays and why, despite their socially disempowered positions and comic representation, they are important to an understanding of how the theater could destabilize dominant cultural discourses, including those of emergent nationalism.

The Boar's Head tavern figures quite prominently in all three plays: *Henry IV, Parts I and II* and *Henry V*. There Prince Hal escapes his princely responsibilities in a place of liberty and experimentation. There he fleets the time with his disreputable "father," Falstaff, and plays at being king, highwayman, and roisterer. The tavern, however, is not just a timeless Saturnalian space, but also the very specific world of contemporary London. A number of taverns bearing that name have been identified in Shakespeare's London,[10] and it is in this place that the realities of sixteenth-century urban life—its theatricality and its commercial vigor—are anachronistically depicted inside an historical narrative detailing the monarchical history of fifteenth-century England. It is in the Boar's Head that the historical Prince meets unhistorical characters who drink anachronistic cups of sack and wear anachronistic ruffs and peach-colored silk stockings. Significantly, this place also contains two women, the whore Doll Tearsheet, and the tavernkeeper Mistress Quickly, who constitute a complex and troubling part of Shakespeare's dramatization of national history. On the one hand the nation's internal outlaws, these women also represent the commercial urban world upon which England's financial power depended and within which the theater had its home. In their depiction of these women the plays repeatedly enact a double move of acknowledgement and repression, celebration and criminalization, indicating the contradictions surrounding the nation-forging project and the usefulness of the figure of the whore, in particular, as an embodiment and partial resolution of those contradictions.

Henry IV, Part II, especially, is haunted by performance anxiety. There is anxiety that the king *cannot* perform his role, and that his son *will not.* What results is a world out of joint, diseased, in which all social distinctions seem to evaporate. Hal, for example, often appears to prefer the company of the gluttonous Falstaff and the impoverished Ned Poins to his own father and brothers, thus devaluing the bonds of blood. Falstaff even accuses Poins of giving out that Hal will marry Poins's sister, which may well be a lie, but which indicates how Hal's behavior threatens to make monarchy "common." Shrinking from court and longing for small beer, the Prince appears less than enamored with his own greatness. Fear of social indifferentiation hangs heavy over the action.[11] In the countryside, Justice Shallow's servant, Davy, o'ermasters his master, pertly telling him what to think and do; in the city Falstaff flouts the authority of the Chief Justice, while Hal assumes the role of a tavern serving man. The endings of both *Henry IV, Part I* and *Henry IV, Part II* attempt to allay fears for the nation occasioned by the king's failure to perform his role convincingly. At Shrewsbury Hal differentiates himself finally from the cowardly Falstaff and from the impetuous Hotspur, emerging as the true Prince who can, if he wishes, play with authority the part his father has often appeared merely to be counterfeiting. At the end of *Part II*, Hal embraces first his own father and then the Chief Justice, casting off his false father, Falstaff. At the same time, the Prince casts off his tavern brothers to embrace his blood brothers in a fellowship founded on their assumed difference from the common rabble.

One function of the tavern and of the tavern women is to localize some of the anxiety thus generated by the royal family's failure to perform, and by the creeping, debilitating sense that in a world where blood and lineage do not secure social distinctions, all can quickly become debased and common. The two women are in that sense scapegoats. As I will argue, tavern prostitution becomes the overarching symbol for all erasures of distinctions between man and man, just as Quickly's pervasive malapropisms erase the distinctions between one word and another. The Boar's Head comes to epitomize the play's obsession with social leveling and disorder. It is a space set apart, an anti-nation, in many ways as foreign as the Welsh borderlands, but existing disruptively at the center of the play and of the territory called England.

The irregularity of this place and the dangers its women pose to the commonwealth are signalled in part by the way the women of the tavern do not fit neatly into the normative categories of maid, wife, and widows marked out for women in the patriarchal economy of early modern England. Each of the categories places women in relationship to men and the marriage state.[12] A woman is either to be married, married, or severed from a husband by death. But if one looks closely, it is the culturally sanctioned position of wife that Quickly can never quite seem to attain or retain. In the course of three plays her marital status becomes increasingly ambiguous. In *I Henry IV*, Quickly is often said to be "an honest man's wife" (3.3.119).[13] Mr. Quickly, however, never appears on stage. In effect, the Hostess appears to preside by herself over a domain clearly connected with lawlessness as well as liberty. It is in her tavern that Hal and Falstaff elude the law after the Gadshill robbery, and there that the two of them turn kingship into a role a "harlotry player" might perform. The feminized world of the tavern stands in clear opposition to the world of masculine power and duty symbolized by Henry IV and his court. At the Boar's Head, disorder and irresponsibility reign. Even Quickly's deformed speech—her cheerfully rendered malapropisms and double entendres—signal disorder at the linguistic level. Neither the King's son nor the King's English is safe in her hands. When Falstaff says of her: "She's neither fish nor flesh, a man knows not where to have her," she replies, "Thou art an unjust man in saying so. Thou or any man knows where to have me, thou knave, thou!" (3.3.127–30). Attempting to establish her integrity, Quickly inadvertently advertises sexual availability.

Part II intensifies the sense of lawlessness, disorder, and disease connected with the tavern world as Quickly is joined in several tavern scenes by her prostitute friend, Doll Tearsheet. Doll's presence in the text makes visible the fourth, socially-*un*sanctioned category into which a woman can fall should she not "succeed" in attaining the status of maid, wife, or widow. The woman not sutured into the patriarchal marriage system always risks being read as a whore. In this play, Doll's presence crystallizes anxieties about the loss of distinctions in a nation in which masculine performance is in doubt, including men's ability to control the sexuality of women and their entrepreneurial energies. As rebellion threatens to fracture the unity of England, and as Hal's disaffection from the duties of kingship threatens further to debase the institution of monarchy, the prostitute embodies a more widespread breakdown of order and social distinctions. Not the exclusive property of one man, Doll sleeps with many, rendering them interchangeable. And she does so for profit, leaving her partners, it is suggested, bonded in a gruesome fraternity of disease. As Falstaff intones: "We catch of you, Doll, we catch of you" (2.4.45–46).

In *Part II*, Mistress Quickly gradually gets assimilated into the discourse of prostitution surrounding Doll. In an example of what we might call "the disappearing husband syndrome," Mistress Quickly no longer seems to have a husband at exactly the time she acquires Doll as a companion. In *Part II* there is no more talk of the hostess's good husband; rather, Quickly pursues Falstaff to make good on a promise of marriage. "Thou didst swear to me upon a parcel-gilt goblet, sitting in my Dolphin chamber, at the round table by a sea-coal fire, upon Wednesday in Wheeson week, when the Prince broke thy head for liking his father to a singing-man of Windsor, thou didst swear to me then, as I was washing thy wound, to marry me and make me my lady thy wife" (2.1.86–92).

There is no concrete evidence to confirm whether, as the Chief Justice assumes, Falstaff has "made her (Quickly) serve your uses both in purse and in person" (2.1.115–16). Quickly's own uncertain control of the English tongue, and the double entendres that, consciously or not, dance through her speech, make determining her degree of sexual activity all the more difficult. To the Chief Justice she says: "Take heed of him! He stabb'd me in mine own house, most beastly, in good faith. 'A cares not what mischief he does, if his weapon be out. He will foin like any devil, he will spare neither man, woman, nor child" (2.1.13–17). It is not quite clear what "weapon" Falstaff has been brandishing. Whatever the truth of Quickly's sexual involvement with Falstaff, certainly her close association with Tearsheet colors the audience's perception of her and of the tavern, now not just a refuge for male criminals and a wayward Prince, but a place, as well, for female criminality: prostitution and, as we learn, female violence. In the last scene, Quickly and Doll, along with Pistol, are accused of having beaten a man to death, perhaps an unruly male consumer of Doll's sexual wares (5.4.16–17). The women of the tavern increasingly appear as predators on the commonwealth, endangering its (male) citizens and diverting its wealth from authorized purposes.

These, of course, are the charges often leveled against the theater, Satan's synagogue, a place accused of making men effeminate and drawing them away from their public duties and their work.[14] To better understand the complex process of disavowal and celebration at work in Shakespeare's depiction of the tavern and its female inhabitants, it is useful to focus for a moment not just on Quickly's criminality and uncertain marriage status, but also on her economic position as mistress of an urban commercial institution devoted to leisure and consumption. *Part II* gives us an increasingly sexualized and criminalized Quickly, but it also demonstrates in a new way her relative economic well-being. Once one begins to notice, signs of her economic independence litter the text. In Act I, for example, she calls in the law to make Falstaff pay his debts to her, an indication she has been able to lend him money. And he insists she has the means, if she wishes, to supply his present needs as he sets off for war. She has, for example, plate and tapestries to sell or pawn for more cash (4.2.1.140–42), and the wherewithal to summon a whore, Doll Tearsheet, to entertain Falstaff when he is about to depart (2.1.163–64). She also has, if the beadle in V.iv is to be believed, a dozen cushions for the seats of the tavern, one of which has been used to pad Doll Tearsheet's stomach in order to fake a pregnancy to avoid punishment for her various crimes (5.4.14–15). In addition, Quickly has employees such as the hapless Francis under her control. In *Part II* the tavern is thus rendered as a sexualized scene of female entrepreneurship in which Doll, the *sexually* independent woman, and Quickly, the *economically* independent woman, form a threatening combination. They challenge both gender ideology and the system of social stratification distinguishing man from man. Predictably, the punishment meted out to these women is severe. Unlike Falstaff, they are not just banished from the King's presence; rather, they are sent off to prison to be whipped. As Barbara Hodgdon observes, when Doll and Quickly are arrested in V.iv, "... the potential threats Carnival represents are displaced on the play's women." They are "the first to be demonized as corrupt, set aside and excluded from the commonwealth."[15] It is not clear what place, if any, they will have in the reordered state that is about to follow from Hal's assumption of the throne. Hardly good wives, these women become the detritus of the commonwealth.

The closing scenes of *II Henry IV*, which include the imprisonment of Doll and Quickly, look forward to *Henry V* where the king attempts to construct a renewed sense of national identity and purpose. The success of this project depends in part on casting out of the commonwealth all those who do not assent to the king's logic, a logic that makes the interests of some men—king, aristocrat, and churchman—the interests of all. Bardolph and Nym are excluded from the band of brothers for putting their own material interests before those of the king, and Pistol undergoes a mock castration for pursuing a similar path. The place of women in the renewed nation is also precarious. While there is a space for Katherine in the marriage arranged between Henry and the French king, the old inhabitants of the tavern fare less well.

Criminalized at the end of *II Henry IV*, Quickly remarkably emerges at the beginning of *Henry V* once more a wife—but now she is not wed to some unseen "good husband," nor to Falstaff, but to the disreputable Pistol. As Pistol's wife, Quickly's entrepreneurial activities threaten to move her ever deeper into illicit territory. At one point she laments: "We cannot lodge and board a dozen or fourteen gentlewomen that live honestly by the prick of their needles but it will be thought we keep a bawdy-house straight" (2.1.32–35). Perhaps the lady protests too much. Her comment suggests that she does indeed now keep a bawdy house and that while her husband is being a horseleech abroad, she is being one at home. It is therefore not too surprising when the last thing we hear of Quickly is that she died a whore's death. Or is it really Doll who dies this death? The humiliated Pistol says:

> News have I that my Doll is dead i' th' spittle
> Of a malady of France,
> And there my rendezvous is quite cut off
> (*Henry V* 5.1.81–83)

Textual editors have a variety of ways of explaining the "curious reference" to Doll Tearsheet which, to quote the Riverside editors, "properly should be to Mistress Quickly, Pistol's wife."[16] But the momentary textual conflation of the two women—whatever its source—merely underscores the symbolic conflation of the two types of "public women," the entrepreneurial tavern keeper and the prostitute, that has been underway since *II Henry IV*. Quickly can't simply be a "good man's wife" because her visibility, her volubility, and her economic independence clash with the imperatives governing wifely behavior. Quickly's remarkably unsteady relationship to the marriage state signals the gender trouble she embodies. There seems, finally, no way for the entrepreneurial urban woman to exist in the nation forged within Shakespeare's history play except on terms of criminality. Quickly exits the play world as a common whore. The woman left within the play world is Katherine, who has acceded to the will of a father, learned the conqueror's language, and achieved the only position—that of disempowered wife—available to women in the nation birthed by Hal's transformation into Henry V.

What I am arguing, then, is that through the figures of Doll and Mistress Quickly one can discern some of the exclusions, disavowals, and anxieties of Shakespeare's nation-forging drama. In a world in which blood and birth no longer guarantee identity or fix social place, Quickly and Tearsheet are the focus for fears about social leveling and disorder and about the entrepreneurship that forms an inevitable but disavowed aspect of a world premised on performative skill. The ruthlessness of their criminalization and expulsion from the world of King Henry indicates the threat they pose as nonnormative women *and* as the embodiment of a more general anxiety about disorder and the loss of social distinction. The way in which Shakespeare's dramatic narrative positions these women suggests something of the intolerance haunting the early moment of English national identity formation. Sharp lines not only separate English from foreign others, but *some* of the English from their low and disreputable countrymen as well.

One can see, then, that as the plays of the second tetralogy perambulate through the territory of England, visiting the Welsh borders, the provinces, and the darker corners of England's largest city, a sense of the space of the nation is being created in a way quite different from the first tetralogy. Yet within that space, as I hope I have shown, not everyone is to the same degree and in the same way part of that nation. The women of the tavern, and to some extent Pistol, Bardolph, and Nym, define the foreign *within* the emerging nation, the lowness that must be expelled. Yet the story I have been telling thus far about the women of the Boar's Head is both too simple and too ideologically seamless. It falsifies to some extent how theater worked as a unique institution within the early modern cultural economy. Certainly when the tavern scenes anachronistically introduce a new kind of urban woman into the Shakespearean history play, they do so in a way that stigmatizes her. It is as if the playwright, gesturing nervously toward the famed independence of the women of contemporary London, can acknowledge their existence only by transforming that independence into sexual licentiousness and criminality, an emblem of what is sick in the nation at large. Yet, perhaps because of the theater's own involvement in the commercial world of urban London, Shakespeare's representation of these women to some extent undermines or works against the project of exclusion and disempowerment they seem introduced to uphold.[17] To be excluded, these figures have first to be represented and given voices in an entertaining way. Quickly and Doll are endowed, theatrically, with remarkable vitality. Quickly's speech, in particular, is a source of considerable comic pleasure, and it introduces—along with Pistol's bombastic swagger and the dialects of Jamy, Fleullen, and MacMorris—a sense of the linguistic and social differences that the dominant language of the court cannot eradicate or homogenize.

At the beginning of Act II of *II Henry IV*, for example, Quickly urges two officers of the law, Fang and Snare, to lay hands on the fat knight, Falstaff, and bring him to justice.

> I am undone by his going. I warrant you, he's an infinitive thing upon my score. Good Master Fang, hold him sure. Good Master Snare, let him not scape. 'A comes [continuantly] to Pie-corner (saving your manhoods) to buy a saddle, and he is indited to dinner to the Lubber's Head in Lumbert Street, to Master Smooth's the silk-man. I pray you, since my exion is ent'red and my case so openly known to the world, let him be brought in to his answer. A hundred mark is a long one for a poor lone woman to bear, and I have borne, and borne, and borne, and have been fubb'ed off, and fubb'ed off, and fubb'ed off, from this day to that day, that it is a shame to be thought on. There is no honesty in such dealing, unless a woman should be made an ass and a beast, to bear every knave's wrong.
>
> *Enter Sir John[Falstaff] and Bardolph and the Boy [Page]*

> Yonder he comes, and that arrant malmsey-nose knave, Bardolph, with him. Do your offices, do your offices, Master Fang and Master Snare, do me, do me, do me your offices.
> (2.1.23–42)

This is quite a piece of language, at once so plain and yet so mystifying to those who seek in the King's English a standard of authoritative communication. In Quickly's world there is on the one hand an absolute correspondence between people and the concrete objects and occupations by which they are known. A silk merchant is named Smooth; officers of the law are called Snare and Fang; Bardolph is characterized as a malmsey-nose; Falstaff is an infinitive thing upon Quickly's score. Yet as that troubling word, *infinitive*, suggests, there is static in the communicative circuit, a potential duality, in a great many of the things Quickly says. When she calls Falstaff an "infinitive" thing upon her score, the playgoer probably silently translates *infinitive* to *infinite*, thus imaging Falstaff as an endless series of chalk markings on a board on which Quickly keeps track of credit extended. But at the same time the grammatical term, *infinitive*, is not simply wiped from consciousness; it has its own resonances, pointing exactly to a domain, that of grammar, where Quickly is no master and in which, in fact, she can be read as comically deficient by those who "know better."

The same duality is reflected in the rest of her speech, making its reception unpredictable. Falstaff is *indicted* to supper, the domain of hospitality entangled in Quickly's speech with the domain of legal punishment, social fact and Quickly's desire running together indiscriminately. He has been *invited*, but Quickly would like him to be *indicted*. Similarly, even as she calls for the law to vindicate her rights as tavern keeper and virtuous woman, one who will not be a "beast and an ass, to bear every knave's wrong," her iterations, "do me, do me, do me your offices," make her the unintentional solicitor of sexual favors, so that her status as victim seeking legal redress for wrongs done her is made uncertain by the way her speech continually sexualizes her. Is *she* a loose woman and so herself deserving of correction, rather than assistance? Quickly's malaprops jam the communicative networks by which the law does its work of making distinctions and hierarchies, separating criminals from honest men and women, whores from wives, winners from losers, legitimate kings from their theatrical imitations.

Quickly's language is, of course, a means of marking her social unimportance and transforming her into an object of fun. Throughout the *Henriad* the distance of various characters from the culture's center of power and importance is marked by their linguistic distance from perfect command of the King's English. Many of those who inhabit Quickly's tavern—bombastic swaggerers such as Pistol and malaprops such as Quickly herself—are marked as outsiders by their deformed speech. Even the regionals—Fluellen, Jamy, and MacMorris, sturdy officers in Henry's army—often are the butts of a mildly deprecating humor because of their dialects.[18] And the French Katherine, to be England's queen, must learn the King's English and eschew French. In short, linguistic difference is used in the service of social stratification. The women of the tavern enter the national history play on sexualized and criminalized terms, and they also enter by means of a language that infantilizes and culturally disempowers them.

Yet to become the butts of linguistic humor, figures such as Mistress Quickly have to be brought into the circuits of representation. Mistress Quickly's speech renders her comic, but it also pluralizes the languages of the play and denaturalizes the authority and automatic primacy of the speech of dominant groups. In her first act conversation with the Chief Justice, for example, her carnivalized rhetoric provides material resistance to the hegemony of his official speech. Before the law a woman is either a virtuous wife or widow and so worthy of the law's support, or she is a whore and subject to the law's force. Quickly's speech importuning the Chief Justice for aid in apprehending Falstaff makes it hard to determine just which she is. Eventually the law *makes* a determination, and both Quickly and Doll are hauled off to prison, but for much of *II Henry IV* the Hostess's sexual, legal, and marital status remain perplexingly ambiguous.

It is not necessary, in fact it would be unwise, to impute to Mistress Quickly an oppositional, politicized consciousness. She is a fictional creation written to be a humorous butt. But her speech, in the tradition of carnival foolery, makes available a logic and language that can provide an alternative to the logic and language of dominant groups. In the public theater, with its socially mixed audiences, it is not clear how such speech would have been received. Men who wrote against the theater worried that the stage would foster unruliness and licentiousness among its socially diverse auditors. Certainly the linguistic and social variety in these plays enhances the possibilities for "unauthorized" acts of reception. Toward the end of her time on stage, Quickly makes a speech about the death of Falstaff that suggests the disruptive potential of the alternative world view made available through her troubling language.

> Nay sure, he's not in hell; he's in Arthur's bosom, if ever man went to Arthur's bosom. 'A made a finer end, and went away and it had been any christom child. 'A parted ev'n just between twelve and one, ev'n at the turning o' th' tide; for after I saw him fumble with the sheets, and play with the flowers, and smile upon his finger's end, I knew there was but one way, for his nose was as sharp as a pen, and 'a [babbl'd] of green fields. "How now, Sir John?" quoth I, "what, man, be a' good cheer." So 'a cried out, "God God, God!" three or four times. Now I, to comfort him, bid him 'a should not think of God; I hop'd there was no need to trouble himself with any such thoughts yet. So 'a bade me lay more clothes on his feet. I put my hand into the bed and felt them, and they were as cold as any stone; then I felt to his knees, and so up'ard and up'ard, and all was as cold as any stone. (*Henry V* 2.3.9–26)

This speech again fractures the logic of authority by which this jester was banished as a vice. Quickly gives Falstaff a home in Arthur's bosom, a home at once religious and patriotic, calling in question not only Falstaff's damnation, but Hal's exclusive right to the legacy of this mythic Welsh forefather. Moreover, here and in subsequent lines, Quickly inadvertently, or perhaps intentionally, celebrates Falstaff's sensuality: his handling of women, his love of sack—all of which seem in her jumbled speech to qualify him for a holy death. In the language of this common woman the sensual and the spiritual interpenetrate, as do the recording of sin and the promise of salvation, carnivalizing, inverting, and mixing categories elsewhere strictly heirarchized and held in separation. This is very different from the speech and the logic of Henry, King of England, who, in ordering the death of Bardolph, knows who the offenders are and would have them all "cut off" (*Henry V* 3.6.107–08). Quickly's presence in the play makes possible an alternative understanding of what would constitute "justice."

Quickly's presence is important for yet another reason, having to do with the presence of women in the audience watching this play. If the Shakespearean history play is a masculinized genre, the playhouse was not a totally masculine space. As Andrew Gurr has made clear, women of all classes went to the public theater.[19] In the Boar's Head tavern women are also spectators to theatrical entertainments. When Hal and Falstaff undertake "The Arraignment of the Prodigal Son," Quickly proves an avid and involved listener. As Falstaff is about to take a turn at playing the King, Hal's father, the Hostess cries out, "O Jesu, this is excellent sport, i' faith!" (*Henry IV.I* 2.4.390). Then she comments on his performance: "O, the father, how he holds his countenance!" (392); "O Jesu, he doth it as like one of these harlotry players as ever I see!" (395–96). Quickly knows at least enough of theater to have a standard by which to compare Falstaff's performance.

At the end of *II Henry IV* Shakespeare writes an epilogue in which he makes it clear that he knows women are spectators to his plays as well as men. The actor playing the epilogue says that he intends to kneel down and "pray for the Queen" (line 17)—a very special spectator—and in a more general vein opines that "All the gentlewomen here have forgiven me; if the gentlemen will not, then the gentlemen do not agree with the gentlewomen, which was never seen in such an assembly" (22–25). In a nice sleight of hand, Shakespeare makes all the women in the audience into "gentlewomen," thus distancing them from any imputation that they are Mistress Quicklys or Doll Tearsheets. Yet acknowledging the presence of these female spectators is implicitly to acknowledge that the theater constitutes a "public" that consists of more than the elite players of much chronicled history. As Heywood was to argue in his *Apology for Actors*, the theater was one of the most noteworthy London institutions, an ornament to the city, a magnet for foreign visitors, a source of edification for England's people.[20] That theater—communal, inclusive, and dedicated to the mutual pursuit of profit and play—bears more resemblances to Quickly's tavern than to the King's court. Officially denigrated as the seat of vice and disorder, the theater, like the tavern, let foolery thrive, situating the official discourses of chronicle history alongside the less decorous languages of swaggerer, prostitute, and tosspot. If

Shakespeare through his portrait of Quickly's tavern to some extent disavowed his own involvement in the increasingly commercial world of consumption and play, displacing onto the women the burden of the theater's "low" disreputability, the theatrical event tends to contradict that disavowal by placing "the low" hilariously if intermittently in the forefront of our attention where it can, if we let it, destabilize the pre-eminence and the "natural" authority of the "high" players in the nation's drama. The only question to be asked of these plays, then, is not, What were Shakespeare's politics in penning them? Rather, it is just as important to ask, What do my strategies for reading them reveal about my own politics? Or, more concretely, What will I *let* Quickly's malapropisms signify?

In the nation forged in Shakespeare's *Henriad*, women are undeniably less powerful and hence less monolithically demonized than in the earlier histories. The good women dwindle into wives, the category of validation, and as good wives they do not much affect the course of public life, though their presence is required to validate man's proper performance of his masculinity. We see this when Katherine is trotted on stage at the end of *Henry V* to be the object of the King's bluff and manly wooing. Yet the peripheries and subplots of these plays are haunted by other women—whores, unmarried tavernkeepers, effeminating foreigners—who speak or sing in mystifying tongues and who remind the audience of the exclusions through which King Henry's England is to be forged. It is no accident, I think, that it is in the public theater, an impure and polyvocal space, that these other voices are heard, reminding the audience—both men and women—of the possibility of an England in which women are something other than wives and where difference, like copulation, might thrive.

Shakespeare's histories do not tell us what to think about the flourishing of hypernationalism in the present moment. But they provide us materials—if we want to use them—for analyzing the processes of exclusion and marginalization that haunt most nationalist projects and give evidence of the ways in which the very institutions through which the project is advanced can also be used to foil it.

Columbia University

Notes

[1] Benedick Anderson in *Imagined Communities: Reflections on the Origins and Spread of Nationalism* (London: Verso, 1983) argues that nationalism *replaces* religion in the modern world. Present events show the inadequacy of such a formulation, but in sixteenth-century England, as well, Protestant discourses of England as an elect nation were central to the nation-forging project. See William Haller, *The Elect Nation: The Meaning and Relevance of Foxe's* Book of Martyrs (New York: Harper, 1963) and Richard Helgerson, *Forms of Nationhood: The Elizabethan Writing of England* (Chicago: Univ. of Chicago Press, 1992), esp. 249–94.

[2] Thomas Nashe, *Pierce Penilesse his Supplication to the Devil* (1592) in E. K. Chambers, *The Elizabethan Stage* (Oxford: Oxford Univ. Press, 1923), 4: 238.

[3] Phyllis Rackin, *Stages of History: Shakespeare's English Chronicles* (Ithaca: Cornell Univ. Press, 1990), 147.

[4] Thomas Heywood, *An Apology for Actors* (London: Nicholas Okes, 1612), esp. Bk. 3:F3–F3v.

[5] See Rackin, *Stages of History*, esp. 146–247.

[6] Jean E. Howard and Phyllis Rackin, *Engendering A Nation: A Feminist Account of Shakespeare's English Histories* (London: Routledge, 1997).

[7] See Jean E. Howard, *The Stage and Social Struggle in Early Modern England* (London: Routledge, 1994), 129–53.

[8] Rackin, *Stages of History*, 158–61.

[9] For the significance of Renaissance chorographic writing to the project of English nationalism see Richard Helgerson, *Forms of Nationhood*, 107–47.

[10] Chambers, *The Elizabethan Stage*, 2:443–45.

[11] Laurie E. Osborne, "Crisis of Degree in Shakespeare's *Henriad*," SEL 25 (1985): 337–59.

[12] A good investigation of the importance of marriage in English Reformation culture and in works produced for the stage is Mary Beth Rose's *The Expense of Spirit: Love and Sexuality in English Renaissance Drama* (Ithaca: Cornell Univ. Press, 1988).

[13] All quotations from Shakespeare's plays are taken from G. Blakemore Evans et. al., eds. *The Riverside Shakespeare* (Boston: Houghton Mifflin Company, 1974).

[14] See Jonas Barish, *The Antitheatrical Prejudice* (Berkeley: Univ. of California Press, 1981), esp. 80–131, and Jean E. Howard, *The Stage and Social Struggle*, esp. 22–46.

[15] Barbara Hodgdon, *The End Crowns All* (Princeton: Princeton Univ. Press, 1991), 172.

[16] G. Blakemore Evans, "Note on the Text," *The Riverside Shakespeare*, 972.

[17] For the presence of women in the English Renaissance theater audience

see Andrew Gurr, *Playgoing in Shakespeare's London* (Cambridge, England: Cambridge Univ. Press, 1987), 59–64; and for the ideological significance of their presence, see Jean E. Howard, *The Stage and Social Struggle*, 73–92.

[18] Philip Edwards in *Threshold of a Nation: A Study in English and Irish Drama* (Cambridge, England: Cambridge Univ. Press, 1979) discusses this play's role in producing a sense of English superiority vis-à-vis the Welsh, the Irish, and the Scots. In part this superiority is constructed by the deployment of "standard English" against "dialects."

[19] See note 17.

[20] Thomas Heywood, *An Apology for Actors*, Bk 3: F3v.

SARAH HANLEY

Mapping Theory in History: Conceptual Cites and Social Sites in the French Monarchic State

Social Sites and Conceptual Cites

IN 1791, DURING THE FRENCH REVOLUTION, when all manner of reform seemed possible, Olympe de Gouges wrote the *Declaration of the Rights of Woman and Citizen*. She charged the newly elected deputies in the National Assembly, who had written the *Declaration of the Rights of Man* (1789) and were presently writing the *French Constitution of 1791*, with crushing the rights of women. Also in 1791, Etta Palm d'Aelders wrote her *Address from French Citizenesses to the National Assembly*. She demanded that the deputies repeal laws that tyrannized women.

Just what were Gouges and Aelders actually demanding of deputies charged with reordering the monarchic state? Pursuing this query allows one to explore a dragon of social theory: the problem of how to overcome the static separation of structures and events, or system and action, and account for the dynamic long-term relationship between them. Put another way: How to disallow separation of social sites and conceptual cites and to privilege instead relations of practice, wherein interactive structures and events frame an ongoing process of structuration harboring continuity and change.[1]

The pertinent hypotheses are as follows. First, that these political events of the 1790s—the demands of Olympe de Gouges and Etta Palm d'Aelders—must be accorded a different reading than usual, one embedded in a social site structured much earlier, from the 1550s through the 1650s, and well in place by the 1700s; a social site that inscribed those later demands with meaning. Second, that the interpretation presented here could not have emerged by reading just the texts in which the demands were couched, or even by reading those texts situated in their immediate context of the 1790s. Rather, this interpretation emerged only by unravelling the relations of practice observed in a protracted process of social structuration; that is, by assessing the encounters between societal regulations set in place and persons who accepted, manipulated, or rejected them, effecting accommodation, mediation, or collision. These dynamic relations of practice supply the key for unlocking the time-oriented enigma that history is a culturally ordered practice, and culture is a historically ordered practice.[2]

In her challenge, the *Declaration of the Rights of Woman* (1791),[3] Olympe de Gouges addressed men and women. She says: "Man, are you capable of being just?... Tell me, what gives you the *sovereign power* to oppress my sex?" Alongside men, she insists, women must be constituted into a National Assembly" in order to privilege equally the "authoritative acts of women and the authoritative acts of men," because in the past the "scorn" of men for the "natural, inalienable, and sacred rights of woman" has been the cause of "public misfortunes and the corruption of governments...." At this moment of potential structural change enabled by the legislation of a new constitution, she delivers a warning: "Women, wake up ... discover your rights!... What advantage have you received from the Revolution?" Then she poses the critical leading question: "Do you [women] fear that our [new] French legislators, correctors of that [old] *morality,* enshrined in *political practices* now *out-of-date,*" will say to you once again: "Women, what is there in common between you and us?"[4] Here it is important to note that Gouges likens marriage (for women) to the condition of slavery and appends to her *Declaration* a new model social contract between man and woman that governs the marital condition.[5]

In her challenge, *Address of French Citizenesses to the National Assembly* (1791),[6] Etta Palm d'Aelders addressed the deputies elected to the National Assembly, who were making new laws at that very moment. She says: "You [deputies] have restored to man the dignity of his being by recognizing his rights; [now] you must no longer allow woman to groan beneath *arbitrary authority....*" "Justice... calls all individuals to the *equality of rights,* without discrimination of sex...." At this moment of potential structural change, she indicts present laws governing society, warning that "For too long, alas, the imprescriptible *rights of nature* have been misinterpreted; for too long, *bizarre laws*, the worthy product of centuries of ignorance, have afflicted humanity...; for too long, the most *odious tyranny* [over women] was consecrated by *absurd laws*" still in force. Then she makes the crucial leading plea: "Gentlemen, [the proposed law now before the Assembly] Article 13 of the code of civil order [the *Police Code*],... is a refinement of *despotism* [designed] to render the constitution *odious to the female sex...*," [because] it will "*degrade* [women's lives]" as surely as the chains of "*slaves*." Here it is important to note the precise challenge posed when she says: "Legislators, [in the future] *conjugal* [marital] *authority* should be only the consequence of the *social pact* ..., [in which] *the powers of husband and wife must be equal and separate.*" "Representatives of the nation ... vote down the *unjust* and *unpolitic* code [Article 13]...." "Consult only your hearts ...," which "will instruct you better than the *maxims of the jurists of preceding centuries.*..."[7]

At this point a pertinent question rightly intrudes: What were the provisions of the allegedly infamous, odious, tyrannical, unjust Article 13, which lay at the heart of both these demands? This study comes back to that question after a foray into past centuries to identify the political and social practices, maxims and laws, that Gouges and Aelders castigated as being misinterpreted, out of date, despotic, and injurious to women.

Constitution of the Male Right to Rule in Household and State

It is clear that the many women who wrote letters, memoirs, novels, and philosophical tracts in the 1600s and 1700s,[8] and especially those involved in marital litigation and the production of legal briefs transmitted to "the public" in the same period,[9] struggled to understand a phenomenon that even we have not yet quite fathomed. That is, how *male authority* had come to be politically and socially constituted—not only in the French monarchic state (where male rule prevailed by Public Law), but also in the French household (where male rule prevailed through Civil Law). As in the legal case studies below, many of those women were on the right track but could not finish the run without archival access to official state documents. Armed with that access and documents these centuries later, I have been able to identify *patterns of law* (a structure set in place over time) and to reconstruct *lawsuits* (events enacted in time) from the 1500s through the 1700s, which trace the interrelated processes of state building and family formation. In those centuries political theorists, politicians, lawyers, and judges in Parlements—from Jean Bodin in the 1570s to Robert-Joseph-Pothier in the 1750s—formulated a French Law Canon, which instituted a *marital regime* system of male governance empowering husbands and kings as rulers in household and state.[10] It is important to note first, how this *marital regime* system applied politically to state building; second, how the *marital regime* system applied domestically to family formation; and third, how male authority sustained by *marital regime* male governance was challenged, first in lawsuits over marital position and possession in households, then in political suits over monarchic power in the state.

From the mid-1500s through the 1650s during the era of nascent state building, the French monarchic state attained a new juridical base for the male right to rule at a very critical juncture in history: the moment when the Salic Law, which allegedly excluded women from rule in the French kingdom from time immemorial, collapsed under the weight of forgery and fraud.[11] When lawyers and historians trained in the French *mos qallicus* method of modern historical scholarship recovered original copies of the ancient Salic Law in the mid 1500s, they were staggered by the enormity of that fraud and rejected Salic Law.[12] Committed to female exclusion but bereft of Salic Law, they moved to institutionalize the principle of male right (and its corollary, female exclusion) on more dependable juridical grounds even though female monarchs and regents were not the exception in Europe but the rule in this era.[13] Legists and theorists formulated for the monarchic state a French Law Canon, which underwrote a *marital regime* system of governance legitimizing the male right to rule in parallel realms, household and state. That French Law Canon was composed of the following rubrics: *Public Law* (instanced in a French custom favoring male monarchs); *Natural Law* (instanced in a seminal theory of authority linked to male generative capacity); *Civil Law* (instanced in French edicts favoring male rule in households); and *Moral Law* (instanced in moral lessons defaming women).[14] Crossing a wide cultural purview, those rubrics gave form to an early modern monarchic state in which political identity was defined in male terms difficult to transcend.

First, the French Law Canon rubric on Public Law and state governance was explained, in part, through a new political maxim employed to exemplify *marital regime* governance in a male monarchic state. From the 1520s jurists and governors invented a powerful new metonymic device: a French marital maxim (for the state), which encapsulated (through analogy and mimesis) a juridical marital model of male authority articulated in the following linked passages. The marital maxim and its extended analogic equivalencies contractually united king and kingdom in a political marriage, which was likened to a civil marriage of husband and wife: it reads—"The king is the husband and political spouse of the kingdom." As extended to encompass assets, the marital maxim equated the royal domain of the kingdom (which was ritually brought to the king in the Coronation ceremony by Public Law and declared inalienable), with the female dowry of a marriage (which was ritually brought to the husband in a marriage ceremony by civil law and could not be alienated). It reads—"The kingdom brings to the king the royal domain as a dowry of his crown, which dowry kings at their Coronation solemnly swear never to alienate." As further extended to include male reproductive replication, the marital maxim identified the sons of kings as political progeny born of king and kingdom. It reads, "They [the sons] are the children of the French people and of the kingdom (*chose publique*)." The glaring absence of women from these politicized marital contracts, transactions, and generative acts anticipated the related Natural Law grounds for male rule also articulated.[15]

Second, the French Law Canon rubric on Natural Law, metaphysical grounds for governance, was explained by reference to a politicized biogenetic seminal theory of male authority. Although historians have missed the strategic connection here, from the 1550s to the 1650s jurists and politicians, such as Jean Bodin, Louis Turquet de Mayerne, Cardin Le Bret, Antoine Loysel, and Charles Loyseau developed a political theory of male right by advancing (under the rubric of Natural Law) a seminal theory of governance that conveyed the masculine nature of authority itself. In an important treatise on legitimate governance in the 1570s, one anonymous political theorist explained this seminal theory of male authority and its biogenetic consequences.

He argues that human authority in household and state derives not from original sin but from nature. Then he locates the right to govern in males by politicizing an Aristotelian metaphysical, or pseudo-biological, notion of *male reproductive replication*, hence *male monarchic replication*. According to this view, nature dictates that males (who transmit active seed) generate, or propagate, familial heirs who continue households; likewise kings generate successors who perpetuate the state. Nature also dictates that females (who lack seed and contribute only passive matter) cannot seminally create; hence, a French queen may reproduce but cannot "generate" royal progeny.

The message stands out: If the monarch was a queen, male monarchic replication, hence the monarchic state that kings embody, would naturally die. In this politicized Aristotelian view of male-to-male reproductive replication, the author declares the rule of men (as propagators) natural and legitimate; the rule of women (as non-propagators) is unnatural and forbidden. For good measure, he confirms male right by reference to the sexual and moral perversity of woman that makes women unfit to govern households or states.[16]

From the 1570s and through the 1600s, legists and writers beholden to seminal theory, such as Bodin, Turquet de Mayerne, and Le Bret, juxtaposed legal and illegal forms of state governance: "monarchy" and "gynecocracy." They allege that a state governed by a woman is not a monarchy but a gynecocracy, which is a type of rule both unnatural and illegal in France. A woman-governed state is illegal because French Public Law (beholden to Natural Law) rightly prohibits female rule. It is unnatural because a gynecocracy (modeled on the female body and bound to the seminal theory presumption that "the Queen dies" through default of generative seed) spells the imminent death of the state; whereas a monarchy (modeled on the male body and symbolized by the seminal theory maxim, "the King never dies") is immortal.[17] In the 1570s Bodin encapsulated this Natural Law, seminal theory, principle in his political maxim, "The king never dies, inaugurating the French theory of *The King's One Body*."[18] In the 1600s when others inscribed that maxim in poems, which likened successive French male kings to lilies that reseed themselves, and in engravings and sayings, which likened a series of French progenitor kings to a phoenix and cast them as mediators between Natural Law and French Law,[19] they wrote seminal theory into Natural Law, the state constitution, political practice, and aesthetic sensibility. Thenceforth Natural Law, biogenetic gender contraries supposedly replicated in the human body, separated men (capable of generative acts) from women (incapable of generative acts); that generative disconnection situated women as aliens, or outsiders, within the household and by definition within the state. These Public Law and Natural Law rubrics of the French Law Canon, which underwrote male rule in the state, were connected with the rubric of Civil Law, which underwrote male governance in the household.

Third, the French Law Canon rubric of Civil Law and household governance was explained, in part, by a marital compact of Civil Laws governing society. From the 1530s through the 1640s and beyond, legists, councilors in Parliament, and other government officeholders acting in consort with kings and royal governments, promulgated a Family-State Compact of civil laws that regulated family formation through edicts and case-law precedents on marriage regulations, reproductive customs, marital separation arrangements, and inheritance rules. As legists such as Jean de Coras, Jérôme Bignon, and Pierre Séguier argued from the 1530s to the 1640s, secular control over family formation through Civil Law (as opposed to Catholic Church control through ecclesiastical law) should be mandated by the French state for the public good. That it was, even though this shift of venue, removing marital cases from church courts into state courts, contravened articles drawn up in the 1560s by the Council of Trent, which the French refused to sign.[20] Family formation and state building were intimately connected in France because of the existence of a unique sociopolitical system of venal-hereditary officeholding. Rapidly institutionalized from the mid-1500s, that system sanctioned not only the purchase of offices by families, but also inheritance.

By the 1570s judges were treating government offices as negotiable property (*immeubles*) transmitted in family estates. By 1604 the Paulette edict, which was a prime piece of inheritance legislation in the Family-State Compact, made purchased offices lineage property regulated by Civil Law.[21] In the 1580s the jurist Georges Loüet suggested the way Civil Law brought male dimensions to family property (including government offices) when he argued for advantaging sons since daughters (through marriages) moved family possessions into "alien" families.[22] The Natural Law, Public Law, and Civil Law rubrics on male rule in the French Law Canon were accompanied by Moral Law dictates that favored male rule by defaming women as unfit for governance.

Fourth, the French Law Canon rubric of Moral Law was articulated through female defamation lessons linking law and popular culture. Female defamation actually was incorporated into the texts of laws that made up the Family-State Compact. The legal intent of such lessons, repeatedly alleging female presumptive blame, is etched on two fronts. First, the edicts in solemn tones effect the pretense that women are responsible for the serious misdemeanors that the laws must address. Second, the edicts in shrill tones directly charge women with the wreckage of the family and, by analogy, the state. The edicts forming the marriage pact and regulating reproduction recall intellectual and moral character defects inherent in woman, decry the many detestable female vices that ruin women and their families, and purport to define for women true female honor. The edicts on inheritance insist that widows are courted only for their goods, never for their personal attractions, and accuse married women and widows of being potentially disloyal to family and patrimony. Various edicts trumpet a litany of women's worst excesses, such as demeaning the entire family by consorting with or marrying men of lower status, introducing illegitimate children to unsuspecting families, providing donations (estate shares) larger than warranted to non-blood relatives in second marriages, and committing one of the worst acts of sexual license and family treason, adultery. In tenor, the edicts would lead one to presume that men did not commit any of these infractions; yet in practice, many of these laws were applied to both women and men in litigated court cases. This rhetorical move to bypass men and target women indicates how loath jurists were to criticize publicly male heads of households (and by reference, male rulership), and how loath they were to indict men whose male authority they were actively engaged in strengthening. As a result, the language of the law, along with the law itself, positioned women as cultural symbols for the misdeeds that corrupted families and states, a theme translated into popular culture. The cultural force of philosophy, political theory, law, legal language, and iconography that legitimized male rule should not be underestimated, especially as it spread through popular culture.²³ Yet the system itself contained dangerous collision courses that women and men had to negotiate over generations. As collisions escalated, so did lawsuits.

Turning from the French Law Canon, which structured state and society through natural, public, civil, and moral law, to the daily business of litigants and lawsuits, which were events wrought from collisions with that structure, the pivotal place of lawsuits commands attention. From the 1600s on, many of the legal cases heard by judges in courtrooms were taken by litigants to the streets in printed accounts hawked by vendors, posted on walls with public notices, sold in bookstalls, and recounted by readers to non-readers, accomplishing wide dissemination. As a result, some litigants secured one hearing from judges in a courtroom and another from what they called "the public" in the streets, and the effects on public opinion were sometimes dramatic.²⁴ It is the collisions, more than the accommodations, that reveal the ways marital rule, hence male right, was contested. In general, the study of lawsuits helps assess why the relations of practice observed between structured regulations (the Family-State Compact of laws) and human actions (the litigated court cases) led to collisions. In particular, the study of two lawsuits for marital separation brought by wives against husbands in the 1680s and early 1700s discloses the social conditions that first prompted some women to criticize the marital regime system, then provoked Gouges and Aelders to demand constitutional reform.

Case Study 1: Antoine Du Bois du Plessis— Marie-Anne Rainssant

In October 1680 Marie-Anne Rainssant brought a lawsuit for marital separation (domicile *and* property) against her husband, Antoine Du Bois du Plessis, as she put it: "to conserve [my] liberty and [my] life." This household marital regime ruled by Antoine was particularly threatening for Marie (subjected to marital rule), who suffered repeated beatings from a husband whose jealous tirades were indiscreetly launched in front of witnesses. The minute Antoine realized he was going to lose the case, he interrupted the court proceedings by filing his own countersuit: that is, he filed a suit charging Marie with adultery and produced three servants as witnesses. As a result of

Antoine's adultery countersuit, Marie's original separation suit was put on hold while the adultery charge was heard. Five months later, in February 1681, the adultery countersuit was quashed when evidence showed that Antoine's witnesses were lying and more than likely had been bribed. Only then, when the adultery suit was over, could Marie's original marital separation suit be resumed in court. Seven months later, in August 1681, the judges brought forth a verdict quite unusual in these times: they decided for Marie and granted her a separation of both domicile and property (including child custody). Marie and her young son went to live with her parents, who had supported her lawsuit throughout. This verdict should have been the end. It was just the beginning.

Over the next three years, Antoine, who was determined to reverse the legal decision, plotted and planned. He hired lackeys to spy on Marie all over Paris, including at the church at Saint Sulpice, in the gardens at Luxembourg, at fairs, and even in the homes of friends. For four months (around November 1683 to February 1684), he spread rumors among acquaintances all over Paris that Marie was pregnant. Then on 6 March 1684, around 7 pm, Antoine carried out his well-planned move. As Marie came out of evening services at Saint Sulpice, three men armed with swords grabbed her. While she screamed for help to a throng of onlookers who made no move to stop them, the armed men threw Marie into a closed carriage and abducted her. Suspecting the worst, Marie's father, Henry Rainssant, quickly brought an abduction suit against Antoine, using as grounds a threatening letter sent by him to the family some months before Marie's disappearance. Four months later, in July 1684, just as evidence was being presented in the abduction suit, Antoine arranged to have Marie released. Blindfolded, she was put out of a carriage in the rain at midnight on the outskirts of city. Thoroughly shaken by the ordeal but all the more determined, Marie pressed the abduction charges will full parental support. They all went back to court.

In his court testimony Antoine made a second adultery charge, which had been his plan all along. According to him, Marie had become pregnant from a longstanding adulterous affair and had hidden the pregnancy for some months. Then she feigned her own abduction, he said, in order to give birth secretly without his knowledge or that of her parents. In her testimony Marie charged Antoine with her abduction and also with having defamed her reputation before "the public" through gossip, rumor, and false accusations that caused "scandal in Paris." That is not all. Marie directed bold criticism against the legal system itself: She bitterly complained that Antoine stood as the accused in both her first suit (for marital separation) and her second suit (for abduction), but the law allowed him (by inserting a charge of adultery) to reverse the entire docket. That is, he was allowed to displace her lawsuits (even though they were brought first), he was able to turn her into the accused (rather than the accuser) through his adultery charge, and he was able to be heard in court first (while both her suits were put on hold).[25]

Case Study 2: Marguerite Aurillon—François de Sorny

One of five children, Marguerite Aurillon was destined by her surgeon father, Guillaume Aurillon, for life in a convent, which required less dowry funds than a marriage, and her adamant refusal to take the habit as ordered strained their relationship. Then François Sorny, a captain in the King's Regiment, appeared on the scene. An older man with a past that did not pass muster, he seems to have been under pressure to marry in order to salvage a disintegrating reputation that had become anathema to the honor of his regiment. Marguerite's father dowried her (with minimal funds), and she married François in July 1699.

From the start in this marital household ruled by the ever absent François, marital relations were disastrous. As François later admitted, he had become a husband without reflecting upon the conjugal obligations entailed, and Marguerite's presence in his life reminded him of his old "aversion" to the marital condition. Away for long periods on military duty, François never did establish a home. Instead, in an odd arrangement, he left one-third of Marguerite's dowry funds with her father in whose household she had to reside, though a married woman. On rare occasions when he chose to visit, she testified, François either ignored her or treated her with contempt. As she put it, "I did not gain a husband but only a master."

Caught for a decade in this limbo (seemingly neither wife nor daughter) and subjected to physical abuse for complaints, Marguerite decided to bring a suit for marital separation (domicile and property).

To that end, she notified François and offered to take up residence in a convent until the separation suit was decided in court. She requested that François suggest a reputable convent and agree to pay the board costs from her dowry funds. Because he acquiesced in such an agreeable manner, she failed to remain on guard.

To discuss the pending convent arrangements, François invited Marguerite for supper at the house of a friend. As it turned out, she was hoping to instigate a reconciliation and behaved accordingly. But following their supper when she was disrobed, François swiftly left the house just moments before police officers noisily entered with a warrant (signed by him) for her arrest as a "disorderly woman." To the police, as well as a throng of neighbors now made witnesses, it appeared as if Marguerite had been caught in the act of adultery with a partner who had fled. Taken by force in this humiliating manner (naked but for a bathrobe) to the dreaded Parisian Convent of La Magdeleine where prostitutes were incarcerated, Marguerite attempted again to pursue her separation suit. But by bringing a suit for marital separation after her husband's accusation of adultery was set in motion, and without any parental support, the odds in her favor were not good.

When she went to court in 1711, Marguerite maintained that her marital separation was absolutely necessary given the scorn, abuse, and duplicity she had endured. Alluding to the risks for women in this legal system, she said: "At stake in my case is my reputation and even my life." That is not all. Marguerite made a bold negative judgment about the legal system itself: The law, she said, has allowed "my husband [to be] my adversary, my judge, and my executioner [that is, the one who carries out the sentence]."[26]

Reconstructing many of these cases has been necessary: first, to figure out what legal procedure was followed in settling disputed marital separation cases up to 1791, and second, to figure out how legal practice affected women and men. Oddly enough, the Civil Laws of the Family-State Compact, which regulated so many areas of marital concern, did not provide edicts on marital separation, but left the disposition of such cases, on the whole, in the hands of judges and husbands. As a result, judges and husbands created law, case by case, through legal practice over time. Judges were notoriously loath to indict husbands (as household heads) for faulty governance; however, wives were prejudiced unduly in such suits and in most of the legal decisions that set precedents.

My study of legal practice drawn from case law shows that during the 1600s and 1700s the following procedure on marital separation was followed. First, in the simple cases of voluntary marital separation (of domicile, *not* property), the corporate family assets remained intact. The husband continued to disburse the combined resources; and the wife had access (albeit quite limited) to those resources (through his permission). Second, and more important for the cases here, in the more complex cases where lawsuits were brought for marital separation (domicile and property) great difficulties ensued. In the event that the wife sued and won a separation, she could legally withdraw her dowry funds from the corporate family assets and live on her own, as Marie was able to do and as Marguerite hoped to do. She retained legal entitlement to her dower funds, if widowed, as well as a share of community property. But in the event that the husband sued or countersued and won a separation for adultery, he legally appropriated the principal and interest from the wife's dowry funds, withdrew the dower, and negotiated terms for her confinement in a convent, where he could leave her for life (paying board from her dowry funds) or effect a reconciliation within two years and bring her home.[27] This summary of precedents from legal practice helps to explain some of the strange events witnessed in the two cases outlined above.

The social consequences of marital separation cases varied greatly for men and for women. One element stands out: Adultery was treated as a female misdemeanor, which was severely punished by the loss of civil rights in society—dowry and dower funds, community property, children, household space for habitation—and then by confinement in a convent, or a prison orchestrated not by the judge but by the husband. As a result, the minute wives suggested they might sue for a separation, or long before it ever crossed their minds, or even in the middle of such suits, husbands often sued (or launched countersuits) charging them with adultery. Real or imagined, adultery charges provided men with the legal power to maintain marriages and keep limited control of women's assets, or to break marriages and gain total control of assets. This situation is exemplified in the Du Bois-Rainssant and the Aurillon-Sorny cases. First, Antoine and François had to secure adultery convictions against Marie and Marguerite. Otherwise, they were deposed as husbands from household rule and incurred tarnished reputations. In addition they lost control of their wives' assets and suffered grave financial losses. It is clear why many husbands concocted wild schemes to prove adultery, whether or not adultery had ever been committed: Case law as practiced invited such schemes. Furthermore, arrests of wives were made relatively unhindered in society. The bystanders who witnessed Marie's violent abduction and screams for help outside the church of Saint Sulpice, as well as the neighbors who witnessed Marguerite's humiliating arrest in a bathrobe at a domicile not her own, stood still and mute. As they later reported in court, they did not intervene because the abductors in the one case and the police in the other told them that a husband was having his wife arrested for "disorderly conduct." Obviously male heads of households could arrange and secure clandestine arrests, and the law as practiced condoned and aided those surreptitious actions. Placed in such danger, women voiced complaints.

And finally, when women spoke boldly and bitterly of their lives being at stake in these cases, as did Marie and Marguerite, they surveyed the risky situation surrounding marital separation and adultery suits quite correctly. Confinement of a wife in a convent for adultery (should a husband decline reconciliation) removed her from civil society with a life sentence that might last even beyond the husband's death. Marie and Marguerite both aptly stated the egregious nature of those female life risks. They complained that the legal system privileged the husband's suit by allowing his accusation to be heard first, and that husbands were legally empowered to act as the accusers of their wives, their judges, and their executioners (that is, the persons who ultimately determined the particulars of their sentence). That is why, in the face of such risks, women engaged in the social process of "counterfeiting culture"; that is, in the social process of fashioning, utilizing, and sharing strategies, legal or illegal, that would enable them to avoid, or at least to cushion, built-in life risks sanctioned by law.[28] Women manipulated the system precisely because the French Law Canon made marital regime governance and male rule almost impermeable to criticism and change. Yet over time, as such cases escalated, it was the marital separation suits brought by women that posed the greatest threat to male governance.

The marital separation suits brought by women in courts, and sometimes taken to the streets as well, undermined the social and economic stability of households, tarnished the reputed authority of the male heads, frayed the sociopolitical tie that bound husbands and kings as male governors in this marital regime system, and eventually called the system itself into question. That is why, despite many collisions and criticisms repeatedly voiced by women such as Marie and Marguerite, marital regime rule privileging male right was steadfastly and righteously defended. As late as the 1750s, the jurist Robert-Joseph-Pothier, still employed marital-political terms to comment on "the power of the husband" and the propriety of male rule unshared in the household (akin to the power of the king and orderly state governance). He declared the husband as ruler of the family, the wife as subject, and warned that "It is not the place of the woman who is an inferior to inspect the conduct of her husband who is her superior...."[29]

Wedded to the rubrics of the French Law Canon created in earlier centuries, Pothier's unyielding views of male authority took no cognizance, for instance, of Montesquieu's cautionary "Persian" tale of the 1720s, which featured the tragic effects of despotic male rule unshared in a household, or his political theories of the 1740s, which recommended the salutary effects of a "separation of powers" in the state (posthumously adopted in the Constitution of 1791). This powerful notion—separation of powers—had a double life, one social, the other political, and the social notion articulated by women from the 1600s pre-dated the political theory articulated by Montesquieu later.[30]

Women's Constitutional Demands for a Separation of Powers

What were some of the consequences of these increasing collisions between structures (laws set in place) and events (human agents who ran afoul of them) over two centuries? That question brings us full circle back to the proposed law, Article 13, discussed by the deputies in the National Assembly in 1791. It is instructive to review the contents of that purportedly odious, degrading, tyrannical, unjust Article 13, which in fact the deputies discussed but did not promulgate as the

Law of 1791 (in the Police Code), which reads (in part) as follows:

> [In a marriage] the [legal] charge of adultery can be pursued *only by the husband* and only through the correctional police. . . . [First] A *woman* convicted of this [adultery] offense will be punished, depending on the circumstances, by 1 year, or 18 months, or 2 years of *imprisonment* and by *forfeiture of matrimonial arrangements* established in her favor [by the marriage contract]. [Second] the [wife's] *dowry* will not be confiscated; [but] *the husband will have control of it* no matter what clauses [protecting her dowry] are contained in the marriage ceremony [contract], on the condition, however, that he provide an allowance for board [at the place of imprisonment], at the judge's discretion. [Third] the *husband* at any time can put an end to the [wife's] legal sentence by stating his willingness to take his wife into his home.[31]

In general, these were the same stipulations on female adultery that had been put into practice, case by case, by judges and husbands in the preceding two centuries but never actually written into law. Now in 1791 those old stipulations, instead of being reformed, were being discussed as a full-fledged law applicable only to women. The provisions of this projected Law of 1791 infuriated and confounded Gouges, Aelders, and others who sought equal civil rights before the law for women, just as those stipulations practiced for two centuries earlier had confounded women who were not able to transcend marital regime rule, women who angrily decried a system wherein husbands were "masters," and wives "slaves."[32] There is no doubt why Gouges and Aelders brazenly castigated the revolutionary deputies for their limited vision of reform. While the deputies applied the vaunted principle of "separation of powers" to king and state, they did not apply that principle to husband and household. At the moment they mediated unshared political authority; therefore, they paradoxically confirmed unshared marital authority. Gouges said it all. In her *Declaration*, Article 16, she states that "No society has a constitution without the guarantee of rights and the *separation of powers* . . . ;" and she exemplifies that separation of powers in her guarantee of equality between husband and wife set forth in the model "social contract between man and woman."[33] Aelders said as much. In her *Address*, she declares forthrightly that *"the powers of husband and wife must be equal and separate."*[34] Appropriating theories of governance born of women's separation suits but applied by Montesquieu only to the state, Gouges and Aelders moved them into the civil sphere and thus addressed social problems neglected, on the whole, by "enlightened" *philosophes*.[35]

Olympe de Gouges reckoned astutely that if women failed to obtain equal civil rights in law as members of households, they would fail to qualify as citizens in the state. That is why she pointedly redefines the "natural rights" of humanity linked with Natural Law, which surely criticized the old French Law Canon rubric on Natural Law, biogenetic seminal theory, that endowed man alone with generative capacity. That is why she refers to "that [old] morality, enshrined in political practices now out-of-date," which surely indicted the Family-State Compact of Civil Laws that privileged male authority in the household. That is why she strikes a chilling chord, surely aimed against Moral Law injunctions on female inferiority, when she suggests that women are afraid that men might say again, "Women, what is there in common between you and us?" Most especially, that is why Gouges appended to her *Declaration of the Rights of Woman* (1791) a model social contract guaranteeing equality between husband and wife as co-governors in the household, a social contract that enabled a political one, citizenship, for women.

Etta Palm d'Aelders also understood the political consequences of disavowing a "separation of powers" in the family. That is why she speaks of women enduring "arbitrary authority" for so long, advocates "equality of rights" now, and reminds deputies that the "rights of nature" and Natural Law have been misinterpreted in the past; criticism aimed no doubt at the marital regime system of male governance long underwritten by the French Law Canon and its Natural Law seminal theory. That is why she points directly to the inherent problem of "conjugal [marital] authority" and the necessity for a "social pact" in marriage that guarantees "equal and separate powers" for husband and wife. And most especially, that is why in her *Address from French Citizenesses to the National Assembly*, she furiously refers to Article 13 on female adultery as "barbarous," "despotic," akin to "slavery," "degrading for women's lives," and "odious to the female sex." When she asks the deputies to listen to their hearts, rather than to the "maxims of the jurists of preceding centuries," she calls for repeal of the French Law Canon with its attendant Public Law maxims, "The king is the husband of the kingdom" and "The king never dies," and for repeal of the Family-State Compact of Civil Laws that in her ken tyrannized women by giving men the marital power to remove them from civil life in society.

Why was the tocsin sounded for women in 1791? Why should women wake up? Because by leaving adultery (with its serious penalties) as a female offense and husbands as ultimate arbiters of that offense, the deputies in the National Assembly made three announcements to the public. First, that they intended to reform governance by disassociating civil law and public law, family law and state law; that is, they negated the marital regime system of rule that linked social and political spheres. Second, that they intended to reform state government by maintaining male rule (monarch or regent) but mediate the power of the ruler; that is, they instituted an executive, legislative, and judicial separation of political powers. Third, that they did not intend to reform household governance but would maintain marital regime male rule there unmediated by a separation of powers; that is, they continued to empower husbands as accusers, judges, and executioners. The appeals of Gouges and Aelders for equal civil rights were aimed, as were criticisms of their predecessors in the 1600s, at the burning issue of civil law defining marital rights in the household for very good reason: Because the reform of marital rights through shared powers in the household was absolutely essential before women could transcend subjected status, claim liberty, and seek political citizenship in the state.

In early modern France, the unravelling of these relations of practice from interwoven structures and events, system and action, forces historians to recognize the harbingers of change that hovered all along. In retrospect, for example, there were the passionate discussions of Descartes's mind-body dualism from the 1630s and 1640s, which challenged Aristotelian biology and female inferiority and provoked treatises by women on the subject;[36] the demise of the popular French fable of the bees in the 1670s when the "King bee," who governed the hive so well, turned out upon scientific scrutiny to be a "Queen"[37]; the suppression of Aristotelian views of nature in the 1690s when the "Ovists" successfully challenged the "Spermaticists" on scientific views of generation;[38] the repeated charges made public by women from the 1600s through the 1700s, who brought lawsuits to the streets and indicted husbands before "the public" as despotic "masters" ruling over wives as subjected "slaves;" and the political dangers posed by such rhetoric in a society familiar with analogical equivalents that bound husbands and kings in male governance and one attuned to conditions of slavery in the colonies. That is why kings exited from the marital arena (left to husbands) during the early decades of the 1700s and sought political relief in spiritual, rather than legal, axioms for governance connected with God the Father: king as father, subjects as children.[39] In retrospect as well, the sheer audacity and longevity of the cultural enterprise validating the male right to rule and female exclusion from governance is striking: From forgeries of Salic Law in the 1400s to collapse of the Salic Ordinance under the weight of legal fraud in the 1530s; from legitimation of male right through a French Law Canon from the 1500s through the 1700s to public criticisms of male rule in that period and outright challenges in the 1790s; from confirmation of male rule in the state (with a separation of powers) in the Constitution of 1791 and confirmation of male rule in the household (without a separation of powers) realized in the Code Civil (1803), to modern problems of representative government that denied women the right to vote until 1945.[40]

It is worth pondering the fortunes of women made political aliens in the state, men made natural rulers, during this early modern era of state building for what is revealed about the relations of practice in a process of structuration now present. In the French Republic of the 1990s, past traces of male right continue to vex a democratic state committed to political representation in government, yet governing essentially without women.[41] As a result, the political manifesto, *To Power Women Citizens! Liberty, Equality, Parity* (1992), and the Parity Movement political petition (1993) signed by 289 women and 288 men (symbolizing the 577 members in the National Assembly), call for "democratic parity" to be attained through an equal division of elective offices in the Assembly along male and female lines.[42] This bold political solution—gender parity—directly challenges the centuries-old entrenchment of the male right to govern not just from the French Revolution of 1789, when revolutionary women made valiant bids for inclusion,[43] but from the earlier era of monarchic state building, when kings and officeholders, legists and historians, conceived a French Law Canon that established the male right to rule in household and state.

University of Iowa

Notes

¹ My thanks to the Camargo Foundation, Cassis, France. For the application of this method, interweaving cultural categories, see Sarah Hanley, *The Lit de Justice of the Kings of France: Constitutional Ideology in Legend, Ritual, and Discourse* (Princeton: Princeton Univ. Press, 1983; French edition, Paris: Aubier, 1993); "Engendering the State: Family Formation and State Building in Early Modern France," *French Historical Studies* 16:1 (1989): 4–27; "The Monarchic State: Marital Regime Governance and Male Right," chap. 7, in *Politics, Ideology and the Law in Early Modern Europe*, ed. Adrianna E. Bakos (Rochester: Univ. of Rochester Press, 1994).

² For the theoretical exposition of "the relations of practice" involving cultural categories and the relationships they imply, see Marshall Sahlins, *Islands of History* (Chicago: Univ. of Chicago Press, 1985), chap. 1, on history and culture; Clifford Geertz, *Local Knowledge: Further Essays in Interpretive Anthropology* (New York: Basic Books, 1983); Pierre Bordieu, *Outline of a Theory of Practice* (Cambridge, England: Cambridge Univ. Press, 1977); Anthony Giddens, *Profiles and Critiques of Social Theory* (Berkeley: Univ. of California Press, 1982); as well as Gabrielle M. Spiegel, "History, Historicism, and the Social Logic of the Text in the Middle Ages," *Speculum* 65:1 (1990), 59–86. For the way cultural categories are interwoven in early modern France, see Hanley, "Engendering the State," 4–6, 21; "The Monarchic State"; *The Lit de Justice of the Kings of France*; and *State Building in Early Modern France*.

³ *Les Droits de la Femme* (Paris, n.d. [1971]), Bibliothèque Nationale, E 5568; see this document in the very important collection and commentary of Darlene Gay Levy, Harriet Branson Applewhite, Mary Durham Johnson, eds., *Women in Revolutionary Paris, 1789–1795* (Champagne: Univ. of Illinois Press, 1979): *Declaration of the Rights of Woman and Citizeness*, 87–96 [hereafter cited as *Declaration*]; my translation differs slightly.

⁴ Gouges, *Declaration*, 89 and 92. All brackets and italics in this chapter are mine.

⁵ Ibid., 93; and 94–96, "Form for a Social Contract Between Man and Woman."

⁶ *Adresse des citoyennes françoises à l'Assemblée nationale* (n.d. [summer,

1791]), Bibliothèque Historique de la Ville de Paris, 12,807, Vol. 1, no. 15: 37–40; see this document in Levy, et al., *Women in Revolutionary Paris: Address from French Citizenesses to the National Assembly*, 75–77 [hereafter cited as *Address*]; my translation differs slightly.

⁷ Aelders, *Address*, 75–77.

⁸ On the ways writings (for and against women) reflected social change, see Carolyn C. Lougee, *Le Paradis des femmes: Women, Salons, and Social Stratification in Seventeenth Century France* (Princeton: Princeton Univ. Press. 1976), chap. 1, whose astute recognition of women as central to the process of social mobility, hence targets for attack, still stands. On the way literature, correspondence, and philosophical exegeses, 1600s–1700s, contained social and historical critiques, see Faith E. Beasley, *Revising Memory: Women's Fiction and Memoirs in Seventeenth-Century France* (New Brunswick: Rutgers Univ. Press, 1990), chaps. 2–5; Michelle Longino Farrell, *Performing Motherhood: The Sévigné Correspondence* (Hanover, NH: Univ. Press of New England, 1991); Joan DeJean, *Tender Geographies: Women and the Origins of the Novel in France* (New York: Columbia Univ. Press, 1991), chaps. 1–3; Erica Harth, *Cartesian Women: Versions and Subversions of Rational Discourse in the Old Regime* (Ithaca: Cornell Univ. Press, 1992), chap. 4; and Joan Hinde Stewart, *Gynographes* (Lincoln: Univ. of Nebraska Press, 1993), chaps. 5–6, and 10; as well as the earlier Ian Maclean, *Woman Triumphant: Feminism in French Literature, 1610–1652* (Oxford: Clarendon Press, 1977), introduction; Paul Hoffman, *La Femme dans la pensée des lumières* (Paris: Ophyrs, 1977), 45–52.

⁹ For the way law cases, wherein litigants argued both sides, were set in print, taken from courts into public space, and fired public opinion over social entitlements and then political practices, from the 1600s on, see Sarah Hanley, "Social Sites of Political Practice in France: Lawsuits, Civil Rights, and the Separation of Powers in Domestic and State Government, 1500–1800," *American Historical Review*, 102: 1 (1997): 27–52.

¹⁰ The important legal distinction between the marital regime system empowering husbands (as opposed to a vague notion of a "family model" featuring fathers) was drawn by jurists, who considered the marital model indigenous and French but criticized the family one as foreign and Roman; Hanley, "The Monarchic State", 112, denying the historical efficacy of a concept of "family romance" in this period.

¹¹ For this political debate over female political exclusion (1350s–1530s) and the fraudulent Salic Law introduced in the early 1400s by Jean de Montreuil in a desperate attempt to refute the powerful arguments of Christine de Pizan validating rule by women, see Sarah Hanley, "Salique," *Encyclopédie Politique et Historique des Femmes*, ed. Christine Fauré (Paris: Presses Universitaires de France, 1997); and for a fuller account, see Hanley, "The Politics of Identity and Monarchic Governance in France: The Debate Over Female Exclusion," chap.

13, *Women Writers and the Early Modern British Political Tradition* (Cambridge, England: Cambridge Univ. Press, 1997) ed. Hilda L. Smith.

[12] On the *mos gallicus* method, emphasizing the indigenous origins of French law as opposed to Roman law, and the embarrassment of legists over the collapsed Salic Ordinance, see Donald R. Kelley, *Foundations of Modern Historical Scholarship: Language, Law and History in the French Renaissance* (New York: Columbia Univ. Press, 1970), chaps. 5–8; and for the parliamentary context where those notions were articulated in the new *Lit de Justice* assemblies, first convoked in 1527 and 1537, constitutionally distinguished from ordinary Royal Seances held in the Parliament of Paris, and provided with fictional origins in the medieval past of the 1300s, see Hanley, *The Lit de Justice of the Kings of France*, chaps. 2–4 and Table 1.

[13] The monarchs are Isabella in Spain, Mary Tudor and Elizabeth I in England, Mary Stuart in Scotland, and later, Christina in Sweden; the regents in France, Anne of France, Louise of Savoy, Catherine de Médicis, Marie de Médicis, and later, Anne of Austria. The aggressive behavior of these French regents, determined to take a place in Parlement, is recounted in ibid., chaps. 7, 10, 12, and 13.

[14] See Hanley, *State Building in Early Modern France*; "Engendering the State" on Civil Law in the Family-State Compact, and "The Monarchic State" on public law.

[15] Ibid., 110–13, for further exposition of this *French Law Canon*; and 110, n. 7, on the difference between this powerful early modern French marital maxim sexually tied to male generative capacity, which disallowed rule by women; and the non-sexual limited medieval precursor, the marriage metaphor, likening the ruler of a terrestrial kingdom to the bishop of a spiritual church, which later proved adaptable to female rule as used by the celibate Elizabeth I in England. For the parliamentary context in which these Public Law precepts were articulated, embellished, and refashioned in Lit de Justice assemblies, and especially the most extraordinary one of 1610, see Hanley, *The Lit de Justice of the Kings of France*, chaps. 2–9, Table 1, and engravings.

[16] See *Discours politiques des diverses puissances establies de Dieu du monde, du gouvernement legitime d'icelles, & establies de Dieu du monde, du gouvernement legitime d'icelles, & du devoir de ceux qui y sont assujettis* (anonymous, s.l. 1574), published in Simon Goulart, ed., *Mémoires de l'estat de France, sous Charles neufiesme* (Geneva, 1579), Vol. III, fols. 147v–213r: political power issues from nature, fols. 147v–158v; men as "the source from which children originate" (i.e., semen the source of progeny, fols. 149r–52v, 170r–71v; alien elements introduced by a queen, fol. 171v; the demise of a state with a female ruler, fols. 166v, 193v, 197v; on female defamation, fols. 169v–72r, 182v; and note that "biogenetic seminal theory" the term I have applied to these notions. This tract is further analyzed by Sarah Hanley, "The French Constitution Revised: Representative

Assemblies and Resistance Right in the Sixteenth Century," chap. 2, in Mack P. Hold, ed. *Society and Institutions in Renaissance and Early Modern France* (Athens, Ga: Univ. of Georgia Press, 1991).

[17] See Hanley, "The Monarchic State in Early Modern France," 119–21.

[18] On Jean Bodin, who invented that new maxim in 1576, and others such as Charles Loyseau, Antoine Loisel, Nicolas Bergier, and Pierre Dupuy, who incorporated it into the French Law Canon during the early 1600s, see Hanley, "The Monarchic State," 111–16; and for the parliamentary context, ibid., The Lit de Justice of the Kings of France, chaps. 7, 9, 11, and 13.

[19] Ibid., chap. 11 and plate 9 on the "French Phoenix" (the bird that arises instantly from the ashes of its progenitor).

[20] Consult, "Family and State in Early Modern France: The Marriage Pact," chap. 1, in *Connecting Spheres: Women in the Western World, 1500 to the Present* (New York: Oxford Univ. Press, 1987), eds. Marilyn J. Boxer and Jean H. Quataert, on the procedure of *appel comme d'abus* used by Parliaments to evoke marriage cases from ecclesiastical courts and the French edict (requiring parental consent to marriages) that overrode the church precept (denying a consent requirement).

[21] On the unique French office-holding phenomenon and the Paulette, see Hanley, "Engendering the State," 6–7; and "The Monarchic State," 113–16.

[22] Ibid. 114.

[23] For a full exposition of early modern Moral Law, lessons on female defamation, including engravings related to lawsuits, see Hanley, *State Building in Early Modern France*. For female defamation in general, see Laure Beaumont-Maillet, *La Guerre des sexes; XVe–XIXe siècles: Les albums du Cabinet des Estampes de la Bibliothèque Nationale* (Paris, 1984), and Sara F. Matthews Grieco, *Ange ou diablesse: La représentation de la femme au XVIe siècle* (Paris: Flammarion, 1991).

[24] For the full study of legal cases, see Hanley, *State Building in Early Modern France*, emphasizing the much earlier emergence of public opinion from the 1600s in public spaces and connected with lawsuits brought to "the public," as opposed to the view of Jürgen Habermas, *The Structural Transformation of the Public Sphere: An Inquiry Into a Category of Bourgeois Society*, trans. Thomas Burger (Cambridge, Mass.: Massachusetts Institute of Technology Press, 1989; German edition 1962), chaps. 2–3, who locates that phenomenon much later in the 1750s and specifically connected with salon culture.

[25] Hanley, *State Building in Early Modern France*. The case of Antoine Du Bois du Plessis, seigneur du Plessis-Gastebled versus Marie-Anne Rainssant, daughter of Henry de Rainssant, sieur de Vieux-Maisons is a huge one with over 50 pertinent documents, because Antoine brought another suit against René Choppin [Chopin], seigneur d'Arnouville, Lieutenant Criminel in the Châtelet, also Prévôt and Vicomté in the city of Paris, whom he accused as the partner in adultery, and who in turn brought a suit for defamation against Antoine.

[26] Hanley, *State Building in Early Modern France*. The case of Marguerite Aurillon versus François de Sorny, First Captain of the Grenadiers in the Regiment of the Crown. Here Marguerite recounted the case while imprisoned at the Convent of La Magdeleine.

[27] The procedure is recounted in Hanley, "Engendering the State," 13–14.

[28] Ibid., 15–21, on "counterfeiting culture."

[29] Quotations in Hanley, "The Monarchic State," 122.

[30] For further discussion of Montesquieu's *Persian Letters* (1721) and *Spirit of the Laws* (1748), see Hanley, "Social Sites of Political Practice in France," 40–43.

[31] For the text of Article 13 (*Code de Police*); see *Projet de Loi sur la police municipale et la police correctionelle presenté par le Comité de Constitution; imprimé par ordre de l'Assemblée nationale* (Paris, 1791) as cited in Levy, et al., *Women in Revolutionary Paris*, 76, n. 1, including another provision, "[Fourth] The woman's accomplice [in adultery] will be condemned to a fine of one-eighth of his fortune and to a prison term of three months."

[32] On husband-wife as master-slave, see Hanley, "The Monarchic State," 121–22: In the play of Pierre Matthieu, *Vasthi* (1589), the wife questions the tyrannical rule of husbands, as well as the marital family-state analogy that supports it; among others, Madeleine de Scudéry in her novel, *Artemène ou Le Grand Cyrus* (1649–1653), has the heroine decry marriage as a "long slavery;" as pointed out in Lougee, *Le Paradis des Femmes*, chap. 1, writers in the mid 1600s noted that salon women liken marital subjection to slavery; and Hanley, *State Building in Early Modern France*, especially women who brought court cases to the streets.

[33] Gouges, *Declaration* 92; the contract, 49–96.

[34] Aelders, *Address*, 76.

[35] Hanley, *State Building in Early Modern France*, expands on this argument.

[36] Londa Scheibinger, *The Mind Has No Sex? Women in the Origins of Modern Science* (Cambridge, Mass.: Harvard Univ. Press, 1989), chaps. 6–7; and Harth, *Cartesian Women*, on the women *philosophes*.

[37] See Jeffrey Merrick, "Royal Bees: The Gender Politics of the Beehive in Early Modern Europe," *Studies in Eighteenth-Century Culture*, ed. J. Yolton, 18 (1988), 7–37.

[38] Maryanne Cline Horowitz, "The 'Science' of Embryology Before the Discovery of the Ovum," chap. 4, in *Connecting Spheres*, recounts the arguments.

[39] See Hanley, "The Monarchic State, 121–25, on the expeditious exit and the spiritual rhetoric suggested by Bossuet in the 1680s and soon put to use. For a study of lawsuits in France, which were brought and won by slaves, see Sue Peabody, "*There Are No Slaves in France: The Political Culture of Race and Slavery in the Ancien Regime*" (New York: Oxford Univ. Press, 1996).

[40] Ibid., on the *Constitution of 1791*, tit. 3, chap. 2, sec. 1, art. 1 (constituting

male monarchs and male regents); and the *Civil Code*, art. 213 (citing "laws of nature" to dictate male domination, female subjection in the family).

[41] Christine Fauré, *Democracy Without Women: Feminism and the Rise of Liberal Individualism in France*, trans. Claudia Gorbman and John Berks (Bloomington: Indiana Univ. Press, 1991; French edition, 1985), chaps. 4–6, treats this problem.

[42] See Anne Le Gall, Claude Servan-Schreiber, and Françoise Gaspard, *Au Pouvoir. Citoyennes! Liberté Éqalité, Parité* (Paris: Éditions du Seuil, 1992); and see *Le Monde*, 10 November 1993, for the Parity petition, "Non à l'Assemblée Nationale—Oui à la Parité Hommes\Femmes," on the problem of a National Assembly in which only 6% of elected deputies are women.

[43] Read documents in Levy et al., *Women in Revolutionary Paris*; and Paule Marie Duhet, ed., *Cahiers de doléances des femmes en 1789 et autres textes* (Paris, 1989). For the way the revolutionaries deliberately structured the first French Republic to exclude women, see Joan B. Landes, *Women and the Public Sphere in the Age of the French Revolution* (Ithaca: Cornell Univ. Press, 1988); and for the paradoxes inherent in "natural rights," which subverted attempts to discuss equal rights thereafter, see Joan Wallach Scott, *Only Paradoxes to Offer: French Feminists and the Rights of Man* (Cambridge, Mass.: Harvard Univ. Press, 1996).

DAVID QUINT

Dueling and Civility in Sixteenth-Century Italy

1

THE DUEL IS PART OF THE *LONGUE DURÉE* of the Western cultural imagination. The weapons may change: guns have succeeded if they did not always replace swords. But the fight between individuals to settle private scores has remained a defining ritual of aristocratic identity from the Middle Ages to the present, an identity which the duel defines precisely as individual. The long life of the duel makes it difficult to describe as a historical phenomenon, but it is possible to locate the emergence of its modern form in the sixteenth and seventeenth centuries as doctrines spelling out the grievances of honor, the procedures of challenges and responses, and the rules of combat were codified, largely in Italy, and spread to the rest of Europe. The duel as we know it, as it has entered and shaped a vision of aristocratic or would-be aristocratic culture, is the product of the late Renaissance.[1]

A series of factors determined the way noblemen of this period understood the duel. The military revolution brought about by artillery and massed infantry encounters rendered increasingly obsolete the heavily armored knight on horseback and offered fewer occasions for the gentleman soldier to distinguish himself in single combat. Though the form of the duel followed the new military technology and changed in the course of the sixteenth century from combat on horseback in full armor and knightly regalia to the more lethal, if not necessarily less formal and ceremonial fencing with rapier on foot and everyday clothing, it nonetheless remained colored by chivalric nostalgia, and allowed noblemen, even those whose families had not experienced warfare for several generations, to assert their membership in a traditional military caste. It gave young and sometimes older nobles the chance to prove themselves and experience the excitement of man-to-man fighting with their own peers; the dueling ground might be a more appealing and exclusive arena than the battlefield, where one risked being killed by a pikeman or a stray bullet.[2] The greatest literary treatment of the duel, Corneille's *Le Cid*, contrasts the occasion which the hero Rodrigue has to manifest his personal valor and prowess in his private duels to his conduct in actual warfare, where he plays an executive role as commander of his followers and where individual acts of fighting are lost in the darkness of night and in the anonymity of battle.[3]

The ideology of the duel also reflected the pressure being felt by an aristocracy coming to terms with the emerging power of Early Modern states. Kings and princes sought to curb the old feudal prerogatives of their nobility—not least the prerogative of violence. The gradual transformation of magnates with their own private armies of retainers and clients into pacified courtiers dependent on royal favor has become a familiar story in the historiography dealing with the sixteenth and seventeenth centuries, whether one speaks of Lawrence Stone's period of aristocratic "crisis," or Norbert Elias's longer-term "civilizing process."[4] State and eccclesiastical authorities condemned the duel and punished duelists. But for that very reason, the duel could be attractive to the aristocrat who, through recourse to private violence not so much above as outside the law, could assert a sense of independence that was beginning to disappear in his other power relations with the crown. The duel represented an individual right and equally a psychological disposition that noblemen found hard to give up.

Furthermore, the modern duel was the product of the printing press. A flood of treatises on honor and the duel—and treatises on honor are usually much devoted to the duel—flowed from sixteenth century presses, mostly in Italy. These books, loaded with the terms and methods of scholastic argument which distinguished gradations of insult that are famously lampooned by Shakespeare's Touchstone and which dictated punctilios of combat and fair play—if you are fighting a one-eyed man, should you wear a patch over one eye of your own?—seem highly unreadable now, but they enjoyed a tremendous vogue.[5] They did so not least as a response to the literature on courtesy and civility, Castigione's *Courtier* and della Casa's *Galateo*, that emerged in the same period and that spelled out the new decorum of the nobleman as subject and servant to his prince. At court the nobleman might behave one way, but he had another code, now spelled out for him as elaborately as della Casa's table manners, that told him how to afffirm his honor as an individual and licensed him to defend it, if necessary, with his sword.

But the paradox of this literature and the paradox of the duel as one studies its representations in Renaissance literary texts and in contemporary documents of real duels and challenges, is that violence itself has manners. The duel was as much inside as outside a civilizing process, for it gave a kind of ceremonial containment to the aristocratic violence it simultaneously sanctioned. By individualizing conflict, the duel replaced larger scale encounters between noblemen and their respective retinues of friends and servants—and it is for this reason, Stone has suggested in the case of England, that the crown generally tolerated the duel and pardoned duelists. The elaborate and public exchanges of challenges could, moreover, allow the King and Privy Council to step in and mediate quarrels before they actually came to conflict.[6] The duel also, and this may be much the same thing, replaced the vendetta, as in the history of the Savorgnan and Colloredo families that Edward Muir has studied; their century-old feud came to an end in 1568 when representatives of the families met—and killed each other—in an arranged duel.[7] Even the swordsmanship of the duelist was formalized as the new balletic fencing positions of the Italian masters came to be adapted throughout Europe.

Some nobles grumbled that these ceremonial features robbed fighting of its naked aggression and mayhem—taking the fun out of a pastime that shared features of those other aristocratic diversions, gambling and the blood sport of hunting. Such complaints may have been most frequent in France, where, according to Francois Billacois, combatants were wont to strip down the duel's formulaic procedures to their basics and to seek to fight on the spot, perhaps to avoid interference from the authorities.[8] We may hear a similar impatience in Mercutio's complaints about Tybalt in *Romeo and Juliet*.

> O he's the courageous captain of compliments. He fights as you sing prick-song, keeps time, distance, and proportion; he rests his minim rests, one, two, and the third in your bosom: the very butcher of a silk button, a duelist, a duelist; a gentle-

man of the very first house, of the first and second cause. Ah, the immortal *passado,* the *punto reverso,* the *hay!*[9] (II.iv.18–26)

Tybalt fights by the book, as if he were sight-reading music from the page: he knows the forms of a quarrel and all the fancy moves of swordsmanship. Mercutio almost appears to confuse the deadly serious Tybalt with an impostor like Jonson's Captain Bobadill, and he expresses, as he subsequently appeals to his "grandsire," a horror at Italianate newfangledness (however odd it may sound coming from an Italian) that would seem to associate the duel not so much with old nobiliar values as with an emergent culture of courtly civility.[10] It is significant, perhaps even surprising, to note in the case of Shakespeare's Verona, still caught in the world of the vendetta, of violent encounters between whole households, lords and servants alike, that irate Tybalt may be the representative of a civilizing process still to impose itself, while loveable Mercutio, no less spoiling for a fight and committed as he to an old-fashioned violence untrammeled by the duel's formalities, is the greater threat to civic peace.

2

The paradox inherent in the duel—a kinder, gentler way of killing—was already appreciated by Ariosto in a pair of linked episodes of the *Orlando furioso* (1516) that further examine the relationship between the duel and nobiliar identity. Even as he depicts the duel as part of the system of chivalry—and it would be to the *Furioso* and other chivalric romances that later theorists of the *scienza cavalleresca* would turn for authority as they thought to perpetuate chivalry in the duel[11]—Ariosto subjects both to his famous irony.

At the beginning of Canto 31, Rinaldo of Montalbano and his brothers—the famous four sons of Aymon of the French and Italian romances of chivalry—as well as their cousins are all riding to the aid of Charlemagne, besieged in Paris by the pagan army of King Agramante. On their way they encounter an unknown knight who challenges Ricciardetto, riding in front of the rest, to a joust. Ricciardetto gladly and confidently accepts, but is quickly unhorsed, and he is followed in succession by Alardo and Guicciardetto who similarly end up on the ground. (8–10) Rinaldo now takes the field himself, eager to get the fighting over so that he and his men can get to Paris. In their encounter, neither knight is removed in the least from his saddle and their lances shatter into pieces; but following this equal exchange of blows, Rinaldo's superior horse, Baiardo, collides with and breaks the back of the horse of the unknown knight. To avenge his dying steed, the knight challenges Rinaldo to battle.

> Disse Rinaldo a lui:—"Se 'l destrier morto,
> e non altro ci de' porre a battaglia,
> un di miei ti darò, piglia conforto,
> che men del tuo non crederò che vaglia.—
> Colui soggiunse:—Tu sei malaccorto,
> se creder vuoi che d'un destrier mi caglia.
> Ma poi che comprendi ciò ch'io voglio,
> ti spiegherò più chiaramente il foglio.
>
> Vo' dir che mi parria commetter fallo,
> se con la spada non ti provassi anco,
> e se non sapessi s'in quest'altro ballo
> tu mi sia pari, o se più vali o manco."[12]   (31.16–17.1–4)

[Rinaldo said to him: "If the dead horse and nothing else should get us to battle, I will give you one of mine that, you may take comfort, I do not believe will be worth less than yours." The other replied, "You are not very clever if you think that I care about a horse. But since you don't understand what I want, I will more clearly explicate the page for you. I want to say that it would seem to me to commit a failing if I did not try you as well with a sword, and if I did not know whether you are my equal in this other dance, or whether you are worth more or less than me."]

The stranger knight spells out, as a kind of literary critic glossing a text, the logic of mimetic desire that motivates all the knights of the *Furioso* and that transforms all the objects of their quests—horses, ladies, swords, shields—into so many pretexts for competitive rivalry. It is not the horse that matters, but rather the question of who is the greatest fighter of all, and that question, in turn, boils down to being "more or less"—"*più . . . o manco*"—than another.[13] By the same token, the act of measuring his or her prowess against others' places the knight inside a chivalric code whose adherents may mutually recognize one another.

The issue of recognition is central to Ariosto's episode, where Rinaldo, a full participant of the code, courteously agrees to the single combat requested by his adversary—both of them unknown to one another—and sends his brothers and cousins on ahead of him in order to ensure a fight on equal terms. The two then battle to a draw, each marveling at the other's valor and wondering how he can extricate himself from an encounter fought only for *"disio d'onore"* (22.8) with his honor intact (23.7; 25.3). Darkness at last intervenes, and Rinaldo invites the stranger knight to put off fighting until the following day and meanwhile to join him and his brothers in their pavilions. It is here that the latter realizes that he has been fighting none other than Rinaldo and reveals his own identity: He is Guidon Selvaggio, the bastard brother of Rinaldo, and thus one more son of Aymon, who has come to France precisely to be reunited with his kindred (31). Rinaldo repeatedly embraces (32) this new addition to the family and notes that

> per certificarne che voi sete
> di nostra antiqua stirpe un vero ramo,
> dar miglior testimonio non potete,
> che 'l gran valor ch'in voi chiaro proviamo.   (31.33.1–4)

[to certify that you are a branch of our ancient stock you cannot give better testimony than the great valor that we have clearly experienced in you.]

Guidon has not only shown that he belongs as a knight, but as a member of one of the great chivalric lineages. The episode conflates the idea of a brotherhood of arms—what will allow Shakespeare's Henry V to address his army at Agincourt as "we band of brothers;/ For he to-day that sheds his blood with me/Shall be my brother" (4.3.60–62)—with literal brotherhood and a mystifying notion of aristocratic pedigree. If the first case suggests a kind of blood brotherhood, the second argues for a blue blood that will tell in martial prowess and honor. As *Mad* magazine once commented on a modern incarnation of the chivalric clan in the television western—the Cartwright family in *Bonanza*, where each of the sons of Ben Cartwright was born from a different mother—"the family that slays together, stays together."[14]

Ariosto pairs this episode with another that concludes the same Canto 31. Rinaldo, Guidone, and their kindred have reached Paris and their intervention is decisive in routing the pagan army of Agramante and driving it in retreat from Paris all the way to Arles. In the midst of the fighting, Rinaldo is confronted by the pagan king Gradasso (90f.), who reproves him for not having shown up to fight a prearranged combat in an episode near the opening of Boiardo's *Orlando innamorato* (1.5.7f.), the predecessor poem to the *Furioso*; the winner was to have obtained possession of Baiardo, Rinaldo's wondrous steed. Now, some 95 cantos of poetry later, Rinaldo seeks to explain his absence and asserts that he will give Gradasso the lie if the pagan champion claims that he, Rinaldo, ever shirked his chivalric duty—*e sempre che tu dica mentirai,/ch'alla cavalleria mancass'io mai* (31.99.7–8). Here the poem specifically invokes the terms of the dueling code, according to which the man who is given the lie is required to fight to wipe away the imputation of dishonor. Gradasso is content to accept Rinaldo's explanation, whatever doubts he may harbor about it (103), in order to return to their earlier quarrel over Baiardo. Rinaldo has promised to fight for possession of the horse just as they had originally agreed. He now invites Gradasso to lodge with him that night (106), much as he had earlier offered lodging to Guidon Selvaggio; although Gradasso refuses, the two knights show the greatest signs of courtesy to each other when they meet the next morning alone at a chosen field.

> s'accarezzaro, e fero a punto a punto
> così serena et amichevol fronte,
> come di sangue e d'amistà congiunto
> fosse Gradasso a quel di Chiaramonte. [31.110.3–6]

[they embraced and indeed each showed such open and friendly countenance as if Gradasso were joined to the lord of Chiaramonte by blood and amity.]

Where Rinaldo discovers his half-brother Guidon Selvaggio through fighting him, here he treats the pagan enemy Gradasso, whom he is about to fight, like family or at least like an old family friend. The juxtaposition of the two episodes, linked by their positions at the beginning and end of the canto, is typical of Ariosto's procedure in the *Furioso;* his interlace technique allows for ironic similarities and relationships to emerge among apparently independent narrative strands within the poem. In both instances, the paladins are fighting over a horse—Guidon Selvaggio's horse killed by Baiardo and then Baiardo himself—but the horse is relatively unimportant. What interests the fighters is the fight itself and the occasion it gives them to enter into the system of emulation and competition that is chivalry—where even enemies of rival faiths can recognize their underlying kinship. Ariosto's attitude towards this aristocratic ideology is, as usual, distanced and potentially satiric. For if his knights may discover that their prowess and allegiance to chivalric norms make them all brothers, chivalry and its duels turn into fratricide.

Through his chivalry, Ariosto's Guidon Selvaggio demonstrates that he is, although a bastard, a true son of Aymon: the willingness to fight in the duel's honorable mode of single combat becomes the badge of noble identity. We may find a real-life parallel to the fiction of the *Furioso* from the poet's Duchy of Ferrara in a letter written by Count Galeotto Pico, lord of Mirandola, to his lord, Duke Ercole II d'Este in 1548, some sixteen years after the third and final version of Ariosto's poem. Beginning with the legal formula, *Dico e per li presenti faccio fede*, the letter is an affidavit describing an event in the streets of Mirandola involving the Count's cousin through an illegitimate branch of the family, the similarly named Galeotto d'Ettor Pico.[15] It is preserved in the collection of documents concerned with affairs of honor under the heading *Duelli e sfide*, in the Este archive in the Archivio di Stato in Modena.

> I say and I give faith to those present that the case was of this sort, that as Battista Signoretto was walking beneath the Palace with Leandro dell'Usana, Messer Galeotto d'Hettor Pico who had come there began angrily to say to him, "Are you that wretched, rascally coward" [*triste furfante poltrone*], with other similar insulting words, "who has been ordered to send a killer to my house?" To which Battista responded that he was a man of honor [*uomo da bene*] and that it was not true

that he had sent a killer to his house. When Messer Galeotto continued to say the same thing to him, Battista gave him a lie [*gli diede una mentita*], whereupon Galeotto, having put his hand to his sword, advanced upon him to strike him. Battista, who also had his sword in hand, went ever backing away and saying that he did not want to have it out with him because he bore him respect [*per avergli rispetto*], at which time, Messer Galeotto, seeing that he could not strike him because he was backing away, hurled his sword at him. The sword was repelled by Giovanni Trinco with his own, which he removed from its scabbard in order to separate them, and there was a danger that Messer Galeotto would have hit Battista if Giovanni Trinco had not intervened. After this as Messer Galeotto continued to insult him and to say to him "poltroon, you are running away," Battista who was already outside of the portico of the Palace, gave him the lie [*lo mentì*] another time. Shortly afterwards, after Messer Galeotto had withdrawn inside the workshop of Francesco Zalotto while Signoretto went into the house of Leandro, Signoretto returned beneath the palace while Messer Galeotto was walking, whereupon Messer Galeotto, seeing him turning to go home, said to him certain words that indicated that he was superior to [*era di più del*] Signoretto, to which Signoretto replied, "Yes, in riches." To which Messer Galeotto answered him, "In riches and in blood, and in every other thing, you coward," and put his hand to his sword and ran towards him, but he turned his back to him without drawing his sword, and fleeing, bumped into a bench and fell with his hands on the ground, during which time Messer Galeotto was grabbed, kept apart, and restrained by Messer Pagano.

Galeotto Pico, Count of Mirandola
May 11, 1548[16]

Whatever truth may lie behind Galeotto d'Hettor Pico's suspicion that Battista Signoretto is involved in a possibly murderous conspiracy against him, their public quarrel turns into a defense of personal honor—of Signoretto who claims to be a *huomo da bene* and therefore above underhanded means, of Pico, who twice given the lie, demands the satisfaction of wiping this slur against his honor away with his sword. Signoretto backs out of the fight, depending on the intervention of bystanders and friends, because he claims to have respect for Pico—and because, we may assume, he knows better than to fight a Pico, even an illegitimate one, in Mirandola. The connected issues of respect and illegitimacy emerge when the quarrel ignites a second time after the two men have apparently cooled off indoors. Like Ariosto's Guidon Selvaggio, Pico wants to measure himself against his adversary and to establish that he is worth more: "*di più;*" he reaches for his sword again when Signoretto is willing to concede that Pico is his superior only in a wealth that might belong to a merchant or tradesman: "and in blood," cries the irate Pico, asserting the nobility of his lineage. The drawing of his sword, his engaging in this public display of his fighting disposition, in fact, demonstrate—and demand recognition from others—that he is a real Pico. The letter from his cousin the Count, his namesake, that describes the events for their mutual superior, the Duke, may be a token of just such recognition. As Rinaldo welcomed Guidon Selvaggio into the family, Count Galeotto testifies to the noble behavior of his relation—at the comic expense of the retreating, stumbling Signoretto. These stories of bastard brothers revealing their innate nobility may be emblematic of the legitimizing role the duel played for the aristocracy at large. The function of the duel as a form of conflict resolution was at least balanced in importance by the occasion it gave for the ritualized display of those qualities—fighting skill, courage, reckless exposure to risk—that were supposed to define membership in a noble class.

3

If the duel revealed the nobility of those who fought it, it also set a standard for honorable fighting in the aristocratic imagination. Other forms of violence were assessed by how closely they approximated the situation of the duel: its single combat on equal terms. The model of the duel lies behind the verdicts that Bernardo Canigiani, the Florentine ambassador to Ferrara in the latter part of the sixteenth century, delivers on the protagonists of two contrasting anecdotes concerning honor and vengeance that he reports in his typically chatty diplomatic letters to the Medici Grand Duke Cosimo I. On the 30th of June, 1572, he relayed the latest gossip of the city.

> On Thursday evening, when he was returning from court at two at night, the Cavalier Gualengo found in his house a young brother of Doctor Quaresima, who went hiding himself from room to room, and in the last, instead of answering who he was, drew his sword, which he carried naked, at the Cavalier, who parried it with his left hand, protected by a glove, and answered him with so many swordthrusts [*stoccate*] that he died: then they say, he wanted to kill his wife, who is well on in years, ugly, and crippled, and mother of five or six children, two of whom already have beards [*assai ben vecchietta, brutta, et storpiata, et madre di 5 o 6 figliuoli che 2 hanno la barba*]; but she had fled next door into the house of Count Palla Strozzi. Others save her honor by telling it in some other way that has likelihood. The Cavalier immediately presented himself [to the Duke] at the Castle, and will be absolved of the homicide in a few days: he is truly a gentleman of many virtues and honorable qualities.[17]

This vignette of violated honor and deadly vengeance reads like an attempted "Divorce, Italian Style" of the sixteenth century. Canigiani is suspicious: Why would the unfortunate brother of Doctor Quaresima be interested in the Cavalier's old and unattractive wife? Had he been set up in a plot that had for its true aim the killing of Lady Gualengo? In a letter two days later on July 2, the ambassador can jokingly refer to the younger Quaresima's death by "mal di punta" as he recounts that Gualengo had wounded him no less than thirty-two times, but he also notes that there is something wrong with Gualengo's story: "The warp does not correspond with the rest of the cloth."[18] Nonetheless, much as Canigiani had predicted, Gualengo was absolved by his lord, the Este Duke Alfonso II, to whose justice he had immediately surrendered himself and appealed. And Canigiani himself cannot help but admire the prowess and honorable qualities of the Cavalier Gualengo, especially when the Cavalier employs them to defend his person and his honor.

Almost a year later, in a letter of June 22, 1573, Canigiani reports another episode of honor affronted and redeemed.

it happened that as the Cavalier Malvagia of Bologna, together with his son, was talking inside the courtyard with a Bolognese soldier, he unwarily came to blame and criticize a certain Bolognese gentleman who was the creature of the Malvezzi family: whence the soldier, when he found Malvagia outside the courtyard, said to him that he lied in the words that he had spoken in freedom [*in Franchigia*] shortly before to the prejudice of the honor of his friend. Malvagia answered that he did not want the lie and that he was speaking in jest: Later, being rebuffed by the Duke, and told that he did not want him in his household with such a mark of disgrace, he was helped out by Signor Cornelio [Bentivoglio] and by Contugo, the head of all the militia of the city, so that his opponent was attacked all in a flash in the courtyard by two men with cudgels and blows, and also received a sword wound to the head from Malvagia, who had for a shield all of the household of Signor Cornelio and one hundred and fifty swords. I would rather wish to be the wounded victim than Malvagia, who brought about this vengeance with such unfair odds [*superchieria*] and cowardice.[19]

Canigiani's story is striking for the way in which the courtyard [*Cortile*] defines a private space where talk is supposed to be free and candid. But Cavalier Malvagia finds that such talk has consequences once it is reported outside the courtyard in the public world. We are made to feel something of the often-noted paranoia of the Renaissance court, where the courtier was under the constant scrutiny of others and it was impossible to trust the confidentiality of one's interlocutor: Malvagia has his son along with him and he makes the mistake of extending a familiar conversation to a third party. Malvagia is first branded as a coward because of his attempts to dismiss his talk as a joke in order not to be given the lie, and hence be obliged to challenge his opponent to a duel. Since the opponent in this case is a soldier, Malvagia looks unwilling to take on a professional swordsman. The soldier may also be too far beneath Malvagia's class to merit the recognition of a duel; Malvagia at least seems to treat him this way in the vengeance he metes out on him in the form of a beating. But this vengeance only confirms the charge of cowardice, since Malvagia is backed by two thugs and a large troop of armed retainers. The attack on the poor soldier takes place back *inside* the courtyard, that is, as a kind of private ambush rather than as a public requital for the public affront of the lie. It is as if Malvagia and his backers know that the overwhelming odds they use should be kept hidden. The facts, nonetheless, come out, and while the blot on Malvagia's honor may be officially washed away by violence, he may still be a coward in the court of public opinion, at least in the opinion of Canigiani.

Canigiani's response in the two cases is instructive. He may suspect Gualengo's story and have some sympathy for Malvagia whose confidence was betrayed; but it is Gualengo, drawing his sword and fighting hand-to-hand in single combat, who wins his admiration. Gualengo's fight looks like the duel on honorable terms that Malvagia should have fought.

In both anecdotes, however, the final arbiter of honor is Duke Alfonso, who, it appears, not only condones Gualengo's killing of the armed intruder in his house, but also virtually orders Malvagia to remove his stain of dishonor if he wishes to remain at court, a command that the captains of his military forces, Bentivoglio and Contugo, promptly help to carry out. Malvagia may in fact have had little choice in how he fashioned his revenge. By sanctioning such settlements of cases of honor, the prince exerts his control over the individual use of violence in his state.

We may get some idea of the official ideology of honor and the duel in late *cinquecento* Ferrara, and of the relationship of the duel to the authority of the prince and state, in the *Discorsi* of Annibale Romei, published in 1585, translated into English as *The Courtiers Academie* in 1598.[20] The week of seven daily dialogues that comprise the work are set in the court of Alfonso II and feature notable court figures as their speakers. The speaker of the third and fourth days, which treat respectively of honor and the duel, is none other than the Cavalier Camillo Gualengo, the gallant avenger of his honor and would-be wife-killer. Gualengo was, in fact, a long-time crony and servant of the Duke; he had been his ambassador to Spain, where he was awarded the order of Santiago, hence his title of "Cavalier," and to Rome, where his contacts aided him to retain position in Ferrara after the death of Alfonso and the devolution of the city to the States of the Church; he was appointed to the position of tutor to the Aldobrandini nephews of the Pope. According to an early seventeenth-century historian, Gualengo "managed arms with great art, agility, and courage. He was a most beloved companion to Duke Alfonso II...."[21] It is little wonder that the Florentine ambassador expected his quick release from ducal custody after his killing of the intruder in his house in 1572.

The few documents that survive about Gualengo suggest, moreover, that he had a life-long engagement with matters of honor. In a letter from his early years, sent from Venice in September 6, 1553, he writes to Duke Ercole II of a run-in with the law.

> These most lofty gentlemen have expedited my case, and because it has seemed to them that I committed an error in putting a hand to my arms in defense of my honor they have banished me for a year from Venice and my servant for three years with the usual protestations, which since it has thus been determined by their most prudent council and state, I too will say that it has been excellently done....[22]

Gualengo can scarcely conceal his contempt for the *altissimi signori* of Venice and for their prudence—a normal attitude of Italian gentlemen towards the Venetian merchant patriciate—and we sense that the city magistrates were wise to get rid of this young aristocratic hothead spoiling for a fight and chafing at their control:[23] The honor he seeks to defend is identical to his freedom to defend it.

Later in Gualengo's life, this sense of honor appears to have taken a more refined, less impulsive turn. As the mature counselor of Alfonso II, and when he had perhaps reached an age where he was no longer fit for combat, Gualengo had become an expert on *materia dell'honore* and *stile cavalleresco*; in 1595, he prepared for Duke Alfonso a memorandum about the precise language to use in deciding disputes of honor between the Duke of Parma and the Duke of Mantua, and between the Duke of Parma and the Marchese del Vasto. Such disputes were in the fullest sense formal, since these princes were not about to descend into the field to fight one another: Gualengo's role was to bring about a peaceful reconciliation which satisfied the honor of all parties. He considered the formula that put the blame on "the lying reports of some persons" that had "given birth if not, as they are wont, to exacerbations and hatred, at least to suspicions and disdain in the minds" of the princes; he objected to the verb "given birth" [*partorito*] because it suggested that the disdain was bred inside and was thus partly the product of those princely minds, leaving their owners still accountable.[24] This punctilious attention to verbal detail shows that Gualengo had read through the dueling treatises of the sixteenth century, most notably the *Dialogo dell'honore* of Giovan Battista Possevino and *Il duello* of Girolamo Muzio.[25] It is as just such another authority on the formulas of the duel, of insults, challenges, and, most importantly, of reconciliation that Gualengo is presented in Romei's book, where he cites these and other treatises, and which is itself one more such treatise.

These few episodes from the life of the historical Gualengo suggest, in their contrast of youth and age, also a divergence between rival concepts of honor and the duel: honor as the property of a fiercely independent individual ready to uphold it with violence, honor as subject to elaborate pseudo-legalistic codes of comportment that work to contain violence and that connive with, if they are not promulgated by, state power—roughly the divergence between the emphases of Billacois's and and Stone's accounts of the duel in France and England. This divergence and the conflict in aristocratic ideology it makes manifest can be traced through the views that Romei's fictional Gualengo expresses on the duel on the fourth day of the *Discorsi*.

Gualengo begins by asserting unequivocally that duels are "no longer in use, having been removed from the Christian republic by the supreme pontiffs and Christian princes," by 1585 an almost obligatory nod to the condemnation of the duel at the Council of Trent.[26] In 1573, Alfonso II had himself passed an edict against dueling that was renewed in 1578. The fictive Gualengo of the *Discorsi* goes on to spell out the political logic that lies behind the efforts of the authorities to suppress the duel.

> It is contrary to both civil and divine laws, because it is permitted by neither one nor the other of these laws that an individual should dispose either of his or of another's life, since the law considers the individual not as his own, but as belonging to his country and to the prince to whose rule he is subject.[27]

In an argument that parallels religious and civil injunctions against suicide, Gualengo asserts that one's life is not one's own, and neither, it appears, is one's honor. The injured party is instructed to take his case to the magistrates and lawcourts: "this battle between individuals, which is called a duel," says Romei's Gualengo, "will never be licit, as long as the individuals have a prince, laws, and magistrates, to whom belong the avenging of injuries, and the ending of all the differences that may arise among individuals."[28] Recourse to higher authorities prevents and takes the place of the risky and undesirable violence of the duel that appears to receive Gualengo's categorical condemnation: "Nobody in their right mind would choose to put his life, honor, and soul in jeopardy as do the combatants in the *steccato* [the dueling lists]."[29]

Yet the ritual language of the duel may still have its uses: It can help to defuse conflicts that might lead to violence, as Romei indicates in an added subsection to the dialogue, "On the Way to Make Peace and Reconcile Quarrels." Gualengo gives the following example.

> Let us take the case that the injurer has said to the injured: you are a traitor, and after having received the lie, has given him a slap or done some other offensive deed; should he wish to restore honor, he will say: having been misinformed, I entered into the opinion that you were a traitor, and therefore some days ago I called you such, and I also struck you: now, having been satisfied of the truth, I confess that you are not a traitor, whence esteeming you a man of honor [*uomo da bene*], and a man to revenge yourself on me, as much because of the injury I have done you by words as that by deeds, and having repented my offense to you, I ask you to be my friend.[30]

As was the case in the real-life Gualengo's memorandum to reconcile the quarreling princes, misled as they were said to have been by the "lying reports" of certain unnamed persons, here, too, the disputant backs out of the quarrel by claiming to be the victim of misinformation. Especially important is the formula whereby he acknowledges that the party he has injured is capable of revenge, *uomo da risentirvi contro di me*—a phrase that restores his honor to him without necessarily constraining him to act on that capability. Romei's Gualengo remarks that "suppose that in making peace, one cannot distribute honor equally, and that therefore some deception is necessary, these words are most proper; because since they can be interpreted in different ways, they are most apt to satisfy."[31]

This last bit of casuistry, frankly admitted, suggests just how far the dueling code could become an instrument in the "civilizing process": how a code ostensibly dedicated to an older ethos in which the nobleman's honor was only as good as his word and the defense of that word justified any recourse to violence now promotes the compromise of the white lie. The duel is itself outlawed, but its verbal formulas survive to allow peace with honor: They consitute an extra-legal code by which the society of honor can peacefully regulate itself and as such parallel the civic laws themselves. The authorities who adjudicate honor become much like lawyers. Romei's Gualengo remarks, "the matter of duels belong to jurists and not to moral philosophers,"[32] and he points out that Muzio and other writers on the duel had been lawyers.

But the Gualengo of Romei's treatise leaves open certain loopholes that qualify this vision of gentlemen peacefully redressing personal affronts either in the court of law or the court of honor. Aristotle, he says, does not, like the stoic, deprive man of his affections, but rather wants him to moderate them with reason and to bring them to a state of mediocrity or balance:

> it is necessary therefore that in the instant when a man is offended that he will become angry; and therefore it will be licit for him in that moment to feel and act upon his resentment to the extent that he can and that is honorable; not to do so is to fall into the vice of insensibility or stolidity.[33]

It is only natural for the offended party to become angry and to strike back then and there, and the laws acknowledge as much. But, by the same token, once he has had a chance to cool off and reason has regained control over his emotions, a recourse to arms is no longer appropriate: "Once the occasion is past, it is not right that in cold blood, as one would say, that one do anything further by one's own valor."[34] This distinction rules out the formal duel, fought after the fact—and it suggests the logic of the behavior of those Frenchmen described by Billacois who sought to dispense with the ritual procedures and get down to fighting. Gualengo spells out the sequence of possible redress.

> His resentment will be just who, in the instant that he is offended, seeks to repel the injury with his own valor: and it is just, because he does what is permitted by the laws of nature and civic laws, which make it lawful to repel force with force, and when he cannot do so, either because of the unfair advantage of his opponent or because of some other impediment, he is obliged after the fact to have recourse to the magistrates, and to seek vengeance from them rather than from the duel, so that the magistrates and laws will not seem to have been created in vain in the city.[35]

The man of honor can freely resort to violence as long as he doesn't waste any time about it. Under the cover of legality, Romei's Gualengo sanctions the most lawless behavior, the act of rash, unthinking anger. It is perhaps similar to the behavior of the historical Gualengo reaching for his sword in Venice, repelling force with force against young Quaresima, seeking to kill his wife in a *delitto di passione*.

This concession to what Gordon Braden, following Shakespeare's Kent in *King Lear* has called "anger's privilege," what we may see as the class privilege of the aristocrat to anger, is followed by an even more dramatic reversal on the part of Romei's Gualengo—in the very section of the dialogue devoted to making peace and reconciling quarrels.[36]

For he notes that while the victim of an affront to honor should have recourse to law courts, he who seeks his own redress, even after the moment of anger has past, will find his deeds sanctioned by public custom and opinion:

> but this sin is so much warranted by custom, that the man who returns injury, even if he takes revenge in cold blood, is held in much more honor than he who has recourse to the magistrates, since recourse to the magistrates, according to the common abused perception, arouses the suspicion of little valor and impotence: and to take vengeance by oneself demonstrates the contrary.[37]

Gualengo's opinion wins ready assent from his interlocutors in Romei's dialogue, because, one of them replies, "it does not depart from the common usage of noblemen [*cavalieri*] and of those who make a profession of arms, who would think themselves stained, rather unworthy to bear arms, if for the vengeance of a received injury, they availed themselves of the laws and magistrates rather than of themselves."[38] But to acknowledge the claims of aristocratic honor and of its time-honored customs of expression is tantamount to licensing the custom of the duel itself, the private combat arranged and fought in cold blood against which Gualengo and Romei's treatise have taken such an unequivocal stand. It is no wonder that the other Ferrarese gentlemen of the *Discorsi*, who have listened to him so far with a certain amount of skepticism, are now relieved to find that Gualengo is one of the boys after all.

What then is one to make of Romei's contradictory positions on the duel, which seem to parallel the contrasting positions of the historical Gualengo as hotblooded young swordsman and as older and wiser peacemaker? Set in the confines of the court of Alfonso II, Romei's dialogue suggests the contradictory impulses and problems of identity felt by the noble class in the period of early-modern state-building. Romei continues to recognize and consent to the indulgence in violence and anger that had been a traditional hallmark of aristocratic selfhood, while he nonetheless argues for the submission of cases of honor to the jurisdiction of the laws and magistrates, to the authority of prince and church. It is as if the Ferrarese noblemen of his dialogue wish to feel that they always have the option of fighting for their honor—for fighting seems to be the only means by which the noble individual can authenticate his personal honor, which is, if not identical to, at least inseparable from his belonging to a class that has the honor of fighting. At the same time, this rugged individualism already seems somewhat nostalgic in an increasingly civil and law-abiding society whose aristocratic members may, in fact, be disinclined to risk their lives in single combat: You would have to be out of your mind, says Romei's Gualengo. Similarly, the nobleman who envisioned exercising violence above or outside the law might feel that he still belonged to a world of feudal independence even as he recognized his changed role in a new political formation that wrested power away from local magnates and vested it in the prince, whose rule of law sought to replace custom and prerogative—including the custom of the duel. The duel that Romei condemns and condones can, in fact, be seen as a kind of social compromise. If on the one hand it allowed the aristocrat to enjoy an ideal self-image as the defender of his honor and his class, on the other it conferred upon the actual practice of violence a ritualization and quasi-legal form that allowed for mediation both by higher authorities and by the combatants themselves—who might find the proper formulas by which to back out of fighting with their respective honors intact. It was equally important to have the right to a duel in order to vindicate one's personal honor and to know that a duel need not lead to a fight to the death.

4

Similar ambivalences—the duel as the assertion of the nobleman's independent right to violence, the duel as aristocratic violence carefully ritualized and subject to princely supervision—can be read into accounts of highly formal and ceremonial duels fought in Italy a few decades before the *Discorsi* and to which Romei's work seems to hearken back. These duels were fought before the edicts of Trent had been adopted, when the authorities—often minor lords—were still willing to offer a field of battle to the contending parties. One celebrated combat, attended by a large viewing public, took place in 1558 between Count Camillo Forni, a subject of the Duke of Ferrara, and Signor Lanfranco Fontana.[39] They had been granted a field of battle within the neighboring Duchy of Mantova by the lord of Gazzuolo, Federico Gonzaga, head of a lateral branch of the Gonzaga family. It was this Federico Gonzaga who offered a report of their encounter to the Ferrarese Duke, and who repeatedly attempted to act as peacemaker in the affair.

> Being conducted into the lists in my domain of Gazuolo, where I had granted them a free field, since I was desirous that these gentlemen should make peace together, I went before Signor Lanfranco, warmly beseeching him, that he would be content to remit his differences to me, who accepted them on my honor. He answered me that Captain Camillo had requested the combat, and that he was here to that effect. I returned to beseech him again as before, and he answered me to a greater degree, that I was not his man, and that I should speak with his sec-

ond; I, leaving the said Fontana still inside the lists, went to Captain Camillo, who was in his lodging next to the lists, he, too, armed and on horse, in the same way that the aforementioned Fontana was, and there I began to exhort him and persuade him to make peace with Fontana, remitting to me his quarrels and differences on my honor. He answered me that he was my servant, but that he could not, and would not, neither for me, nor another, since he had not wished to consent to the Most Excellent Lordship the Duke, his master.

I then gave him license to enter into the lists, where he had his back to the sun, and Fontana was facing it, who wished to know if he was supposed to be standing there; I answered him that it had been decided by lot, whereat he was appeased. The signal given at once by the drum (as is the custom), they both courageously came to blows in combat, in which assault Signor Fontana had a wound and a little blood, and one heard him say, disconcerted on horseback, "Alas." I then went forward to them and began to speak to them of peace and accord, with the most illustrious Signor Ludovico, brother of the Most Excellent Lordship the Duke of Mantova, the most illustrious Signor Andrea Gonzaga, and Signor Alfonso Gonzaga of Catelgifreto, who were with me inside the lists, exhorting and beseeching them many times, one and the other, to remit their difference to me, which I accepted on my honor.

They remained obdurate, rather they besought us to let them proceed, whence, knowing them so determined, we gave place to them, and with as much heart and boldness as any Cavalier in the world can show, they both intrepidly came to blows in combat, most valorously and with great courage, and stayed fighting for a good space with this assault. And then as they drew apart somewhat in order to return to close with each other and renew their struggle, I, with those most illustrious aforementioned lords, entered between them, beseeching and exhorting them in the best way that I knew and could, those most illustrious lords who were together with me doing the same, now with one, now with the other, that they should be appeased and remit their quarrels and differences to me. Neither of them ever wanted to do or say it; nonetheless, I never ceased trying, saying that they were most honored cavaliers, and that they had shown to all the world their heart, bravery, and valor. But for all that they never were content to remit to me their said quarrel and differences.

While they stood in these parleys, it happened that the nail of the right shoulder armor of Captain Camillo had been prised loose, whereat Signor Lanfranco said to him "Captain Camillo I am content to do you a courtesy: have that right shoulder-plate nailed."

He answered, "I am grateful to you, and I accept it." Then Fontana, showing that the guard of his sword was bent so that he could no longer use it as he intended before, said to me, "Signor, my sword is broken." And I answered, "One cannot call this sword broken." Then Captain Camillo said to me, "Signor, since he has done a courtesy to me, I am content to use another to him: Let him be given a new sword." Immediately the most illustrious Signor Andrea gave another sword to Fontana, but not for this did I and these most illustrious lords stop beseeching them to make peace, and to remit their said quarrel to me, nor with all this did either of them ever consent to do so.

While we were in this interval of the parley, the most Excellent Lord Duke of Mantua, who was at a window to see this combat, sent to tell me through the most illustrious Count Francesco of Nuvolara that I should detain them until His Excellency came into the lists, and so it was done. When the Duke arrived, he began with words to beseech one and the other of these combatants and valiant Cavaliers, that they should give to him their differences and quarrels, since they had given a good account and glorious taste of their prowess and valor; in the same manner as before, they did not want to hear of it. Nonetheless His Excellency did not stop beseeching and exhorting them once more that they remit their differences to him, who took them upon his honor. His Excellency was answered by Captain Camillo that he could not do so because he had denied this to his Most Excellent Lordship the

Duke his lord and master. His Revered Excellency answered him that this did not matter at all: Even though he had not gratified that lord of his, he nonetheless must do what he was asked, for he knew that the Duke of Ferrara would be satisfied and would hold it dear, since they were such valiant cavaliers.

Even for this the said Forni did not make other answer, whereat, the affair standing in this manner, his Excellency now with one, now with the other, and neither of them resolved, the Duke returned to beseech them once more. Then, since neither wanted to speak before the other, he made them content both at one time to raise their swords, which they held in their fists in the sign of peace and faith. Then the said Signor Lanfrano and Captain Camillo, at those exhortations and prayers of His Excellency, raised their swords in the same moment. The Duke immediately dismounted from his horse and ordered that they too dismount, and so they did, whereupon he made them both embrace in the sign of peace, since they could not make any other sign.

After this, Captain Camillo, having emerged outside the lists, was found himself to be wounded by a nothing wound, from which a little blood had issued. In this way the combat came to a glorious end, in which the said Cavaliers spoke to one another with such modesty that no Cavalier in the world could speak with more, nor will anyone henceforth be able to say that one or the other fell short in any way, for in effect both have fought similarly with great courage, and as valiant Cavaliers, and as greater faith and witness of the truth the present will be affirmed by our own hand and sealed with our greatest seal.[40]

This account, as formalized as the event it reports, appears to describe the duel as it should be, satisfactory to all parties, a duel with a happy ending. The noble antagonists were mounted on horseback and dressed in full armor, like characters from the romances of chivalry; they fought with heavy dueling swords. While it was possible to be badly injured in such combat—as happened to one Galeazzo Casaburri della Cava, as well as to his horse, wounded respectively in the throat and in the eye, in a duel fought in front of the Duke of Ferrara at San Martino—the heavy armor and weapons protected the duelists and slowed down their attacks on one another. Rather than a quick and skillful exchange of rapier strokes between lightly clothed combatants, the form that the duel would take by the end of the century, this fighting took the form of a deliberate, ritualized exchange of blows.

Such prolonged combat both allowed for the reciprocity between the two fighters upon which the account insists and, because it required them to pause to rest, presented occasions for the mediation of peacemakers. Forni and Fontana both receive small wounds, both have the opportunity to show their courtesy in battle to the other, both stubbornly reject offers of peace from the presiding lords, both refuse to be the first to stop fighting. Only the intervention of the Duke of Mantua himself, whose presence as an outside observer is revealed as a kind of surprise, can bring their fighting to an end—but not before both noblemen are allowed to assert their autonomy in matters of private honor from the prince.

We would probably be right to suspect that Forni and Fontana had been counting on the eventual mediation and cessation of the duel by the authorities. This is what the authorities were there for: The great scandal of the famous 1547 duel of Jarnac in France was caused by Henri II's failure to stop the duel before Jarnac's defeated victim, La Châtaigneraye, bled to death.[41] At the duel in San Martino the Duke of Ferrara stepped in to save the wounded and bleeding Galeazzo Casaburri—"the most illustrious Duke, who had intervened to reconcile them before they fought, entering onto the field on horseback, and withdrawing a space most justly wishing not to prejudice either one of them, and knowing at last that Signor Galeazzo was growing weak for the great effusion of blood said to him, 'surrender yourself to me, man of honor [*homo da bene*],' *and he did not want to consent to it....*"[42] (My emphasis.) The injured Galeazzo's initial refusal of ducal mediation is, I would suggest, a key ritual gesture of the duel, and it points up the duel's double political nature. The duelist was not just fighting his adversary; both were declaring themselves independent agents, and they seem to be united together against the mediating peacemakers.

While the duelist may have wished to fight before his prince's watchful eye to help his chances of survival, he valued equally the occasion the duel afforded to deny any external control over his quest for honor: the thrill of saying "no" to one's prince. Yet the prince in the end assures the honor of the duel's participants. "Surrender yourself to me, man of honor" says the Duke of Ferrara here, just as Federigo Gonzaga repeatedly vindicates the honorable comportment of Forni and Fontana, who ultimately bow to the similar princely authority of the Duke of Mantova. The prince confers honor on the nobleman at the price of the nobleman's surrender to the prince of the authority over honor itself: it is a surrender to which the duelist alternately refuses and accedes.

The mediation of the peacemaking lords succeeds, whether positively by enforcing the deference of Forni and Fontana or negatively by creating a solidarity between the two duelists against the lords' interference, or by a combination of these two effects. The two combatants fight to a draw and may thus mutually recognize themselves as brothers at arms. The exchange of courtesies in the midst of their battle is a further step towards such recognition. Both the actual fighting of the duel and the efforts of the peacemakers lead ritually to the happy ending of reconciliation. The duel is so well-mannered that it almost becomes possible to forget that Forni and Fontana were trying to kill one another.

5

The combat between Forni and Fontana suggests how the duel might actually limit violence and provide peaceful conflict resolution. Such elaborate and ceremonial duels nonetheless involved bodily risk, and they were expensive; Ercole Varano complained in 1541 to Ercole II, Duke of Ferrara, about the "intolerable expenses" that he was incurring in trying to arrange a much-delayed duel between his son Camillo and Paolo Vitelli.[43] Another ritual of the sixteenth-century duel allowed adversaries to fight virtually without violence at all; it was cheaper, too, if hardly less elaborate and ceremonial. These duelists fenced on paper and spilled ink rather than blood.

It had been a long established practice, reaching back into the fifteenth century, for offended parties to issue challenges in the form of short written documents—*cartelli di sfida*—that they posted in public.

Around the middle of the sixteenth century the *cartelli* began to be printed instead of handwritten and became more embellished, spelling out the causes for the duel and often provoking written responses from the challenged parties. The exchange of such documents, which, since they were printed, could have a wide distribution, might go on for some time, constituting a kind of publicity campaign before the duel or—as I suspect was most often the case—replacing the duel itself, since many of the *cartelli* accuse the other party of delay, of failing to live up to stipulated conditions, or simply of not showing up on the appointed day.

Giovanni Vincentio Capece did not appear for his slated duel in Anghiari in 1560, whereupon his opponent Don Francesco Guevara printed up a *cartello* informing the world that he had gone through with the duel anyway—one-sided though it had been—and had ridden in triumph through the lists. "Lo," he said to Capece "how quickly in chivalry are boasters discovered, those who offer to fight every kind of quarrel that may please their adversary, the bravos who threaten that they want to have their own way, and who then back out under the pretext of having been so advised by their friends."[44]

The *cartelli* and their replies, as well as the letters and other documents that had passed between would-be duelists, could even be published in little booklets, spelling out to the public the nature of the disputes and the behavior of the adversaries, each of whom, of course, was assured of his own honor and of the failings of his opponent.

One such published exchange took place in 1568 between Francesco Varese, a gentleman of Piacenza, and Count Carlo Thiene, a resident of Florence.[45] According to Varese's version of the story, he had come to Florence and had set out, as a good tourist, to see the city, especially "some of its leading courtesans." In the company of one Count Germanico Hercolani, he had come before the door of La Tancia, who had appeared above at her window in the company of Count Carlo Thiene, a gentleman from Vicenza; when they asked admittance to her house, La Tancia refused and went inside. Thiene, however remained at the window, and said "to Count Germanico that if he wished to enter alone, they would open up only to him." Varese took offense at being excluded.

Perturbed by this, and thinking that woman hardly courteous, I could not restrain myself from saying some words that were of this sentiment that I, with the forbearance of Count Carlo, had little esteem for her, at which he in the same manner answered, that she had little for me, and I answered that I paid no attention to the words of that woman. Then, doubting lest Count Carlo had formed that answer himself, I added that if there were anyone who wanted to take it up for her, that I would settle the question with him, and with arms to be chosen by mutual consent, and he said, "Yes, yes, wait until I come downstairs." And as I waited for him to come, thinking that we could not settle the proposed question since I was alone and unarmed, here he came armed with sword and dagger and accompanied with many others also armed and, as I think, his dependents and not casually in his company. I then asked for a sword, and could not obtain one; and while Count Germanico put his hand on the sword of Count Carlo, I wound my cape around my arm, and as we neared one another, Count Carlo delivered two punches that I parried on my arm, and I gave one to him, and then many intervened and separated us.

The situation was a classic occasion for the duel, a quarrel over a woman of ill repute, where sexual tension exploded into an equally pleasurable aggression against a male rival. Varese went his way, but expressed his desire to settle the question. He subsequently sent his challenge to Thiene from Bologna, noting that he would have fought in Florence, had "the strict ordinances of that city not prevented me." He also repeated his initial terms that they fight with weapons to be decided by mutual consent and added the condition, "as equals": "*del pari, & con armi usate, & da eleggersi communemente tra noi.*"

Thiene, to Varese's exasperation, resorted to a number of delays, first questioning whether the challenge actually came from Varese, then asking Varese's appointed procurator to define exactly what they were quarrelling about: "For I am ready to settle the question, provided that there is a question to deal with, and I have said to you that it is necessary that you specify the quarrel that Signor Varese claims to have with me, as the law of honor requires." Moreover, Thiene insisted, as the challenged party, to have the choice of weapons. This was not a minor technicality, for were Varese cast in the role of challenger, it would imply that his honor was at stake, that there was some stain that needed to be washed away. Varese vigorously protested that this was not so, that he was merely repeating the terms he had offered Thiene beneath the window of La Tancia, and that his original sense of being insulted, either by La Tancia or by Count Thiene, had not been satisfied by their exchange of fisticuffs. He accused Thiene of only being willing to face him with the advantage of arms and numbers; as for himself, he had defended himself on that occasion in an honorable manner against superior odds.

> Now let Count Carlo esteem himself, and usurp, and tell the affair as he likes, if his two blows were not taken by me on the arm in my defense, if I did not fail to hit at and strike him, nor did I commit any base act, when all is taken into account, that I was without Arms and he was Armed, and accompanied, as I said, and almost in his own house; I do not have to prove to him, nor is there any reason to put into question such a manifest case, in which I did not feel any obligation on account of honor.

Thiene did not budge on his demands and, in Varese's words, finished the comedy [*finì egli la comedia*], by wishing Varese's procurator a good trip back to Bologna.

These events took place in February and March. In July Varese published in Piacenza a ten-page manifesto, which included his narrative of the affair and the correspondence with Thiene. He concluded that Thiene had backed out of the duel and "had recourse to the [technicalities of] the duel, and shows himself to wish that this affair should subtly weigh upon me, and would wish that something come out of it to my prejudice: let him be satisfied as it suits him, for I am most satisfied in my conscience of having maintained what I proposed and to be out of any obligation to propose anything else; I will be most ready to make peace with him, to which I invite him with good heart; so that he will the better perceive, how much I am tranquil in my own Conscience." He gives Thiene a month to make peace, after which he feels himself no longer under any obligation: "I will leave it to the world to judge our cause."

It was Thiene, however, who had the last word, for he reprinted Varese's manifesto together with a fourteen-page response (so the booklet now totaled 24 pages.) Thiene's version of what had transpired between the two of them in Florence was rather different. Calling on witnesses, Thiene stated that the exact words that Varese had uttered when he was denied a visitation by La Tancina—now given an endearing and proprietary diminutive—were "we shit upon her [*gli ne incachiamo*]." And "I," Thiene asserts "replied, 'the lady says she returns it in your face.'"

> See Readers how the said Varese perseveres nonetheless in wishing to show that I formed this response from my own head, and see how the said witnesses make it clear that I always answered in the name of the said Tancina, and that the beginning of the discourteous speech came from him, and not from me, nor from Tancina, who had no obligation at all to open to him.

Furthermore according to Thiene, Varese never issued the formal challenge specifying the choice of arms: "Consider please, readers, even if we didn't have the testimony of the gentlemen who were in his company, does this seem to you the occasion or the time that Varese would have in any likelihood spontaneously said those words about choosing arms by mutual consent?"

Finally, Varese misrepresented the scuffle between them: "I gave him slaps, and he didn't strike back. I offered him and presented him the sword of my servant, as the witnesses testify, and he did not want to accept it, not being at any disadvantage at all, as will be seen below; whereupon I do not rest under any obligation with him, for the affair that passed between him and me in Florence." It was true, Thiene acknowledged, that Varese had asked for a sword from his own servant—and so, it turned out, Varese had had an armed servant of his own with him—but had been refused, and Thiene of course implies that the servant had known enough to refuse it. "I understanding that he asked for a sword, immediately drew one from the scabbard of a servant who was with me, and said to Varese, 'Take this sword.' And he responded, 'This is not the time now, but we'll see each other again.'"

As for Varese's claim that he had gotten in a punch against Thiene, "this is a most solemn lie ... having given him many slaps, he made no response except to shield himself and to turn his face away and to cover himself with his cape." Thiene, in fact, adduces a series of affidavits from witnesses, who back up his side of the story. Varese, according to Thiene, had been dishonored by being slapped around the street and by refusing to defend himself even when a sword was offered to him. Thus Varese was obliged, as he well knew, to offer a challenge and to allow Thiene the choice of weapons, and it was Varese who was using the formalities of the duel in order to avoid fighting, "for it is the same thing to offer to settle a question with another, and not to observe the terms that are required, as not to wish to carry it out."

Varese was only posturing: "Whence I deem that Varese, being jealous of his honor, and having forgotten the slaps he received, has through his procurator proposed a new quarrel as a fantasy, in order to be esteemed a bravo and a roarer."

Varese's face, still, Thiene implies, marked by the imprint of his hand, "ought at least to show him the way along which he should travel, knowing, as will appear from the affidavits below, the ending of the last act of his Tragedy which he put on in the middle of the Scene of Florence, on the day of the question that he had with me." But, Thiene concludes with magnanimous sarcasm, since Varese is "indeed tranquil in his Conscience as he says he is, I will accept the invitation that he extends to make Peace with me."

We may feel a little sorry for the imprudent Varese who got himself in over his head in Florence: he may have felt that La Tancia was slighting both his manhood and his rank and that both required vindication. But once his challenge was taken up, he could well have feared that he was outnumbered in a strange city—like the poor Bolognese soldier beaten up by Count Malvagia's retainers in Ferrara—and that resistance might be fatal. Perhaps he had not been as cowardly as Thiene portrays him: Count Germanico, who may have been the most reliable witness, attested to the slaps Varese had received and to Varese's asking his servant for a sword, but he does not mention Thiene's having himself offered Varese a sword— although Thiene found many other witnesses who confirmed that he had done so. Varese nevertheless had been made a public spectacle, having been slapped about in the Florentine streets, and he had perhaps only left himself open to further humiliation by pleading his case in print and leaving it to the world to judge him. For Thiene, too, had access to the printing press and to the court of public opinion, and he was a better writer than Varese.[46]

Thiene had in fact written Varese's story as a kind of drama, obviously a comedy rather than a tragedy, played out in the theater or street scene of Florence; Varese had been cast in the role of the would-be bravo and *huomo da brighe,* a kind of impostor or braggart soldier like the Spanish *capitani* of cinquecento comedy and their later descendant, Jonson's Captain Bobadilla in the first version of *Every Man in his Humor,* the expert on the *duello* who boasts his prowess as a swordsman, but who lets himself be beaten without defending himself or his honor on the same streets of Florence.[47] Thiene implies that Varese failed the real test of honor beneath La Tancia's window and that the challenges he has since issued in his *cartelli* are sham posturings that can be easily seen through. Thiene nonetheless plays along with the charade in order to expose it to the ridicule it deserves—but also because Thiene himself does not care to fight. Here, too, the duel and its formulaic rituals have become the means to a peaceful resolution of conflict, though perhaps these very rituals have come to look faintly ridiculous: a resource for the comic stage. Thiene may come off better than Varese in their paper battle, yet in the substitution of that battle for the violent duel that they never fought—what represents an indisputable gain for the civilizing process—aristocratic honor has lost some of its sheen.

6

In the exchange between Varese and Thiene, the bookish nature of the sixteenth-century duel turns it literally into a book, letters taking the place of arms and combat. The duel's general bookishness, modeled on the romances of chivalry and codified by the literature of *scienza cavalleresca,* tended to diminish its violence and fatalities, even if it did not remove them altogether. The bookish, ceremonial character of these duels was reinforced by their public nature: Forni and Fontana fought before princely spectators in the lists; Pico and Signoretto squabbled in the piazza of Mirandola where bystanders could step in and separate them; Varese and Thiene traded courteous insults in the public arena of print. But already in the sixteenth century, Italian gentlemen were finding more private and secluded venues to settle quarrels of honor. Romei cites, if only to condemn, the "diabolic invention" of the duel *alla macchia*, the combat waged in the wild that he acknowledges has come into wide use; his Gualengo asserts that fighting in the woods or in other isolated places is behavior appropriate to "thieves, assassins, and ruffians," and cannot be called a duel, which a man of honor wages in the presence of his prince and other gentlemen competent of judging his honor.[48] Once princes, however, began to refuse to condone, let alone preside over duels, noblemen were increasingly obliged to fight on their own. A century later, the Duke of Saint-Simon would recall how his father and his adversary had resorted to the subterfuge of arranging a traffic accident between their carriages and an ensuing mêlée among their servants, under the cover of which the two nobles could fight their duel against one another.[49] The idea that the duel was a matter of private honor that belonged to the contending noblemen alone confirmed itself more and more in practice; it began to resemble those lone combats that Ariosto's Rinaldo wages, sending his entourage ahead so that he can battle Guidon Selvaggio, inviting Gradasso to fight *"in solitario lato"* (*OF*.31.100). As the duel was removed from public view, it lost some of its ceremonial and formal trappings and some of its bookishness. By the end of the sixteenth century, the flood of books on the duel had slowed to a trickle in Italy. And the duel, especially with the introduction of the rapier and the pistol, may have become correspondingly more deadly.

And yet the ritualized and formulaic aspects of the sixteenth century duel—those aspects that tended to contain, diminish, or even displace its lethal violence and that made it a potential institution of civility—remained alive in cultural memory. Duelists in subsequent centuries were still expected to fight according to the book. Although the rules of combat and the etiquette of challenges became simplified,[50] the duelist internalized the watchful public eye that scrutinized his behavior and accorded him honor. The sense that even the most impetuous combat was performed under controlled conditions, especially under the duelist's own self-control, continued to inform the duel even after it had seemed to outlive its social formation in the late Renaissance. It survived as a vestigial practice of aristocratic culture into later periods that were apparently committed to the rule of law and civility. On the one hand, the duel kept alive an idea of the autonomous individual whose honor and integrity were his own to defend and lay outside the jurisdiction of lawcourts and the state. On the other it provided its own code of laws through which even private honor was to be adjudicated, laws that extended to the conduct of violence itself. The codification of the duel thus partook of, even as it contested, the growing legalism of modern society.

The duel survived, however, well past the point where it might be seen simply as a transitional institution in a civilizing process, an institution that would fall away once its historical function was done; it belonged to an aristocratic culture that embraced politeness, but never fully agreed to be civilized.[51] In distinguishing the way a gentleman fights from the everyday violence and casual aggression of the lower social orders, the duel held out, or was supposed to hold out, the possibility of mutual respect between antagonists, of fair play, and of the means, through its ritual procedures, of honorable reconciliation.

From the outside these rituals continued to look faintly silly, precisely because they might lead to bloodless conclusions incommensurate with apparently deadly intentions. Mark Twain quipped that the great French duel was "one of the most dangerous institutions of our day. Since it is always fought in the open air the combatants are nearly sure to catch cold."[52] Yet the idea of a gentlemanly violence employed to limited, private ends has proved deeply appealing to the cultural imagination, perhaps as a compromise between plebeian lawlessness and the impersonal authority and extensive coercive force of the state. Its inevitable corollaries, however, are the mystified concept of violence as a class prerogative and the still more regressive notions that violence ennobles, and is itself ennobling—it may even, on some occasions, be good manners to fight. The duel's long-term survival attests both to the persistence of the *ancien regime* and its habits of mind and, not least, to the pleasures, real and vicarious, of violence. If the duel was in part the product of a process of civilization, it is also a measure of its discontents.

Yale University

Notes

[1] On the sixteenth-century duel, see Francesco Erspamer, *La biblioteca di Don Ferrante: Duello e onore nella cultura del Cinquecento* (Rome: Bulzoni, 1982); Frederick R. Bryson, *The Sixteenth-Century Italian Duel* (Chicago: Univ. of Chicago Press, 1938) and *The Point of Honor in Sixteenth-Century Italy* (New York: Columbia Univ. Press, 1935); Enrico Musacchio and Giuseppe Monorchio, *Il duello* (Bologna: Cappelli, 1985). On the larger history of the duel, see V. G. Kiernan, *The Duel in European History* (Oxford: Oxford Univ. Press, 1988); Lorenzo Sabine, *Notes on Duels and Duelling* (Boston: Crosby, Nichols, and Co., 1859).

[2] Edward Muir makes this argument in *Mad Blood Stirring: Vendetta and Factions in Friuli During the Renaissance* (Baltimore and London: The Johns Hopkins Univ. Press, 1993), 263. For the change in warfare, see Geoffrey Parker, *The Military Revolution: Military Innovation and the Rise of the West, 1500–1800* (Cambridge, England: Cambridge Univ. Press, 1988). See also François Billacois, *The Duel: Its Rise and Fall in Early Modern France*, trans. Trista Selous (1986; English trans. New Haven and London: Yale Univ. Press, 1990), 190–94, 217–19, for remarks on the duel and warfare. For the change in the weaponry of the duel, see Billacois, 63–64, and Lawrence Stone, *The Crisis of the Aristocracy 1558–1641* (1965; abridged edition London, Oxford and New York: Oxford Univ. Press, 1967), 118–19.

[3] *Le Cid*, vv. 1301f.

[4] Stone, *The Crisis of the Aristocracy*, esp. 96–134; Norbert Elias, *The History of Manners (The Civilizing Process, Volume I)* (1939; English trans. New York: Pantheon Books, 1978); *Power and Civility (The Civilizing Process, Volume II)* (1939; English trans. New York: Pantheon Books, 1978); and *The Court Society* (1969; English trans. New York: Pantheon Books, 1983).

[5] For a comprehensive study of this literature, see Erspamer, *La biblioteca*. There is also a fine discussion of the literature of honor and nobility in Stefano Prandi, *Il "cortegiano" Ferrarese: i "Discorsi" di Annibale Roemi e la cultura nobiliare nel cinquecento* (Florence: Leo S. Olschki, 1990), 149–83. On the rules for fighting one-eyed opponents, see Bryson, *The Sixteenth-Century Duel*, 33–34.

[6] Stone, *The Crisis of the Aristocracy*, 118–21.

[7] See Muir, *Mad Blood Stirring*, especially 246–82. I am variously indebted to Muir's account of the duel as part of a civilizing process.

[8] Billacois, *The Duel*, 59–68. Billacois, I think, overestimates the uniqueness of the French duel; he wants to show his countrymen as especially bloodthirsty almost as a point of national pride. Yet the phenomena that he himself cites, including the duel to the first blood (197), suggest that in France, too, the duel could stop short of inflicting death. Billacois acknowledges (71), that the figures for the number of fatalities that contemporaries cited and that have been

accepted by some historians, were greatly inflated. Frenchmen did go in for the practice of fighting with seconds (and thirds and fourths) which increased the level of violence of the duel; Montaigne condemns this practice in "Couardise, mere de la cruauté" (*Essais* 2:27). I suspect that if the French situation were different, it was a difference of degree.

[9] *The Riverside Shakespeare* (Boston: Houghton Mifflin Co., 1974), 1071.

[10] Castiglione had himself linked courtiership with the "art" of fighting in a crucial passage of the *Cortegiano* (2.40). In "Couardise mere de la cruauté" (*Essais* 2:27), Montaigne, like Mercutio, appeals to the example of "nos peres" who tried to avoid reputations as fencers and learned in secret the new Italian art of swordsmanship, which they considered underhanded (though they still learned it!). An Elizabethan defense of the old-fashioned heavy dueling sword as opposed to the newfangled Italian fencing with the rapier repeats similar sentiments. See George Silver, *Paradoxes of Defense* (London: Edward Blount, 1599); the treatise is reprinted, with an introduction by J. Dover Wilson, Shakespeare Association Facsimile No. 6 (London: Humphrey Milford, Oxford Univ. Press, 1933). The analogy of Mercutio's speech to Silver's work is also noted in a recent study of *Romeo and Juliet* and the literature of dueling; see Joan Ozark Holmer, " 'Draw if you be men': Saviolo's Significance for *Romeo and Juliet*," *Shakespeare Quarterly* 45 (1994): 163–89, 185.

[11] Erspamer in *La biblioteca*, 19, cites the 1566 Valvassori edition of the *Furioso* which was commented upon by an anonymous writer's *Pareri in duello*.

[12] All citations of the *Orlando furioso* are taken from the edition of Lanfranco Caretti (Milan and Naples: Riccardo Ricciardi, 1954).

[13] For a classic application of René Girard's concept of mimetic desire to the *Orlando furioso*, see Eugenio Donato, "*Per selve e boscherecci labirinti*: Desire and Narrative Structure in Ariosto's *Orlando Furioso*," in *Literary Theory/Renaissance Texts*, ed. Patricia Parker and David Quint (Baltimore and London: The Johns Hopkins Univ. Press, 1986), 33–62.

[14] A more exact parallel in the television western can be found in *The Big Valley*, a clone of *Bonanza*, where the sons of the Barkley ranching dynasty, Jarrod and Nick, welcome into their family their bastard brother, Heath—whose name recalls the outcast Heathcliff of *Wuthering Heights*. Heath similarly proves himself as a true Barkley by his gun and fists. On the theme of brotherhood, see Billacois, *The Duel*, 214–16.

[15] For the Pico family tree that includes the illegitimate branch of Ettore Pico, see the genealogical tables IV and XII in Felice Ceretti, *Biografie pichiani* vol. IV, *Memorie storiche della città e dell'antico ducato della Mirandola pubblicate per cura della Commissione municipale di storia patria e di arti belle della Mirandola* vol. 20 (Mirandola: Grilli Candido, 1913).

[16] Modena, Archivio di Stato, Archivio Segreto Estense, Cancelleria Ducale, Materie Duelli e Sfide 2.

[17] Florence, Archivio di Stato, Archivio Mediceo del Principato, f. 2892.

[18] Ibid.

[19] Ibid.

[20] The modern edition of Romei's work is found in Angelo Solerti, *Ferrara e la corte estense nella seconda metà del XVI secolo. I "Discorsi" di Annibale Romei, gentiluomo ferrarese* (Città di Castello: Lapi, 1891; 2nd edition 1900). For a good critical discussion, see Prandi, *Il "cortegiano" ferrarese*.

[21] Marc'Antonio Guarini, *Compendio historico delle origini, accrescimento, e prerogative delle chiese, e luoghi pii della città e diocesi di Ferrara* (Ferrara: Vittorio Baldini, 1621), 269.

[22] Modena, Archivio di Stato, Archivio Segreto Estense, Cancelleria Ducale, Particolari 677.

[23] Machiavelli, himself no friend to the nobility, notes that the patricians of Venice are more noble in name than in reality ("piú in nome che in fatto"); see his discussion at the end of *Discorsi* 1.55.

[24] Modena, Archivio di Stato, Archivio Segreto Estense, Cancelleria Ducale, Materie Duelli e Sfide 3.

[25] For the role that Muzio and other writers on the duel played as arbitrators of actual questions of honor, see Bryson, *The Sixteenth-Century Italian Duel*, 156–72.

[26] Solerti, *Ferrara*, 130. And ecclesiastical authorities did intercede to prevent duels in the Duchy of Ferrara, including, as it turns out, the duel that was finally to decide the feud betweeen the Savorgnan and Coloreddu clans that Muir has studied. Canigiani reports in a letter of April 16, 1568, "Here there was expected a little duelling in the *macchia* between one Coloreto and one Savorgnano as usual, and with Coloreto was Pippo da Lotto, but at the last minute, a papal excommunication barring arms was brought to Alessandro, who should have assigned to them a place to fight, and thus the thing will go up in smoke for right now." Florence, Archivio di Stato, Archivio Mediceo del Principato, f. 2891. What Canigiani did not know was that the duel had already taken place two days earlier on April 14 in a remote area in the neighboring Duchy of Mantua; see Muir, *Mad Blood Stirring*, 270.

[27] Solerti, *Ferrara*, 147.

[28] Ibid., 149.

[29] Ibid., 139.

[30] Ibid., 172.

[31] Ibid., 174.

[32] Ibid., 153.

[33] Ibid., 143–44.

[34] Ibid., 144.

[35] Ibid., 144–45.

[36] Braden, *Renaissance Tragedy and the Senecan Tradition: Anger's Privilege*

(New Haven and London: Yale Univ. Press, 1985); see especially Braden's discussion of how *furor*, the property of tyrants and their aristocratic victims, conflicts with the stoic ground of Seneca's tragedies, 1–62.

[37] Solerti, *Ferrara*, 166.

[38] Ibid.

[39] For another account of this duel, see Bryson, *The Sixteenth-Century Italian Duel*, 190–93, which relies on a contemporary treatment of the event in verse by the minor poet Vitale Papazzoni.

[40] Modena, Archivio di Stato, Archivio Segreto Estense, Cancelleria Ducale, Materie Duelli e Sfide, b. 3.

[41] See Billacois, *The Duel*, 48–56, for an account of the duel of Jarnac and La Châtaigneraye.

[42] Modena, Archivio di Stato, Archivio Segreto Estense, Cancelleria Ducale, Materie Duelli e Sfide, b.3. The document describing this apparently mid-century duel is undated.

[43] Modena, Archivo di Stato, Archivio Segreto Estense, Cancelleria Ducale, Materie Duelli e Sfide, b. 2.

[44] Modena, Archivio di Stato, Archivio Segreto Estense, Cancelleria Ducale, Materie Duelli e Sfide, b. 3.

[45] Modena, Achivio di Stato, Archivio Segreto Estense, Cancelleria Ducale, Materie Duelli e Sfide, b. 3.

[46] Varese should have known better than to have crossed pens with Thiene, for he himself republished the following exhange in his manifesto. With considerable rhetorical magnificence, Varese had declared: "I who do not disparage swords, who do not avoid knives, who do not shun Capes and such like things, and who do not fear the cold, just as the heat does not hurt me, am here ready to choose Arms with you, and as a Cavalier, and to treat and decide upon the time and place, and Company, and every other thing that you desire and which is fitting and which will not be lacking from me...." Thiene replied with magnificent disdain at the close of his letter "Finally I tell you that for now I don't need to reply to your Swords, Knives, Capes, Cold, Heat, Readiness, Choosing of Arms, Places, and Times, contenting myself that they adorn your writing and make it very lofty and brave, and be well." Thiene had a satirical sense of literary decorum that Varese entirely lacked—the abrupt wishing Varese good health is a wonderful final dismissal—a sense, too, that, the language and ritual of the duel could easily become ridiculous, especially if they were seen to take the place of actual fighting.

[47] See *Everyman in His Humour*, 4.7.109f. In *La Fantesca*, Giambattista Della Porta doubles the figure of the Spanish *capitano*. The two cowardly bravos, Captains Dante and Pantaleone, back out of the fight they are supposed to have with one another in Act IV, scene vii, and are comically beaten by their respective Italian employers.

[48] Solerti, *Ferrara*, 159–60.

[49] Saint-Simon, *Mémoires*, ed. Yves Coirault, Bibloithèque de la Pléiade (Paris: Gallimard, 1983), I:83–84.

[50] See Kiernan, *The Duel*, 135–51.

[51] Two recent studies have looked at the phenomenon of the duel in nineteenth-century Germany, where the bourgeoisie aped aristocratic habits. See Kevin MacAleer, *Dueling: The Cult of Honor in Fin-de-Siècle Germany* (Princeton: Princeton Univ. Press, 1994); Peter Gay, *The Cultivation of Hatred* (New York and London: W. W. Norton, 1993). For an account of a notorious duel in California with political overtones on the eve of the American Civil War, one that strictly observed all the chivalric niceties of the dueling code, see A. Russell Buchanan, *David S. Terry of California: Dueling Judge*, San Marino: The Huntington Library, 1956), 83–110.

[52] Twain, "The Great French Duel" (from *A Tramp Abroad*), in *Mark Twain: A Laurel Reader*, ed. Edmund Fuller (New York: Dell, 1958), 220.

MARGARET MIKESELL

The Place of Vives's Instruction of a Christen Woman *in Early Modern English Domestic Book Literature*

JUAN LUIS VIVES PUBLISHED HIS *De institutione foeminae Christianae* in 1523; it quickly reappeared as *The Instruction of a Christen Woman* in a 1529 translation by Richard Hyrde. Vives's composition of his treatise was timely, occurring as it did during the early years of a profound and focused reassessment of marriage and family life by humanist scholars and Reform theologians. This scrutiny of the domestic arena shaped the concerns and conventions of many kinds of literature; more pertinently for this study, it engendered numerous sermons, conduct books, and marriage treatises which were published throughout the early modern period. Vives's treatise achieves a kind of simultaneity with these texts, appearing quite regularly alongside them in eight successive sixteenth-century English editions, the last published in 1592. Since the *Instruction* was issued so regularly during the first half-century of the growth of the domestic book, it is important to consider its influence on the genre. Does it have descendants? Is there evidence that it shaped the form and content of later members of the genre?

The answer to the first question is a qualified yes; to the second, a qualified no. The nature of the borrowing, such as it is, is apparent in Robert Cleaver's influential *A Godlie Forme of Household Government* (1598). Numerous passages from Vives's book appear in close copy in Cleaver's manual, although the debt is never acknowledged. In brief, the pattern seems to be this: Cleaver pillaged the earlier work (and Vives's companion *De Officio Mariti*, published in 1529 and translated as *The Office and Duetie of an Husband* in 1553) for specific information for discrete sections of his treatise pertaining to female conduct. But while he draws freely on Vives's prescriptive advice, he ignores most of the earlier author's allusions to a wide range of ancient, patristic and modern texts. In this respect he reflects the common practice of Protestant didactic writers, who look primarily to the Bible for their examples, referring infrequently to the Church Fathers and almost never to classical sources. Moreover, the overall tone and preoccupations of Cleaver's book bear little resemblance to comparable aspects of the *Instruction*.

This pattern is characteristic. Most conduct books do not copy verbatim from the *Instruction*. Rather, they display their authors' willingness to pick up a section of its argument here, an idea there, and its examples, largely the biblical ones. Besides Cleaver's work, important treatises that follow this protocol include Heinrich Bullinger's *The Christen State of Matrimony* (1541), Thomas Becon's *A New Catechism* (1564), Edmund Tilney's *The Flower of Friendship* (1568), and Richard Brathwait's *The English Gentlewoman* (1631).[1]

A consideration of the use made of these borrowings raises a more complex issue: what kind of general influence is apparent between the *Instruction* and later conduct books? This is both a vexing and an important question which can not only clarify the place in history of Vives's text but can also illuminate the key issue that has engaged scholars analyzing the tracts: what continuity may be found from the Roman Catholic ancestors to the Protestant descendants of the conduct book?

In the scholarly literature, a changing consensus on this issue has evolved over the last eighty years. Traditionally, twentieth-century scholars interested in domestic aspects of English Protestantism, including Chilton Powell, William and Malleville Haller, and Roland Frye, have argued that Reformation and specifically Puritan ideologies heralded a significant change in the doctrinal perspective and the prescriptive advice of the conduct books. They cite the celebration of marriage rather than of virginity by Protestants (especially Puritans), and the increased status accorded the "companionate," affective bonds of marriage.[2] Some recent cultural historians locate this "rehabilitation" of marriage with pre-Reformation Christian humanists.[3] Whether these ideas were, in fact, a radical departure from those of earlier writers remains a matter of debate. More recent studies have demonstrated the continuity of the domestic book genre, arguing that apparent changes stem not so much from doctrinal differences between pre- and post-Reformation writers but from what Mary Beth

Rose has termed "significant shifts in prestige, and in emphasis and degree" in marriage ideologies, accompanied by what Kathleen Davies calls the "publishing explosion of the sixteenth century" and the concomitant growth of a literate middle class.[4] As a Catholic humanist document that reappeared regularly alongside some of the seminal Protestant family texts of the period, the *Instruction* can uniquely help us to understand the history of the domestic treatise.

While as we have seen, evidence of direct influence between the *Instruction* and Protestant domestic books is clear, in many areas substantial differences exist between Vives and later writers. One such area is chastity, which is central to Vives's treatise, shaping its pedagogy and informing virtually every chapter. For Vives, chastity is the single measure of a woman's worth. In the Preface he declares that "though the preceptes for men be innumerable: women yet may be enfourmed with few wordes ... a woman hath no charge to se to, but her honestie and chastyte. Wherefore whan she is enfurmed of that, she is sufficiently appoynted."[5] This attitude toward chastity is accompanied by a concomitant attention to unchastity; if a woman loses her chastity she is like a man who has lost "al that he shuld have. For in a woman the honestie is in stede of all."[6] Often these polarities interact in alternate chapters, and as many examples are allotted to show the depravity or grim fate of "whores," as Vives terms them, as to celebrate chaste women.

Many works continue to appear which maintain this concept of chastity as primarily a female ideal.[7] Examples include Edmund Tilney's *Flower of Friendshippe* and Thomas Becon's *A New Catechism*, Thomas Bentley's *Monument of Matrons* (1582), and Dorothy Leigh's *The Mother's Blessing* (1633).[8] And in other kinds of texts, for instance in certain polemical tracts on women and especially in literature, chastity remains the primary signifier determining a woman's worth. In drama, for instance, it is often used as a kind of shorthand to indicate a female character's overall moral probity or lack thereof.[9]

In the domestic book genre, however, this focus on female chastity does not prevail. While later domestic tracts retained chastity as an essential aspect of female character, the authors' formulation of the concept changed, and it was subordinated to other traditional concerns about women which became the primary focus for the prescriptive energies of their authors.[10]

In Cleaver's treatise, Vives's pivotal statement about chastity (quoted above) appears in close copy. The differences between the uses to which the passage is put in each text are instructive, helping to establish the nature of the discontinuities between Vives and many later tract writers. In Vives's work, the passage appears early, in his discussion of the "maid," and it is formative, occurring in a lengthy definition of chastity that shapes almost every chapter of all three sections of the book. In Cleaver's tract, the chastity passage appears in precisely the same place, in the discussion of rearing the daughter. However, that section has been moved to a position, traditional in the Protestant books, near the end of the text, in the "children" section (just before the servant section that closes the book). The passage loses the hegemony it has in Vives; in fact, no further use is made of it. Thus in spite of Cleaver's appropriation of the Vives passage, an important disjunction exists between its power in each text. Understanding more about Vives's conceptualization of chastity and tracing what happens to it in Protestant tracts can help us understand his influence (and the lack of it) on subsequent generations of conduct book writers.

Vives clearly expected his readers to marry, and his definition of marriage—"in dede, wedlocke was nat ordeyned so moche for generation, as for certayne company of lyfe, and contynuall felowship"[11]—is essentially identical to that of Protestant writers. Nevertheless, for Vives the pre-Reformation humanist, chastity is permeated by Roman Catholic notions of celibacy. His counsel accords with the strictures for women found in medieval treatises on education, such as Vincent of Beauvais's *De Eruditione Filiorum Nobilium*, which are heavily indebted to the Church Fathers.[12] Indeed, many of the behavioral prescriptions found in the *Instruction* derive from the advice of Paul, often filtered through Jerome, Ambrose, and Cyprian, to early Christian women committed to continence. Vives quotes extensively from these authors, particularly in his chapters on learning, bodily discipline, clothing, life at home and "abroad," dancing, loving, and, throughout Section III, on the widow.

Significant portions of his advice to maids and wives reproduce, albeit in muted form, the early Christian valorization of celibacy. In his directions to a maid choosing a husband, for instance, the spiritual family of God and the Virgin Mary takes precedence over her biological family, and she is steered ineluctably toward the choice of Christ rather than some earthly suitor as her husband. Similarly, the wives that Vives most lauds are those who renounce sex in favor of a continent marriage.[13] Vives's reliance on sources concerned exclusively with virginity gives the *Instruction* an orientation that allies his treatise firmly with its early Christian and medieval ancestors and marks its greatest distinction from later tracts. His preoccupation with chastity, perhaps the single most complex issue raised by his work, is explained in part by this use of sources.

Questions arise from this disjunction: how is chastity treated differently in the preponderance of Protestant marriage tracts? What replaces it as the key Protestant attribute for female behavior, and why?

Chastity consistently appears in two places in Protestant domestic treatises. Although lingering ambivalence about celibacy remains among the Protestant writers,[14] they reject the valorization of that state, identifying it with Catholic doctrine and often with priestly celibacy. Thomas Becon, who is vitriolic on the issue in *The Booke of Matrimony* (1564), declares that both in the Old and New Testaments, marriage compares favorably with chastity and implores that it may

> overcome her [chastity], and utterly dryve her into exile, and ... bannysh her oute of the bondes of Christianitie, that the most famous and gloryous Empresse Lady Matrimony maye regne in the heartes of all godly personnes, and recover her olde glorie and honoure, whereof she hathe ben certayne yeares moste unjustly deprived thorowe the deuvyll and the Pope, and their Antichristiane adherentes.[15]

For Becon, chastity used in this sense is equivalent to priestly celibacy, a commitment that leads invariably to "whoredome and adultery."[16] Although later Protestant writers are more temperate, their endorsement of marriage often springs, like Becon's, from a rejection of what they label "papist" chastity. In his long compendium on marriage titled *Of Domesticall Duties* (1622), William Gouge, referring to the "ancient heresie, that marriage is of the Divell," comments that if it and celibacy be "duly poised and rightly weighed, wee shall find single life too light to be compared with honest marriage."[17] Becon's explicit equation of celibacy with fornication appears obliquely in Gouge's juxtaposition of "light" and "honest."

In contrast to Vives's presentation in the *Instruction* of chastity as a quality pertaining primarily to women, the emphasis in Protestant tracts is on the couple, where the concept is frequently discussed as the mutual obligation of both husband and wife.[18] It is so presented in Cleaver's *Godly Form of Householde Governement*, and William Whately's *A Bride-Bush* (1619), where it is the announced as the "first dutie" of married men and women.[19] The relationship between marital chastity and love is articulated in Gouge's definition of chastity: "As the man must be satisfied at all times in his wife, and even ravisht with her love; so must the woman be satisfied at all times in her husband, and even ravisht with his love."[20]

In the Protestant treatment of adultery, consistently viewed as the most dangerous threat to marriage, the couple is again exhorted rather than the wife alone; indeed, the husband is more likely than the wife to be selected as the representative perpetrator. The Elizabethan "Homily Against Whoredom" addresses both husband and wife. Gouge typically states that "though the ancient Romans and Canonists have aggravated the womans fault in this kinde farre above the mans ... yet I see not how that difference in the sinne can stand with the tenour of Gods word."[21] Though the comparable passage in Vives runs along the same lines, there is a difference in emphasis that Gouge would identify as "Roman":

> For the man is nat so moche bounde as the woman to kepe chastite, at leaste wayes by the lawes of the worlde, for by godis lawe both be bounde in lyke. Let her consydre that the man lyveth more at libertie than the woman, and hath more to care fore. For she hath nothynge to se to but her honestye.[22]

In Vives's work, where social custom takes precedence, the woman is more blameworthy than the man. Gouge rejects this formulation.[23]

Thus while chastity never loses its importance as an ideal for female conduct in domestic treatises, it does not, in the decades following the *Instruction*, dominate in the same way as a precept directed primarily to women. Its conceptualization as a mutual responsibility binds it not with celibacy, but with the idealization of marital love and the concomitant emerging power of the couple. It becomes, then, an essential part of the companionate ideology of the later domestic treatises. To understand precisely how this change in emphasis fits into the larger project of Protestant marriage ideology, which is to promulgate what Catherine Belsey terms the new, "liberal humanist family,"[24] it is important to explore what replaces chastity as the governing precept of domestic treatises.

The attention that in the *Instruction* accrues to chastity has in most Protestant treatises been transferred to obedience, an essential though secondary ideal in Vives's book.[25] Obedience seems a more worrisome if not a more significant quality to be instilled in girls and women. The Protestant empowerment of obedience is apparent in the intense concern which the subject inspires in William Perkins' Puritan *Of Christian Oeconomie*, where he allots it a double charge:

> Now the duties of the wife are principally two.
> The first, is to submit herselfe to her husband, and to acknowledge and reverence him as her head in all things.
> . . . .
> The second dutie is, to be obedient unto her husband in all things; that is; wholly to depend upon him, both in judgement and will.[26]

This twin injunction is conventional, also appearing, for instance, in Cleaver's and Whately's tracts, and in Gataker's *Marriage Duties* (1619).[27]

The author providing the most striking counterpoint to Vives is William Gouge, who dwells on obedience in *Of Domesticall Duties* with the kind of obsessive fervor that one sees in Vives's treatment of chastity. He uses his introduction in part to defend his lengthy prescriptions regarding this duty, which indeed occupy most of the forty-odd sections devoted to the wife's behavior. Conversely, although Vives allots about fifteen pages to a systematic consideration of obedience (in 2.4, "Howe she shall behave her selfe unto her husbande") and it is an unquestionably important duty for his married woman, his discussion of the subject never runs out of control, as his treatment of chastity so often does.

The difference between Vives's and Gouge's use of "sobriety" reflects their respective emphases. For Vives, sobriety is intimately connected with chastity, as in "shamfastnes and sobrenes be the inseparable companyons of chastite." In Gouge's use of the term, on the other hand, its link with chastity has been largely subsumed into obedience. Gouge says that a wife should behave with sobriety to show that she "respecteth [her husband's] place and the authority which God hath given him.... Contrary to this sobriety is lightnesse and wantonnesse; which vices in a wife, especially before her husband, argueth little respect, if not a plaine contempt of him."[28] "Lightnesse and wantonness" evoke the connotations found in the Vives passage; the preponderance of Gouge's definition, however, is concerned with hierarchy. Similar distinctions are apparent in the two authors' treatment of apparel, speech, and the like.

This shift makes sense. In a fundamental way, Protestant conduct books are defenses of the institution of marriage. As many scholars have noticed, their authors are accordingly preoccupied with demonstrating its centrality within the larger social, religious, and political structures. Picking up on the humanist revival of the Aristotelian trope, they carefully position marriage within one of the most common Renaissance analogic tables: it is like the commonwealth and it is like the Church—and essential to the health of both of these institutions.[29] The roles of husband and wife solidify these connections: the husband is like Christ and king and the wife like the church and body politic. Hierarchy, then, is as integral to the domestic unit as it is to the religious and political units, and the wife's obedience is both symbolic of and essential to that hierarchy—hence its privileged position in the later tracts. As Valerie Lucas argues, Protestant preachers, "the professional ideologists of the period," sought to reconcile women to their legal and political powerlessness by their formulation of obedience as part of their duty to God—and to the state, one might add.[30]

This co-option of the domestic by the religious and political spheres brings all the acknowledged sources of power to bear on keeping the woman—not to mention, reciprocally, the citizen and religious supplicant—in her place. Gouge makes these connections explicit: "inferiours that cannot be subject in a family; they will hardly bee brought to yeeld such subjection as they ought in church or commonwealth...."[31] In an extraordinary tribute to hierarchy, the Elizabethan homily, "An Exhortation Concerning Good Order, and Obedience to Rulers and Magistrates," imbeds husbands and wives deeply within a lengthy list of all the physical, biological, political, and spiritual elements that must be maintained, in all their proper degrees, to insure a "profitable, necessary, and pleasaunt order...." Where such order is absent, "all things shall be common, and there must needs flow all mischeife, and utter destruction both of soules, bodies, goods, commonweales...."[32]

The Protestant concept of chastity is essential to this project. Because it is part of the valorization of the couple and their love—remember Gouge's definition of chastity as the husband and wife being each "ravisht" with love for the other—it is deeply implanted within the ideology of married love. And love, as Belsey argues, is "the solvent of inequality, the source of women's pliability and the guarantee of marital concord."[33] Whately comments in *A Bride-Bush* that while wives are no less subject to their husbands than are servants and children, obedience in their case may be "sweetened" by familiarity. In "An Homilie in the State of Matrimony," it is put more bluntly; if you use "gentle words" toward your wife, "thou shalt not onely nourish concorde: but shalt have her heart in thy power and will."[34] Commenting on Whately's treatise, Lucas observes that "an ideology's effectiveness relies upon promoting its audience's misrecognition of its social reality...." She cites love as such a disguise, one designed to conceal the "true nature of power relations within the couple."[35]

Vives stands as a kind of hinge between earlier Catholic theologians such as Jerome and Ambrose and their medieval descendants, and later Protestant didactic writers, themselves often clerics and sometimes, like Heinrich Bullinger and Thomas Becon, major early Reformation theorists. Substantial though often subtle shifts are apparent between Vives and these earlier and later writers on the subjects of female conduct and matrimony. While Vives's treatise borrows heavily from the earlier tradition and becomes a rich source for the later one, it is distinct from both. Its differentness helps us track a process of domestication—that is, from celibacy to the family—that lies at the heart of the development of the ideology of marriage during the early modern period.[36] And it illustrates the flexibility of domestic book conventions as the genre responds to the exigencies of very different historical epochs.

In this study of difference, it is essential to remember the profound continuity that exists within the long tradition; as Ian Maclean comments, the Christian "marital paradigm, developed long before

Vives and his fellow humanists and persisting long after the Protestant reformers, restricts any fundamental reassessment of woman and her role in society."[37] For both the *Instruction* and the tracts which precede and follow it, chastity and obedience remain crucial; all profess the identical biblical vision of woman as the "weaker vessel", and the advice that prescribes women's dependence on men remains intact, regardless of other changes that occur in the genre.

John Jay College, The City University of New York

Notes

[1] Kuschmiercz has documented the passages that Bullinger and Brathwait appropriated from Vives, and Wayne has systematically tabulated Tilney's borrowings. Ruth Lena Marie Kuschmiercz, ed., "*The Instruction of a Christen Woman*: A Critical Edition of the Tudor Translation," by Juan Luis Vives (Ph.D. diss., Univ. of Pittsburg, 1961), lxviii–lxxxvi; Valerie Wayne, ed., *The Flower of Friendship: A Renaissance Dialogue Contesting Marriage*, by Edmund Tilney (Ithaca: Cornell Univ. Press, 1992), 155, 164–69 passim.

[2] For representative examples of this early analysis of Renaissance marriage theory, see Chilton Powell, *English Domestic Relations, 1487–1653: A Study of Matrimony and Family Life in Theory and Practice as Revealed by the Literature, Law, and History of the Period* (1917; repr. ed., New York: Russell and Russell, 1972), 119–29, for example; William and Malleville Haller, "The Puritan Art of Love," *Huntington Library Quarterly* 5 (1942): 235–72; Roland Frye, "The Teachings of Classical Puritanism on Conjugal Love," *Studies in the Renaissance* 2 (1955): 148–59; James T. Johnson, "English Puritan Thought on the Ends of Marriage," *Church History* 38 (1969): 429–36; and John Halkett, *Milton and the Idea of Matrimony* (New Haven: Yale Univ. Press, 1970), esp. 1–50.

[3] The term is Ian Maclean's. He mentions Vives's *Instruction* along with Cornelius Agrippa's *The Commendation of Matrimony* and Erasmus's *Christiani Matrimonii Institutio* as texts that give new status and power to marriage (*The Renaissance Notion of Woman: A Study in the Fortunes of Scholasticism and Medical Science in European Intellectual Life*, Cambridge Monographs on the History of Medicine [Cambridge: Cambridge Univ. Press, 1980], 19). Elsewhere, however, he argues that "it is difficult to see more than minor shifts of emphasis occurring during the Renaissance" in the conceptualization of marriage itself (66). See also Margo Todd, *Christian Humanism and the Puritan Social Order* (Cambridge: Cambridge Univ. Press, 1987), chaps. 2 and 3, "Christian Humanism as

Social Ideology" and "The Transmission of Christian Humanist Ideas" (22–95). Wayne traces these ideas from Plutarch through the Church Fathers to early Reform theologians (13–38).

[4] Rose, *The Expense of Spirit: Love and Sexuality in English Renaissance Drama* (Ithaca: Cornell Univ. Press, 1988), 3 and 119–20; and Davies, "Continuity and Change in Literary Advice on Marriage," in *Marriage and Society: Studies in the Social History of Marriage*, ed. R. B. Outhwaite (New York: St. Martin's Press, 1981), 61. These issues are also assessed by Linda T. Fitz, " 'What Says the Married Woman?' Marriage Theory and Feminism in the English Renaissance," *Mosaic* 13 (1980): 1–22; Lisa Jardine, *Still Harping on Daughters: Women and Drama in the Age of Shakespeare* (Sussex: Harvester Press, and Totowa, NJ: Barns and Noble, 1983), 37–67; Karen Newman, *Fashioning Femininity and English Renaissance Drama*, Women in Culture and Society (Chicago: Univ. of Chicago Press, 1991), 19–20 and 21–26 passim; and Wayne, 36.

[5] Vives, *Instruction*, sig. B2r. The Vives text used in this paper is the first edition of the English translation by Richard Hyrde (1529). *The Instruction of a Christen Woman*, eds. Virginia Wolcott Beauchamp, Elizabeth H. Hageman, Margaret Mikesell, et. al. (Urbana: Univ. of Illinois Press, forthcoming).

[6] Ibid., sig. G4r.

[7] Ruth Kelso, *Doctrine for the Lady of the Renaissance* (1956; repr. ed., Urbana: Univ. of Illinois Press, 1978), 24–25. Nancy Cotton Pearse argues that the development of the Protestant veneration for marriage was accompanied by a "correspondingly greater emphasis on chastity, particularly as a virtue proper to women" (*John Fletcher's Chastity Plays: Mirrors of Modesty* [Lewisburg: Bucknell Univ. Press, 1975], chap. 3, "Religious and Social Attitudes toward Chastity," 52 and 49–99 passim). Margaret Ferguson argues that of chastity, silence, and obedience, "by far the most important from a socioeconomic point of view was chastity" ("A Room Not Their Own: Renaissance Women as Readers and Writers," in *The Comparative Perspective on Literature: Approaches to Theory and Practice*, eds. Clayton Koelb and Susan Noakes [Ithaca: Cornell Univ. Press, 1988], 97). See also Ann Rosalind Jones, "Nets and Bridles: Early Modern Conduct Books and Sixteenth-Century Women's Lyrics," in *The Ideology of Conduct: Essays in Literature and the History of Sexuality*, eds. Nancy Armstrong and Leonard Tennenhouse, Essays in Literature and Society (New York: Methuen, 1987), 52.

[8] Although Becon does not explicitly stress chastity as a precept for women, *A New Catechism* bears a striking resemblance to the *Instruction* in its pervasive and hostile anxiety about female chastity. Leigh displays a preoccupation with chastity similar to Vives's and, citing his authority, echoes some of his key passages on the subject (*The Mother's Blessing* [London, 1633], 30).

[9] See Valerie Wayne, "Some Sad Sentence: Vives's *Instruction of a Christen Woman*," in *Silent But for the Word: Tudor Women as Patrons, Translators, and*

Writers of Religious Works, ed. Margaret P. Hannay (Kent, Ohio: Kent State Univ. Press, 1985), 24 and 269n16, and Mikesell, "The Formative Power of Marriage in Stuart Tragedy," in *In Another Country: Feminist Perspectives on Renaissance Drama*, eds. Dorothea Kehler and Susan Baker (Metuchen, NJ and London: Scarecrow Press, 1991), 239.

[10] Betty S. Travitsky, a collaborator on the Vives edition, has pointed out that "if one reads 'between the lines,' the relative silence of the Protestant writers does not necessarily imply the relative insignificance to them of chastity, but may instead signify the degree to which they *assume* the centrality of a quality they do not have to mention" (Correspondence, April 2 1993). This useful reminder raises many issues, particularly concerning genre: In the construction of women in early modern England, why is one genre (such as marriage treatises) virtually silent on a subject that another genre (such as drama) subjects to obsessive scrutiny? The analysis of audience and received generic traditions offers two possible ways to understand this difference. Mary Beth Rose works brilliantly with the interactions between domestic treatises and drama, an issue that concerns her straight through *The Expense of Spirit*.

[11] Vives, sig. V1v.

[12] See Mikesell, "Marital and Divine Love in Juan Luis Vives's *Instruction of a Christen Woman*," in *Love and Death in the Renaissance*, eds. Kenneth R. Bartlett, Konrad Eisenbichler, and Janice Liedl, Dovehouse Studies in Literature, vol. 3. (Ottawa: Dovehouse Editions, 1991), 121–24.

[13] Ibid., 113–18; Vives, sigs. F4v–G1r, R2v–R3r, and e4r–v. For consideration of the social and religious roots of this substitution of the spiritual for the biological marriage, see Howard R. Bloch, *Medieval Misogyny and the Invention of Western Romantic Love* (Chicago: Univ. of Chicago Press, 1991), 84–85, and Jack Goody, *The Development of the Family and Marriage in Europe*, Past and Present Publications (Cambridge: Cambridge Univ. Press, 1983), 77–81.

[14] For sensitive discussions of this subject, see the introductory chapters of Rose's *Expense of Spirit* (12–42), and Heather Dubrow's *A Happier Eden: The Politics of Marriage in the Stuart Epithalamium* (Ithaca: Cornell Univ. Press, 1990), 1–41. As Wayne remarks, "the humanist, Protestant, and puritan approaches were not unambiguously pro-sex, pro-women, or even unilaterally pro-marriage" (*Flower*, 29).

[15] *Worckes*, vol. 1 (London, 1564), 572r. See also Heinrich Bullinger, *The Christen State of Matrimonye*, trans. Miles Coverdale (London, 1541), sigs. A2r–A3r.

[16] Becon, 564r.

[17] (London, 1622), 123.

[18] In the *Instruction*, Vives recklessly proclaims about women's chastity that "no man wyl take [it] from her ageynst her wyll, nor touche hit, excepte she be wyllynge her selfe" (sig. G4r). However, in his later treatise on husbands, he

often worries about male desire and physicality, a gendered variation of the chastity anxieties that recur so frequently in the *Instruction* (*Office and Duetie of an Husband*, trans. Thomas Paynell [London, 1553], sigs. A4r–A7v, N5v–N6r, R4v–R5r, S2v, and X6r, for example). Wayne points out that "the shift from a valorisation of virginity to married chastity still depended on women's sexual control" ("Historical Differences: Misogyny and *Othello*," in *The Matter of Difference: Materialist Feminist Criticism of Shakespeare*, ed. Valerie Wayne [New York: Havester Wheatsheaf, 1991], 173.)

[19] Cleaver (London, 1598), 178; Whately (London, 1619), 2ff.

[20] Gouge, 217.

[21] Ibid., 219.

[22] Vives, sig. f2v.

[23] Some authors mention the greater seriousness of the wife's adultery, which is complicated by lineage issues. However, such discussions are brief, and subordinated to the exhortation to marital chastity addressed to both members of the couple. See, for example, Bullinger, sigs. f2r–v.

[24] *The Subject of Tragedy: Identity and Difference in Renaissance Drama* (London: Methuen, 1985), 145.

[25] Newman couches this change in slightly different terms; the Catholic and early Reform manuals, she argues, show an almost obsessive interest in "the destructive power of female sexuality," whoredom, and adultery (20). This preoccupation disappears in later books, which instead concentrate on the depiction of stable family life. Newman sees both orientations as a means of "managing and regulating sexual difference," with changing socioeconomic imperatives accounting for the different emphases (19–27). See also Anthony Fletcher, *Gender, Sex and Subordination in England, 1500–1800* (New Haven: Yale Univ. Press, 1995), 5–10.

[26] *Workes*, trans. Thomas Pickering, vol. 3 (Cambridge, 1613), 692.

[27] Cleaver, 114, 213. Whately divides his bipartite definition into obedience of "word" and "deed" (189), which perhaps explains the seeming repetition in other tracts as well. Thomas Gataker cites women's first duty as subjection and omits discussion of chastity altogether ([London, 1619], 11–12). See also Bullinger, sigs. h1r–h2r.

[28] Vives, sig. I4v; Gouge, 277–78.

[29] This analogy has generated considerable interest among scholars of literature and history. Todd discusses its passage from Aristotle through the humanists and on to the Protestants (100–102). Rose argues that for Puritans it is "the crucial configuration on which all their arguments depend" (120). See also Belsey, 143–46; Susan Amussen, *An Ordered Society: Gender and Class in Early Modern England* (Oxford: Basil Blackwell, 1988), chap. 1, "Political Households and Domestic Politics," 34–66 passim, but esp. 36–39 and 47; and Lena Cowen Orlin, *Private Matters and Public Culture in Post-Reformation England*

(Ithaca: Cornell Univ. Press, 1994), 71–73 and chap. 2, "Patriarchalism and Its Discontents," 85–136.

[30] "Puritan Preaching and the Politics of the Family," in *The Renaissance Englishwoman in Print: Counterbalancing the Canon*, eds. Anne M. Haselkorn and Betty S. Travitsky (Amherst: Univ. of Mass. Press, 1990), 226–29.

[31] Gouge, 17.

[32] *Certaine Sermons by the Queens Majestie* (London, 1595), sigs. J3r–v.

[33] Belsey, 214.

[34] Whately, 193; *The Second Tome of Homilies* (London, 1595), sig. Gg5v.

[35] Lucas, 228–31.

[36] See Wayne's use of "ideology" as it applies to domestic treatises (*Flower*, 12n18). In her study of *Othello*, she warns against viewing "patriarchy as a monolithic and unvarying phenomenon" ("Historical Differences," 154); her nuanced distinctions in the *Flower* Introduction and in her study of misogyny in *Othello* insist on the complexity of changing ideas about matrimony and all its related issues.

[37] Maclean, 86.

KEITH MOXEY

Motivating History

LAST SUMMER I WENT SEARCHING for a book in Avery Library, the art library of Columbia University. This time, instead of looking at the shelves as mere supports for the volumes that contained the information I sought, I became aware that what I was looking at was the architecture (or archaeology) of a particular field of scholarly activity, namely the study of Northern Renaissance art. I was struck, in other words, by the physical presence of an aspect of our discipline's cultural imaginary.

The organization of the volumes arranged on the shelves, I realized, was at least as important as the information contained in the weighty tomes they supported. How had "Northern Renaissance art" come into being? How did this particular category or concept become a topic worthy of scholarly interest? Who or what had determined that there should be more books on certain artists rather than on others? What likes and dislikes do these choices betray? What values went into forming the configuration of books assembled there, and more important, what is it that continues to keep them in place?

The answer, of course, is the canon—that most naturalized of all art historical assumptions. Certain artists and certain works of art that have received the sanction of tradition are unquestioningly regarded as appropriate material for art historical study. Course syllabi are still arranged around artists who are deemed major figures, and the vast majority of publications are dedicated to a consideration of a select number of well-known works. Questions regarding the purpose and function of privileging certain artists and works in this way are rarely raised. Others concerning the esteem in which the canon is held are not regarded as belonging to art history but rather to aesthetics, a

---

"Motivating History" originally appeared, slightly modified, in *Art Bulletin* '77 (Sept. 1995) and is reprinted by permission of the College Art Association Inc.

branch of philosophy, or to the criticism of contemporary art. For the most part, art history's disciplinary work is carried on as if there were no need to articulate the social function it is supposed to serve. The discipline's promotion and support of the canon is all too often still taken for granted. It is as if a consensus had been arrived at some time in the past so that there is no further need for discussion. The library shelves are the physical manifestations of this consensus, the embodiment of an established cultural practice.

In asking for a discussion of the purpose of art history's dedication to the canon, I hope not to be misunderstood. This is not a call for a valuation of works of art, not a call for a more explicit ranking of canonical works, not a request that students be indoctrinated as to which artist is "better" than another. The problem, it seems to me, is that somehow the notion of "quality," that most subjective of judgements, is thought to be self-evident and unquestionable. While some of us may dwell affectionately and pleasurably on certain predictable canonical artists and describe their works in glowing terms, there is usually no attempt to argue, and perhaps even think about, why one artist should be considered more worthy of study than another or why certain moments and places in the history of artistic production should be privileged above others. As it stands now, the history of art could be described as an unacknowledged paean of praise addressed to the canon, and the intensity of this devotion can, perhaps, be measured by the sobriety of our professorial demeanor as we accomplish this task.

The conviction underlying these attitudes, which continue to be widespread—indeed, even prevalent in art history today—is the commitment to tradition. The canon of artists and works discussed in art history courses are those which were once found meritorious by previous generations of scholars responding to very different historical situations from those we currently occupy. Like Mount Everest, the works, the artists, and even the methodologies for interpreting them are simply there, and like mountain climbers, it is our mandate as art historians to climb their peaks and sing their praises to future generations. In doing so, we are often unwittingly engaged in the unthinking reproduction of culture: reproducing knowledge, but not necessarily producing it. As a consequence, the discipline as a whole becomes a powerful conservative force in a rapidly changing society.

The way to start speculating about how we came to this disciplinary moment might be to engage in a cultural history of the discipline, an examination of the classed, gendered, and ethnic values that have marked its development. Such a task, however, is impossible in the time available to me here. What follows is rather a discrete and limited examination of what could be called the founding moment of the canon of Northern Renaissance art, the historical point when a discursive practice first formed around works of art produced in Northern Europe in the fifteenth and sixteenth centuries. In other words, this is not a historiographic account of the origins and development of the appreciation of Northern Renaissance art, so much as an analysis of the political, religious, and emotional sentiments that prompted that appreciation to take place. The analysis is meant to be representative—the northern Renaissance is used here as a test case. A similar study might also be undertaken for what are considered the canonical artists and works of other times and places.

The ideas that led to the historical study of the Northern Renaissance at the end of the eighteenth century will be contrasted with those that inform the way in which the period was studied at the middle of the twentieth century, specifically in the work of Erwin Panofsky. The point of the contrast is to analyze the role of the practice of history in these two very different historiographic moments. How had the function of history changed in the period that separates the late eighteenth and the mid-twentieth centuries? Is there anything we can learn from the different ways in which history was approached, something that might enable us to rethink the function of history in our own time?

Until the end of the eighteenth century, the discipline of art history, founded by Vasari, remained focused on the humanist traditions of the Italian Renaissance as they were codified in the art academies of the seventeenth century. Not only were the styles and artistic techniques of the great masters of the Florentine and Venetian schools regarded as the models to which all artists should aspire, but the academies established a hierarchy of genres, according to which, history painting—meaning the painting of religious and secular subject matter depicting lofty subjects taken from Christian belief and Graeco-Roman mythology and history—was ranked at the top, and mere exercises in mimesis—such as landscape and still life—were located at the bottom. Owing to the dominance of the humanist tradition among the educated elite, there was little significant difference among the artistic aspirations of the schools of artistic production that arose in the regions that were later to become the nation-states of Europe. It was only in the eighteenth century that the dominance of the academy was first challenged by Winckelmann, who proposed that the true source of beauty was to be found in the art of ancient Greece. Later, in the context of the nationalism engendered by the European wars that followed the French Revolution, arguments began to be fielded regarding the aesthetic interest of works of art produced at times and places other than ancient Greece and Renaissance Italy.

The first mention of Northern Renaissance painting as a location for the discussion of artistic issues that had hitherto been associated only with Italy and Greece is found in the curious and delightful writings of the short-lived young author, Wilhelm Heinrich Wackenroder.[1] In his 1796 fictional account, *Confessions from the Heart of an Art-Loving Friar*, Wackenroder makes a compelling case for the relativity of artistic appeal. In doing so, he boldly challenged the accepted canon of his day, according to which Italian art of the Renaissance and the Greek art of antiquity were regarded as possessing greater merit than art produced at any other place and time:

> Stupid people cannot comprehend that there are antipodes on our globe and that they are themselves antipodes. They always conceive of the place where they are standing as the gravitational center of the universe,—and their minds lack the wings to fly around the entire earth and survey at one glance the integrated totality.
>
> And, similarly, they regard their own emotion as the center of everything beautiful in art and they deliver the final judgement concerning everything as if from the tribunal, without considering that no one has appointed them judges and that those who are condemned by them could just as well set themselves up to the same end.
>
> Why do you want to condemn the American Indian, that he speaks Indian and not your language?
>
> And yet you want to condemn the Middle Ages, that it did not build temples such as Greece?[2]

Wackenroder's appreciation for the art of the Northern Renaissance is paraded in a chapter dedicated to the praise of the work of Albrecht Dürer. His melodramatic account makes clear the nationalistic and religious values that underlie his concern to insert this artist into the canon. Dürer is regarded as just as good an artist as those who constitute the canon because of the quality of his inner spirit, an inner spirit that embodies the essence of the German nation:

> When Albrecht was wielding the paintbrush, the German was at that time still a unique and an excellent character of firm constancy in the arena of our continent; and this serious, upright and powerful nature of the German is imprinted in his pictures accurately and clearly, not only in the facial structure and the whole external appearance but also in the inner spirit. This firmly determined German character and German art as well have disappeared in our times ... and the student of art is taught how he should imitate the expressiveness of Raphael and the colors of the Venetian School and the realism of the Dutch and the enchanting highlights of Correggio, all simultaneously, and should in this way arrive at perfection which surpasses all. —O, wretched sophistry! O, blind belief of an age that one could combine every type of beauty and every excellence of all the great painters of the earth and, through the scrutinizing of all and the begging of their numerous great gifts, could unite the spirit of all in oneself and transcend them all![3]

The encomium ends with a description of a dream in which the friar falls asleep in an art gallery and has a vision in which the artists come alive before their paintings and discuss their merits. Among those that appear in this way are the shades of Raphael and Dürer, whom the friar observes holding hands as they gaze in "friendly tranquility" and mutual admiration at the achievements of one another's labors. By pairing Raphael and Dürer in this way, Wackenroder explicitly claims a new status for German painting of the Renaissance.

Wackenroder's argument concerning the relativity of artistic competence seems to depend upon the principle of historicism, which had been introduced into the philosophy of history by Johann Gottfried von Herder a few years earlier.[4] Herder had argued that there could be no objectivity in the writing of history because the historian was himself part of the historical process. On this view, there are no transhistorical absolutes, for all judgements are contingent upon the time and place in which they are produced. Wackenroder's artistic relativism, his capacity to claim that Dürer was the equal of Raphael, finds its basis in Herder's emphasis on the singularity of the historical moment. For Wackenroder, the unique quality of an historical period, that which makes it unlike anything that preceded or followed it, can be put in the service of a national cause. The nationalism of the late eighteenth century, a moment when Germany sought to free itself from the political and cultural domination of France, found in history a means by which its case might be articulated and advanced.

With its emphasis on the spirituality of art and its capacity to embody and transmit religious emotion, together with the conviction that these characteristics were to be found in the art of place and times that had not yet been hallowed by tradition, Wackenroder's book defined the romantic attitude towards the question of artistic quality. Much the same tone is found in the influential criticism of the writer, Friedrich Schlegel, who, during a stay in Paris, was deeply affected by his experience of the Musée Napoleon. It was in the Louvre that Napoleon's artistic plunder, taken from all over Europe, was placed on view as an unprecedented display of his imperial power.[5] Although he shared the admiration for Italian art typical of the taste of the day, Schlegel preferred the early painters of the fourteenth century because to his eyes their work exuded a greater spirituality. It was his admiration for the religious feeling of old master painting that allowed him to extend his appreciation to what he called "old German" painting of the Renaissance, by which he meant not only German but Netherlandish painting of this period.[6] Schlegel's advocacy of the virtues of "old German" painting soon drew the attention of the wealthy sons of a German businessman, Sulpiz and Melchior Boisserée, who traveled to Paris to visit him.[7] After staying at his house as paying guests, they traveled with Schlegel through northern France and the southern Netherlands, visiting Gothic cathedrals before returning to their native Cologne. In the account Schlegel wrote of this journey, he identified the Gothic as the German style of the Middle Ages, extolling its beauties as a manifestation of the age of faith.

Schlegel's views coincided with a significant change of taste, one that assured that his re-evaluation of German art of the Renaissance would be underwritten by capital so as to find a material manifestation in the formation of collections and museums. On their return to Cologne, the Boisserée brothers began avidly collecting German and Netherlandish art. Their passion was aided by political circumstances, for the Napoleonic dispossession of the properties of the Catholic church, enforced throughout occupied Germany as well as France, meant that medieval and Renaissance altarpieces that had been part of the neglected fabric of church interiors suddenly entered the marketplace in large numbers. The Boisserées soon assembled the largest and most important collection of paintings of this period, including some of the most admired works of Stefan Lochner, Rogier van der Weyden, and Hans Memling. After having been made available to the Prussian crown, which was in the process of establishing what would eventually become the national museum in Berlin, this collection was eventually bought by the King of Bavaria in 1827, thus finding an alternative route to the fulfillment of Schlegel's call for a national museum of "old German" painting.[8]

Both Wackenroder and Schlegel had used history as a means of realizing their critical appreciation of art that was emotionally laden with religious values and which could be claimed as glorious manifestations of the German national spirit. In doing so, they laid the foundation for the study of what came to be called Northern Renaissance art. What distinguishes their approach to history from that which still characterizes our own times? What kinds of stories do we tell today and what motivates them?

The other and contrasting end of this analysis of the character of the discourse on Northern Renaissance art is located in what is usually regarded as its apogee, namely in the work of Erwin Panofsky. Panofsky's book, *The Life and Art of Albrecht Dürer*, appeared in 1943, while *Early Netherlandish Painting* was published a decade later, in 1953.[9] Rather than using history in the service of religious, emotional and nationalistic goals, Panofsky's books appear to have no other ambition than to provide the reader with a wealth of information about the subjects under discussion. Both texts are detailed and learned accounts of the available historical evidence, a discussion that is, for the most part, pursued with a relentless "objectivity," with a positivistic desire to evaluate and supercede the nature and quality of the information provided by earlier historians. The introductions to both volumes, however, "betray rather than parade," the ideological agenda behind the works.[10]

In the introduction to the Dürer book, Panofsky declares that he believes the German contribution to art history has yet to be acknowledged. He proposes that the artistic accomplishments of Dürer, whom he defines as a representative of the German national spirit, make him worthy of comparison with the great artists of the Italian Renaissance. While there is an interesting continuity to be traced between the nationalism of Wackenroder and Schlegel and that of Panofsky, the historiographic differences in the way they advance their claims are more significant than their similarities.

The period of 150 years or so that separates the texts of these authors could be said to have witnessed the triumph of history. The historicist principle enunciated by Herder had been developed in the course of the nineteenth century into something resembling a science. The recognition that time is a decisive factor affecting our understanding of the world led to a proliferation of studies affecting all aspects of human knowledge. In addition, the influence of the success of the physical sciences during the same period pushed historical studies into an ever-increasing empiricism. The transformation in the function of history between these two historical moments seems to depend above all else on the elimination of the subjectivity of the historian. Whereas Wackenroder and Schlegel fully articulated that their interest in history depended upon their religious and nationalist beliefs, in Panofsky's case, the historian's agenda is far less explicit.

The nationalism of the introduction to the Dürer book, for example, appears paradoxical in light of Panofsky's forced exile from Germany by the National Socialists. What was at stake in inserting Dürer into the Renaissance canon of Italian artists was much more complicated than an assertion of pride in national identity. As I have argued elsewhere, Panofsky's view of Dürer as torn between the principles of reason and unreason, for which he used the emblem of Dürer's engraving, *Melencolia I*, has more to do with the political situation of Germany in his own time, with a defense of humanism in the context of National Socialism, than it does with the cultural conditions of sixteenth-century Nuremberg.[11] His engagement with politics, however, was not permitted to register as part of the conscious objectives of his historical biography. Political and emotional beliefs were repressed in favor of a "disinterested" account of the historical information on this artist.

The same "objectivist" attitude is found in the introduction to *Early Netherlandish Painting*. Here, Panofsky argues that Netherlandish naturalism, the characteristic quality of this school of painting, is actually indebted to the invention of one-point perspective, an artistic achievement of Italian art of the same period. The canonical status of Netherlandish art is thus underwritten by its incorporation of one of the pictorial devices that serve to distinguish Italian art. Instead of appealing to the notion of artistic relativity on which Wackenroder and Schlegel had based their claim for the interest of "old German" painting, Panofsky attempts to include Netherlandish art under the umbrella of traditional taste for the Italian Renaissance. If Italian painting is part of the canon because of its development of mimetic techniques, such as perspective, that enabled it to achieve more convincing kinds of illusion, thereby heightening the naturalism for which it had been valued, then Netherlandish painting gains status by sharing these characteristics. This is, in other words, a kind of canonization by association.[12] Similarly, Panofsky's analysis of the complex symbolism of Netherlandish painting, which is discussed at length in the text, could be said to represent an attempt to find an equivalent for the complicated religious and secular allegories that are a feature of Italian art of this period. Once again, the artistic merit attached to early Netherlandish art would result not from its pictorial autonomy, not from the principle of artistic relativity, but from its similarity to the southern tradition.

What is it that led to the suppression of the authorial agenda that seems to distinguish Panofsky's treatment of Northern Renaissance art from those of Wackenroder and Schlegel? Why is it that the authorial voice is so much more removed and abstract? What led to the substitution of a colorless objectivity for a passionately argued subjectivity? A full answer to these questions would necessitate a history of the idea of history in the nineteenth and twentieth centuries and would have much to do with the institutionalization of the discipline and the "professionalization" of its practitioners. It is immediately apparent, however, that history served a very different function for Wackenroder and Schlegel than it did for Panofsky. Whereas in the earlier case history is part of a larger cultural rhetoric, in its later incarnation, it seems to be pursued as if it could be an end in itself.

Panofsky's reticence about the larger cultural function of history, his reluctance to articulate the concerns that animate his scholarly work, as well as his conception of history as a positivistic discipline, finds its theoretical justification in "The History of Art as a Humanistic Discipline" of 1955. In this reflective essay, Panofsky suggests that the historian is involved in two very different types of activity. In responding to the work of art (which is defined as a "man-made object demanding to be experienced aesthetically"), the art historian must both "re-create" the work by attempting to intuit the artistic "intentions" that went into its creation and then submit it to archaeological investigation.

The aesthetic re-creation of the work is deemed to depend "not only on the natural sensitivity and visual training of the spectator, but also on his cultural equipment."[13] The difference between a naive beholder and an art historian is the fact that the latter is aware of his cultural predispositions; that is, he is aware of the contemporary perspective he brings to the work of interpretation as a consequence of belonging to a culture different from that which is under investigation, while the naive beholder is not. The point of the historian's awareness of his own cultural values is not to acknowledge them as part of the historical narrative that will result as a consequence of his engagement with the past, not to understand that whatever he comes up with will inevitably be filtered through the peculiar configuration of his own subjectivity, but rather to suppress or eliminate all aspects of his approach to the study of the past that might result from his participation in the historical horizon of which he is a part. It is by means of his knowledge of the past that the historian is to control, if not to extirpate altogether, the affective and valuational baggage he brought to the enterprise in the first place. The goal is to be as "objective" as possible.

> He tries, therefore, to make adjustments by learning as much as he possibly can about the circumstances under which the objects of his studies were created. Not only will he collect and verify all the available information as to medium, condition, age, authorship, destination, etc., but he will also com-

pare the work with others of its class, and will examine such writings as reflect the aesthetic standards of its country and age, in order to achieve a more "objective" appraisal of its quality.

.... But when he does all this, his aesthetic perception as such will change accordingly, and will more and more adapt itself to the original "intention" of the works. Thus what the art historian as opposed to the "naive" art lover, does, is not to erect a rational superstructure on an irrational foundation, but to develop his re-creative experiences so as to conform with the results of his archaeological research, while continually checking the results of his archaeological research against the evidence of his re-creative experiences.[14]

Because of the theoretical elimination of the subjectivity of the historian, the approach to interpretation outlined above has no way of dealing with issues of artistic merit. This method could, for example, be applied to the interpretation of any work of art regardless of its "quality." What is missing is some way of articulating why certain works matter to the interpreter and others do not. The result is an art history absorbed by a positivistic obsession with information.

Panofsky was, of course, fully aware that the discipline could not exist without a means to privileging some works above others. His solution was to claim that "greatness" of works of art was self-evident and artistic achievement would disclose itself to the historian in the course of his investigation. Panofsky's banishment of subjectivity in favor of positivistic objectivity—the sacrifice of cultural judgement in favor of a re-creation of the artistic "intentions" of the past—"intentions" which were to be validated by "archaeological investigation"—proved deeply influential. So far, contemporary art history has concerned itself only with the evaluation and criticism of his methodological concepts of "iconography" and "iconology" that for so long dominated scholarly activity in our discipline.[15] The other side of the coin, the fact that this subtle and effective method of historical interpretation succeeded because it obliterated questions related to the subjectivity of the historian, has yet to be recognized and explored.

Panofsky's bias against the insertion of the concerns of the present into narratives about the past would appear to be part of an historical tendency that has also affected literary studies in the twentieth century. Barbara Herrnstein Smith has pointed out that literary critics have also been more concerned with the development of theories of interpretation than with articulating the rationale that occasions their deployment. She argues that:

> ... while professors of literature have sought to claim for their activities the rigor, objectivity, cognitive substantiality, and progress associated with science and the empirical disciplines, they have also attempted to remain faithful to the essentially conservative and didactic mission of humanistic studies: to honor and preserve the culture's traditionally esteemed objects—in this case, its canonized texts—and to illuminate and transmit the traditional cultural values presumably embodied in them.[16]

Panofsky's relegation of the question of artistic excellence to the realm of the self-evident effectively wove it into the fabric of tradition. One can only tell what is self-evident by consulting what other human beings have considered artistically exceptional in the past. By reading the past we can infer what is appropriate to the present, thus avoiding the necessity of projecting contemporary judgement into the process. The price of interpretive objectivity is the abdication of responsibility for finding in history a means of articulating the cultural dilemmas of the present. The principle of self-evidence is a profoundly conservative one, dedicated to the support of the status quo and ideally suited to the task of providing art history with "scientific" respectability.

Panofsky's equation of canonical value with traditional value was espoused and supported by Ernst Gombrich, arguably the *other* most influential art historian of this century. It is because art historians are the custodians of this tradition that they can be distinguished from social scientists who approach works of art as if they were part of the material of culture. In a 1973 lecture entitled "Art History and the Social Sciences," Gombrich took it upon himself to defend art history's preoccupation with a canon of works that had been recognized as "great" against those who advocated the study of works of art as cultural artifacts. He argued that whereas the study of historical circumstance would significantly affect our appreciation of the art of the past, it was no substitute for the connoisseur's capacity to discern "quality." For Gombrich, the canon

> ... offers points of reference, standards of excellence which we cannot level down without losing direction. Which particular peaks, or which individual achievements we select for this role may be a matter of choice, but we could not make such a choice if there really were no peaks but only shifting dunes.... the values of the canon are too deeply embedded in the totality of our civilization for them to be discussed in isolation....[17]

What was it that led leading art historians of the caliber of Panofsky and Gombrich to dismiss any discussion of the cultural qualities of exceptional works of art on the basis that they were self-evident? What supported their belief that artistic merit was universally discernible? The unstated assumption underlying their position regarding what constitutes the canonical status of a work of art would appear to be a theory of aesthetics. While the notion of the canon and aesthetic theory have everything to do with one another, this is not the place for an extended discussion of their relationship. The following critique of theories that postulate that aesthetic feeling is a universal human response to works of art must suffice for the purposes of the argument of this talk.

According to the most influential theory of aesthetics, that formulated by Immanuel Kant in the late eighteenth century, certain works of art had the capacity to provoke a universal recognition of their extraordinary quality.[18] The existence of the beautiful was thus something located in the human response to objects rather than in the objects themselves. By making the capacity to recognize artistic quality part of the definition of "human nature," Kant's theory offered a basis for the identification of canonical status with the judgement of tradition. Both Panofsky and Gombrich belong to the humanist tradition of which Kant's theory is a part. That is, they share the faith that "human nature" affords human beings an adequate epistemological foundation on which to understand both the world and "man's" place within it. It is for this reason that it is possible for them to assert that the artistic quality of certain cultural artifacts is "self-evident."

The humanist conception of human subjectivity as something stable, continuous, autonomous, and not subject to modulation according to circumstances of time and place, has been subject to devastating criticism in our own time. Psychoanalysis, for example, has tended to emphasize the contingency of the human subject. According to Jacques Lacan, the subject is split on the acquisition of language into that which represents the desires and drives of a pre-conscious condition (the unconscious) and that which represents the codes and conventions that govern social life (the symbolic).[19] On this account, subjectivity is shifting and unstable, constantly under revision as the relation between the unconscious and the social is renegotiated in the light of the ever-changing circumstances of everyday life. This view of the subject clearly militates against the concept of "human nature," against the assumption that all human beings could ever react in the same way towards anything, let alone works of art.

If we accept the notion that human subjectivity is a construction whose shape varies according to the cultural forces that determine its identity, then it follows that human response to cultural artifacts will vary according to the race, gender, class, sexual orientation and nationality of the individual. One of the most powerful critiques of Kant's aesthetic theory has been mounted by the Marxist sociologist Pierre Bourdieu, who used the concept of class to show that the location of individuals in the social hierarchy is crucial in determining their response to works of art.[20]

Anthropologists, like Johannes Fabian and literary critics including Edward Said have also drawn attention to the ideological agenda underlying humanist epistemologies. They suggest that the conception of the human subject as something stable and unchanging, something self-conscious and capable of knowing both the world and itself, is a dimension of Eurocentrism that characterized European culture during the colonial period of the late eighteenth and nineteenth centuries.[21] The age of empire saw a fusion of the desire for knowledge with the world-wide expansion of European power. Not only was the search for knowledge backed by epistemological assumptions that precluded cultural differences, but in the European encounter with other peoples it was always Europe that was used as the canon by which to judge the rest. The result was a subordination of other cultures to a European conception of "civilization" and a reduction of the different ways of understanding the world to what we know as "science."

These critics suggest that the ways in which individuals, classes, and cultures invest objects with social value are so different that such processes cannot be considered to belong to the same category—that is, they cannot usefully be grouped under the rubric of the aesthetic. If this is the case, then the concept of aesthetics, one that is intimately associated with the humanist conception of an unchanging "human nature," is emptied of its content.[22] What becomes more important than trying to reduce the rich variety of human response to a single kind of human experience is the articulation of the grounds on which these different responses attain the status of discursive practices.

Panofsky's attempts to naturalize the concept of artistic quality, or—to paraphrase Gombrich—the claim that quality is one of the implicit value judgements that make up our civilization, were never completely convincing. However, it was not until the advent of feminism that the equation of the art historical canon with tradition received a lasting challenge. More than any other historian or critic, it was Linda Nochlin in her famous 1971 piece, "Why Have There Been No Great Women Artists?," who placed the issue of artistic merit squarely in the foreground of the discipline's attention.[23] She showed just how unsatisfactory the concept of tradition was to a definition of the canonical status of a work of art, by underscoring the extent to which a putative *master*piece serves to articulate and support a hierarchy between the sexes. There was nothing inherently natural about the selection of great artists and works on which art history depended, because that choice was the product of social attitudes that were historically determined. The equation of artistic merit with tradition honored the cultural achievements of men because social forces prevented women from participating fully in the processes of artistic production.

More recently, Adrian Rifkin has used the work of Jacques Derrida to draw out the consequences of poststructuralist theory for the art historical canon, in particular the necessity to recognize that the work of the historian—the historical text—is inevitably colored by his or her position in history and culture. If art history is regarded as a "discursive practice," a socially-sanctioned form of making cultural meaning, then it is susceptible to the type of textual analysis known as deconstruction.[24] Derrida has shown that language is involved in a game of absent presence, that it serves to endow ontological status on what is otherwise only an unstable and shifting system of signs which draw their meaning, not from their capacity to refer to objects in the world, but rather from the cultural attitudes with which they are invested by their users. In such circumstances, the notion of "art" is transformed from being a series of cultural objects distinguished by their capacity to provoke a universal response to their artistic merit, to a series of cultural objects that have been arbitrarily awarded a privileged status by authors whose interests have been served by doing so.[25] The cultural category "art" and the discursive practice "art history" are social constructs rather than eternal constants in the history of civilization.

What conclusions can we draw concerning the function of authorial subjectivity in the writing of history and the nature and status of the art historical canon? First and most startling, is the realization that the type of appreciation expressed for Northern Renaissance art in the work of Wackenroder and Schlegel is more relevant to our conception of contemporary historical interpretation than is the work of Panofsky. As feminist critics have shown, once the concept of tradition has been shown to be historically compromised, laden with the cultural attitudes of a particular historical moment, and once every attempt to make textual meaning has been shown to be less about the world and more about the projection of authorial bias and prejudice as well as insight and understanding, then it seems clear that art historical interpretations must address the question of why they believe the works they discuss are worth talking about. Once there is no longer anything self-evident about the status of the works that are the focus of art historical attention, it is necessary to argue why certain works have been chosen rather than others. The subjective attitudes and cultural aspirations of the art historian become just as important an aspect of the narrative as the works that are its object. This is much the same as saying that there is no canon beyond that which we ourselves construct. Instead of using history to buttress the existence of a traditional canon, instead of making the historical imagination serve the status quo, i.e., the tastes of those whose culture we have inherited, a motivated history can be used to destabilize and call into question the assumptions and prejudices of that culture by insisting on their contingency and relativity.

What are the pedagogical implications of these conclusions? What would happen, in other words, to the educational function of art history, if these reflections were put into practice? In its present configuration as a discipline organized around the study of a canon of artists and works guaranteed by tradition, art history must be considered an agent in what Pierre Bourdieu has called the process of "cultural reproduction." The canonical content of our syllabi serves as a means of transmitting "cultural capital" from one generation of the elite to another.[26] By transferring knowledge about a set of works whose merit can neither be questioned nor discussed, art history plays an important conservative role in contemporary culture.

How can these conditions be transformed? The elimination of a canon seems to be a utopian dream. To suggest that art history could continue as a social institution without making choices between what artists and works should be taught and which should not presupposes that the discipline could operate without a cultural agenda. Such deliberate naiveté would simply reproduce the circumstances that promoted an unquestioning attitude towards the traditional canon in the first place. If we assume in the wake of post-structuralism that there are no disinterested narratives, that all art historical accounts are informed by one bias or another, then it seems wiser to acknowledge that there will always be some works that are considered to be of greater artistic merit than others and that the standards that go into making such judgements differ according to the attitudes and interests of different historical groups and individuals. Rather than assume that the discipline might ever agree on what constitutes "quality," suppose our students were introduced to concepts of artistic merit that responded to different political and cultural beliefs? In such circumstances, they might encounter, among others, a marxist canon, a feminist canon, and a gay and lesbian canon, a post-colonial canon.

Far from assuming that this plethora of ideals of social value could co-exist in egalitarian conviviality, a contest of voices would arise in which a struggle for dominance would result in the hierarchization of contestatory discourses. The value of the existence of such alternatives, as well as of their debate with one another, is that none could henceforth be regarded as a "master narrative." Decisions to subscribe to one or another of their social agendas would be made with a full recognition of the political and cultural implications of that choice. None of the alternatives would be able to mask the contingency of its assumptions behind the naturalizing mask of tradition.

This talk has argued that art history should acknowledge the importance of the subjectivity of the author in his or her account of the past. Rather than legitimating a pre-established canon of artists and works following the principle of "objectivity," historians might pursue their own agendas and articulate their own motives for engaging in the process of finding cultural meaning in the art of the past. Instead of regarding the subject of art history as fixed and unchanging, scholars have an opportunity to define what that subject might be. In doing so, they can display rather than conceal the cultural issues that preoccupy them. The subject of art history thus becomes manifestly an allegory of the historical circumstances that have both shaped and empowered the subjectivity of the author.

This emphasis on the agency of the historian, his or her capacity to subject the values of the past to intense scrutiny and rigorous criticism, as well as to articulate the cultural aspirations of his or her own times, should not be misunderstood. This is not a call for some simple-minded correspondence between interpretation and interpreter, not a suggestion that one should reflect the other. The allegories of subjectivity we call history must inevitably be opaque. We can never be fully conscious of the motives that impel (compel?) us to give one shape to an interpretation rather than another. The unconscious must, by definition, remain beyond our capacity to understand. Not only is the historian's subjectivity partly determined by unconscious forces, but it is also subject to the ideological traditions that are characteristic of its situation in history. Following Althusser, we might define ideology as the unconscious of social life.[27] The historian belongs sometimes knowingly and sometimes unknowingly to a variety of different ways of conceiving of the relations between human beings as members of a particular culture, as well as the way in which that culture relates to other cultures and to the world, and these structures of understanding define his or her subjectivity in relation to all other times and places.

It is only, however, because the cultural codes and conventions that serve to define individual subjectivity also enable it to participate in social life, it is only because the subject is both constituted by and constituting of the circumstances in which it lives, that the active role of history in the creation and transformation of culture can be understood. The call for a motivated history thus does not assume that the historian's motives are transparently accessible, but rather, within the context of psychoanalytic and ideological determination, it insists on the subject's powers of agency to articulate and promote those political agendas that are most relevant to and desirable for the cultural circumstances in which it operates.

Barnard College, Columbia University

Notes

[1] For a fuller sketch of the appreciation of early Netherlandish art in the eighteenth and nineteenth centuries, see F. Haskell, *Rediscoveries in Art: Some Aspects of Taste, Fashion, and Collecting in England and France* (Ithaca: Cornell University Press, 1976) and S. Sulzberger, *La Réhabilitation des Primitifs Flamandes, 1802–1867* (Brussels: Palais des Académies, 1961).

[2] Wackenroder, *Confessions and Fantasies*, trans. M. Hurst Schubert (University Park, Penn.: Penn State Press, 1970), 109–10.

[3] Wackenroder, 115.

[4] See G. Iggers, *The German Conception of History: The National Tradition of Historical Thought from Herder to the Present* (Middletown, Conn.: Wesleyan Univ. Press, 1968), 34–38. The concept of historicism is subject to a variety of different definitions. See, for example, M. Mandelbaum, *History, Man, and Reason: A Study in Nineteenth Century Thought* (Baltimore: The Johns Hopkins Univ. Press, 1971). For an interesting attempt to dissolve the distinction between historicism and history by arguing that all histories share the kind of system-building quality usually attributed to historicist histories on the basis that they are all structured according to rhetorical tropes, see H. White, "Historicism, History, and the Figurative Imagination," *History and Theory* 14 (1975), Beiheft 14, 48–67.

[5] See H. Eichner, *Friedrich Schlegel* (New York: Twayne Publishers, 1970).

[6] Schlegel's views on art are found in F. Schlegel, *Kritische Friedrich Schlegel Ausgabe*, 5 vols., ed. E. Behler with J. J. Austett and H. Eichner (Munich: Paderborn; Vienna: Verlag F. Schöning and Thomas Verlag, 1958–1959), IV, "Ansichten und Ideen von der christlichen Kunst."

[7] For a history of the Boisserée brothers and their collection, see E. Firmenich-Richartz, *Die Brüder Boisserée: Sulpiz und Melchior Boisserée als Kunstsammler. Ein Beitrag zur Geschichte der Romantik* (Jena: Diederichs, 1916).

[8] Sulzberger (as in n. 2), 57.

[9] Panofsky, *The Life and Art of Albrecht Dürer*, 2 vols. (Princeton: Princeton Univ. Press, 1943); idem., *Early Netherlandish Painting*, 2 vols. (Cambridge, Mass.: Harvard Univ. Press, 1953).

[10] The phrase is a quotation from Panofsky, 1955a, 1–25, 14. It occurs as part of the definition of what he called the "iconological" method of interpretation whose purpose was to uncover the cultural attitudes encoded in the "content" of the work of art.

[11] See "Panofsky's Melancolia" in my book, *The Practice of Theory: Poststructuralism, Cultural Politics, and Art History* (Ithaca and London: Cornell Univ. Press, 1994), 65–78.

[12] I have analyzed the introduction to *Early Netherlandish Painting* in, "Perspective, Panofsky, and the Philosophy of History," *New Literary History* 26 (1995), 775–86. Panofsky's text also contains expressions of nationalist views. Some of them were noted by Katherine Crawford Luber in a talk, "Nationalism and Panofsky: Albrecht Dürer, Italy, and *Early Netherlandish Painting*" delivered at the College Art Association Meeting in 1994 in New York.

[13] Ibid.

[14] Ibid., 17–18.

[15] See Panofsky, 1955b, 26–54. For comment and criticism of this method of interpretation, see E. Kaemmerling, *Ikonographie und Ikonologie: Theorien, Entwicklung, Probleme* (Cologne: DuMont, 1979); J. Bonnet, ed., *Erwin Panofsky: Cahiers pour un temps* (Paris: Centre Georges Pompidou, 1983); M. Podro, *The Critical Historians of Art* (New Haven: Yale Univ. Press, 1982); M. Holly, *Panofsky and the Foundations of Art History* (Ithaca: Cornell Univ. Press, 1984) and *Iconografia e Iconologia* (Milan: Jaca Books, 1992); K. Moxey, "Panofsky's Concept of 'Iconology' and the Problem of Interpretation in the History of Art," *New Literary History* 17 (1985–1986), 265–74; S. Ferretti, *Cassirer, Panofsky, and Warburg: Symbol, Art, and History*, trans. R. Pierce (New Haven: Yale Univ. Press, 1989); G. Didi-Huberman, *Devant l'image* (Paris: Minuit, 1990); B. Cassidy, ed., *Iconography at the Crossroads* (Princeton: Princeton Univ. Press, 1993).

[16] B. Herrnstein Smith, "The Exile of Evaluation," *Contingencies of Value: Alternative Perspectives for Critical Theory* (Cambridge, Mass.: Harvard Univ. Press, 1988), 18. It is significant that the book Smith identifies as the most extreme version of the anti-evaluationist stance, N. Frye's *Anatomy of Criticism*, was, like *Early Netherlandish Painting*, published in the 1950's. Smith's book is one of several publications dealing with the question of the canon in literary studies. It is telling that there should be no art historical equivalent. For other contributors, see R. van Hallberg, "Canons," a special issue of *Critical Inquiry* 10 (1983), which included contributions by B. Herrnstein Smith, C. Altieri, J. McGann, J. Guillory, R. Ohmann, and others; Frank Kermode, *Forms of Atten-*

tion (Chicago: Univ. of Chicago Press, 1985); J. Tompkins, *Sensational Designs: The Cultural Work of American Fiction, 1790–1860* (New York: Oxford Univ. Press, 1985); R. Scholes, "Aiming a Canon at the Curriculum," *Salmagundi* 72 (1986), 101–17 and the responses by E. D. Hirsch, M. Perloff, E. Fox-Genovese, and others; C. Altieri, *Canons and Consequences: Reflections on the Ethical Force of Imaginative Ideals* (Evanston, Ill.: Northwestern Univ. Press, 1990); J. Goran, *The Making of the Modern Canon: Genesis and Crisis of a Literary Idea* (Atlantic Highlands, NJ: Athlone Press, 1991); P. Lauter, *Canons in Contexts* (New York: Oxford Univ. Press, 1991); H. L. Gates, Jr., *Loose Canons: Notes on the Culture Wars* (New York: Oxford Univ. Press, 1992); J. Guillory, *Cultural Capital: The Problem of Literary Canon Formation* (Chicago: Univ. of Chicago Press, 1993).

[17] E. Gombrich, *Art History and the Social Sciences: The Romanes Lecture for 1973* (Oxford: Clarendon Press, 1975), 54. Silence was also suggested as the means by which a critic might validate the equation of the canon with tradition by Frye. See Smith (as in n. 19), 24. For a recent defense of the humanist strategy of silencing discussion of the quality of literary text (or works of art) in favor of accepting the verdict of tradition, see Peter Brooks, "Aesthetics and Ideology: What happened to Poetics?," *Critical Inquiry* 20 (1994) 509–23.

[18] Kant, *Critique of Aesthetic Judgement*, trans. James Meredith (Oxford: Clarendon Press, 1952).

[19] Lacan, "The Mirror Stage as Formative of the Function of the I" and "The Agency of the Letter in the Unconscious, or Reason Since Freud," *Ecrits: A Selection*, trans. Alan Sheridan (New York: Norton, 1977), 1–7 and 146–78.

[20] Bourdieu, *Distinction: A Social Critique of the Judgement of Taste* (London: Routledge, 1986).

[21] Johannes Fabian, *Time and the Other: How Anthropology Makes its Object* (New York: Columbia Univ. Press, 1983); Edward Said, *Orientalism* (New York: Vintage Books, 1979) and *Culture and Imperialism* (New York: Knopf, 1993).

[22] See Tony Bennett, "Really Useless Knowledge: A Political Critique of Aesthetics," *Literature and History* 13 (1987): 38–57.

[23] L. Nochlin, "Why Have There Been No Great Women Artists?," *Art News* 69 (1971): 23–39 and 67–69.

[24] A. Rifkin, "Art's Histories," in *The New Art History*, ed. A. L. Rees and F. Borzello (London: Camden Press, 1986), 157–63. See also G. Mermoz, "Rhetoric and Episteme: Writing about 'Art' in the Wake of Post-Structuralism," *Art History* 12 (1989): 497–509.

[25] For a discussion of the way in which works of art are "framed," see J. Derrida, *The Truth in Painting*, trans. G. Bennington and I. McLeod (Chicago: Univ. of Chicago Press, 1987).

[26] P. Bourdieu and J. C. Passeron, *Reproduction in Education, Society, and Culture*, trans. R. Nice (London: Sage Publications, 1990). For an indictment of

the way in which art history serves the process of "cultural reproduction," see Carol Duncan, "Teaching the Rich," *The Aesthetics of Power: Essays in Critical Art History* (New York: Cambridge Univ. Press, 1993), 135–42.

[27] Louis Althusser, "Ideology and the Ideological State Apparatuses," *Lenin and Philosophy and Other Essays*, trans. Ben Brewster (New York: Monthly Review Press, 1971), 126–86.

LAURA MACCASKEY

Tainted Image/Sacred Image: The Wandering Madonna of S. Maria in Vallicella*

THE HIGH ALTAR OF THE CHURCH of S. Maria in Vallicella, known also as the Chiesa Nuova, is surmounted by an altarpiece executed by the Flemish artist Peter Paul Rubens during his second sojourn in Rome (fig. 1).[1] It was a bold move when, in 1606, the brethren of the Vallicella commissioned so prominent a work from this young foreigner, however brilliant. In fact, Monsignor Jacomo Serra (1570–1623), papal treasurer to Paul V and a wealthy Genoese, provided payment for an altarpiece on the condition, stated in the contract, that Rubens execute the painting.[2]

Rubens did not disappoint; the painting he produced is a bravura display of his gift for dramatic and vivid characterization. But the painting now on the altar is not the one executed by Rubens in 1606.[3] The current altarpiece was painted between 1607 and 1608 to replace the one executed under the terms of the 1606 contract. The painting on view in S. Maria in Vallicella emerged from a complex history of three successive schemes involving not only radical changes in iconography, but also in the type of pictorial representation concerned.

Rubens's work at the Vallicella has been addressed by several notable scholars.[4] This paper, however, sets Rubens's response to the commission within the social and religious context of the new congregation of the Vallicella from 1575 to 1620. Instead of focusing on the reasons for the rejection of Rubens's first work, this study will emphasize the appropriation and creation of a cult based on the sacred Vallicella icon of the Madonna, a key feature of the final altarpiece, and the common elements of the successive projects.

The history of the high altarpiece commission is bound up with that of a cult centered on an image of the Madonna and Child

Fig. 1. Peter Paul Rubens. Icon of the Madonna and Child Adored by Angels. S. Maria in Vallicella, Rome, Italy. Reproduced with the permission of Alinari/Art Resource, NY.

originally attached to a wall of a *stufa*, or bathhouse, in the neighborhood of the Vallicella.[5] Bathhouses were notoriously popular in the sixteenth century and were frequently used as meeting places of prostitutes and their clients.[6] Indeed, houses of prostitution, or *cassette*, were located all around the old Vallicella up to the 1540s, and the area was well-known as a working area of prostitutes, procuresses and witches.[7] Sometime in the early sixteenth century, the image of the Madonna began to bleed after being struck in the face by a stone thrown by an impious youth.[8] A cult developed which prompted the icon's removal to the first chapel on the left inside the door of the old church of the Vallicella, which was and is dedicated to the Presentation of Christ and Purification of the Virgin.[9]

The twelfth-century basilica on the site, now dilapidated, was plagued with the unfavorable reputation of being a working area for prostitutes.[10] Furthermore, because of its hot springs and volcanic activity, the area was associated with the pagan cult of the *Dis Pater* and *Proserpina*.[11] The resonances between the stufe, the hot springs, and prostitution are even more apparent through the existence of a marble well that stood in front of the old church. By the fifteenth century, the site was referred to as the Pozzo Bianco.[12] Circumstantial evidence indicates that the Vallicella icon, like Caravaggio's *Madonna di Loreto* of Sant'Agostino, was frequented by the local prostitutes.[13] Indeed, the appropriation of the icon by the priests of the Vallicella may have been connected with a concern to counter sinister associations, not only because of the current reputation of the Vallicella neighborhood, but also because of the ancient designation of the place as the site of a pagan cult.

The Filippini were already a key force within the Roman Counter-Reformation movement when the Vallicella was given to them in 1575. A Florentine by birth, the great spiritual leader Filippo Neri (1515–1595) had become chaplain of S. Girolamo della Carità on the Via Monserrato in Rome in 1551, where his reputation as "the great confessor" emerged.[14] Neri's sermons emphasized charity, piety, and humility as expressed in the gospels and practiced in the Early Christian Church. As an important part of his mission to the people, Neri conducted afternoon sermons in his own rooms, which became so popular they soon had to be moved to a larger facility to accommodate the growing number of devotees.[15] Eventually, the Filippini, or Oratorians as they later became known, had outgrown even this space, and in 1563, when asked by the Florentines to become rector of S. Giovanni dei Fiorentini, Neri sent some of his closest followers to that church, where they were ordained.[16] These men took up residence at S. Giovanni, becoming the core of the future congregation of the Filippine Oratory.[17]

The old church of S. Maria in Vallicella was handed over, quite unexpectedly, to Filippo Neri in the Jubilee year of 1575 by Pope Gregory XIII (1572–1585) to house the newly-created Filippine Order.[18] Neri was prepared to make do with what he had been given—a crumbling old church surrounded by the *cassette* of prostitutes who probably frequented the parish church. At first, Neri suggested that the brethren restore the old Vallicella church, but within the year the decision was taken to rebuild.[19]

Like most late sixteenth-century churches, the new Vallicella comprises a vast, vaulted nave from which open separate chapels. These side chapels contain frescoes of the narrative cycle of the Life of Mary, thematically linking them with the imagery of the remaining, spatially quite distinct chapels. The cycle is read counter-clockwise, beginning at the left chapel (nearest the high altar) with the Virgin's Presentation and continues along the left with the Annunciation, Visitation, Nativity of Christ, Adoration of the Magi, and Presentation of Christ with the Purification of the Virgin (see floor plan, fig. 2).[20] The cycle continues in the upper right chapel with the Coronation, Assumption, Pentecost, Ascension, Pietà and the Crucifixion.

According to the original decorative program of 1575, presumably conceived by Neri, the narrative of the Virgin's life would have begun at the high altar with a representation of her birth.[21] The first scene in the narrative of the Virgin's life, the Nativity of the Virgin, is rarely depicted independently from the cycle and never as the subject of high altar decoration.[22] In the scene, Mary's mother, Anne, reclines on a birth couch and is attended by female servants while her newborn infant is prepared for a bath in a laver.[23] Represented as a human birth, Mary's Nativity prefigures her own future delivery of Christ.[24] In the humble acceptance of her fate, the Virgin was a prime example to the Filippini of the preeminent virtue of humility.[25] As such, the representation of the Nativity of the Virgin carries with it an implication of the stain of birth which levels the Virgin to human status and played into maculist views of the Virgin's conception.

Tainted Image/Sacred Image

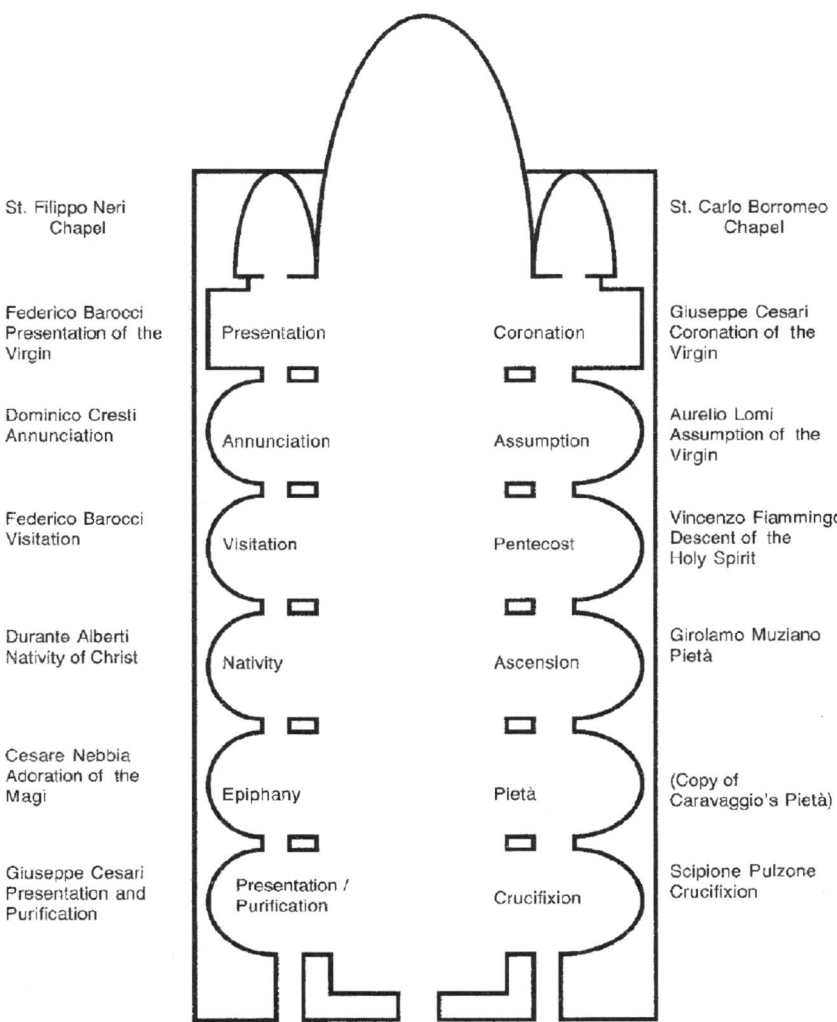

Fig. 2. Floor plan of S. Maria in Vallicella.

In essence a debate over the nature and timing of the Virgin's sanctification, the issue of the Virgin's immaculacy was primarily a matter of debate between the Franciscan and Dominican orders.[26] Defenders of the "immaculist" opinion seized upon the Canticles, particularly Canticle 4:7: "Thou art beautiful, my love, and there is no stain in thee," as proof of the Virgin's immaculacy.[27] Origen (†254) had equated the Bride of the Canticles with the Church in the early third century, and eventually Mary came to be understood as a metaphor for the church.[28] By the sixteenth century, symbols from the Canticles—the *"hortus conclusus"* or enclosed garden, sealed fountain, Rose of Sharon and lily of the valley—were understood as iconographic reference to the Virgin Mary.[29]

In the early sixteenth century, the maculate state of the Church was apparent to all. In the opening sessions of the Council of Trent, the issue of Mary's immaculacy was addressed along with original sin, grace and justification.[30] Canticle 4:7 was frequently cited in sermons delivered at these proceedings.[31] But in 1575, the Bride of the Canticles was no longer the wandering harlot in search of the Bridegroom, as evidenced by the rhetoric which proclaimed the Church's triumph over the stain of heresy.[32] For this reason, a representation of the Virgin's Nativity at the high altar, as envisioned by Filippo Neri in 1575, would have contradicted the notion of triumph prevalent in Rome at the time of Neri's decorative program.[33]

At the time of Filippo Neri's death in 1595 there was still no decoration at the high altar of the Chiesa Nuova. The ecclesiastical historian and influential member of the Filippine Oratory, Cardinal Cesare Baronio (1538–1607), replaced Filippo Neri as Provost-General on July 23, 1593.[34] As late as 1606, the Filippini were trying to decide what to put at the high altar; more specifically, they were still debating over what to do with their precious Vallicella icon.[35]

What were these reservations concerning the icon of the Oratorians? Probable considerations must take into account the issue of clerical celibacy as ruled upon by the Council of Trent earlier in 1563.[36] In an atmosphere of particular concern with the chastity of priests—their abstention from sexual taint—the icon's position of the entrance signalled its association, however benign, with sources of taint that needed to be kept at a distance.

In 1605, Canticle 4:7 was engraved on the façade of the reformed pilgrim church. "*Tota pulchra es, amica mea, et macula non est in te,*" is inscribed in two separate tablets over the left and right portals of the Vallicella.[37] In Filippo Neri's original program, one way of realizing the text would have been through the representation of the Nativity of the Virgin, a more demotic image relating to women. What remains clear is that by 1606, the Filippini no longer felt compelled to represent the Virgin's Nativity, featuring the washing of a new-born infant, at the high altar.[38] More specifically, the placement of the icon appears to be the issue of debate within the Oratory.

In 1606, the Oratorians signed a contract with Rubens to produce a completely different altarpiece.[39] It was undoubtedly Cesare Baronio who informed the iconography of Rubens's first work, as his titular saints, Maurus and Papianus, as well as Pope Saint Gregory the Great, Domitilla, Nereus and Achilleus, were included in the painting.[40] Rubens completed the painting in June 1607, but before it was installed, Baronio died, and the painting was never installed.[41] The Vallicella icon remained in its original chapel, and there was still no altarpiece on the high altar.[42] Rubens's first work was eventually rejected in 1608 and he quickly offered to do another painting according to the terms of the contract.[43] Rubens's second painting, executed *in situ* on slate in three separate panels, marginalizes Baronio's saints on two separate panels (figs. 3 & 4).[44] The Vallicella icon was then inserted into the central panel and concealed by Rubens's own interpretation of the Madonna and Child (fig. 1).[45] Thus framed, the image is accessible only to the priest performing the mass at the high altar.

To summarize, the old Vallicella was given to Saint Filippo Neri and his followers in 1575. Neri envisioned a decorative program for the Vallicella dedicated to the Mysteries of the Blessed Virgin Mary and planned to commission a Nativity of the Virgin at the high altar. After his death in 1595, his predecessor, Cesare Baronio, wanted his own titular saints incorporated into the high altarpiece along with the Vallicella icon, and Peter Paul Rubens was commissioned to interpret this intent. The façade was inscribed in 1605 with the Canticle text which removed the implication of stain from the high altar. Baronio died the same month that Rubens completed his first work in 1607. Still undecided as to where the icon should be located, the Oratorians rejected Rubens's first painting in 1608, and Rubens offered to execute a second work which he quickly finished that same year.[46] The second

Fig. 3. Peter Paul Rubens. Saints Domitilla and Nereo and Achilleo. S. Maria in Vallicella, Rome, Italy. Reproduced with the permission of Alinari/Art Resource, NY.

Fig. 4. Peter Paul Rubens. Saint Gregory the Great, Saints Maurus and Papia. S. Maria in Vallicella, Rome, Italy. Reproduced with the permission of Alinari/Art Resource, NY.

work incorporates the icon into the center of three separate slate panels, and includes a replica of the Vallicella icon which serves as a cover for the icon itself. Ruben's copy of the Vallicella icon conceals and simultaneously reveals the sacred icon-relic possessed by the Vallicella. While Rubens's first solution celebrated the Vallicella icon, the second and final solution merely alludes to the sacred icon. Through Rubens's invention, the Virgin's status, as represented, was displaced from the subject of a narrative scene, as in the Virgin's Nativity, to an object of veneration. The framed and enclosed icon, less apparent than in Rubens's first version, is checked and controlled by Rubens's Madonna and Child and the viewer's access to the mystery, and presumably, to its power, is also checked and controlled.

Thus transformed, the wandering Madonna of S. Maria in Vallicella was transferred from a neighborhood wall to the front chapel of the old building and finally immured within Rubens's painting. In this sense, the Filippini not only rescued, purified and controlled the old Vallicella, but the icon as well. In Rubens's second painting for the high altar, the focus was shifted from a literal, pictorial representation of Mary's cleansing to a hieratic and hierarchical expression of the Canticle 4:7 text. The high altarpiece and decoration program of S. Maria in Vallicella serve therefore as a microcosm for the theological concerns within the Vallicella that in turn reflect the greater polemics of the Catholic faith during the period of the Counter Reformation. In this way, Rubens's altarpiece for S. Maria in Vallicella marks an important transition from the art of Catholic Reform to the art of the Counter Reformation in Rome.

State University of New York at Binghamton

Notes

* This paper has grown out of my dissertation research addressing Nativity of the Virgin imagery in late sixteenth-century Roman painting. I am most grateful for the help and advice of Barbara Abou-el-Haj, Barbara Wisch, Charles Burroughs, and especially for the continued support and advice of Regina Stefaniak.

[1] Photo: Art Resource. Rubens was employed by the Oratorians between 1601 and 1608; Michael Jaffé, "Peter Paul Rubens and the Oratorian Fathers," *Proporzioni*, 4 (1963) 209–51.

² For a facsimile copy of the original, handwritten contract, see ibid., figs. 38–41. The document was first published by Giovanni Incisa della Rocchetta, "Documenti Editi e Inediti sui quadri del nella Chiesa Nuova," *Atti della Pontificia Accademia Romana di Archeologia*, 3rd Series, *Rendiconti*, 35 (1962–63) 161–83.

³ For a reproduction of the 1606 work presently in the Musée des Beaux-Arts, Grenoble, see Frans Baudouin, *Pietro Pauolo Rubens*, E. Callander, trans. (New York: Harry N. Abrams: 1977), plate 12.

⁴ See, most recently, Steven Ostrow's suggestion that the Chiesa Nuova commission had its direct precedent in the Pauline Chapel of S. Maria Maggiore in *Art and Spirituality in Counter-Reformation Rome. The Sistine and Pauline Chapels in S. Maria Maggiore* (Cambridge, Mass.: Cambridge Univ. Press, 1996), 174–80. For discussion of the substitution, see Volker Herzner's suggestion that Rubens's first altarpiece was rejected because it would have cloistered the icon, in "Honor refertur ad prototypa. Noch einmal zu Rubens' Alterwerken für die Chiesa Nuova in Rom," *Zeitschrift für Kunstgeschichte*, 42 (1979) 117–32. This view, however, does not take into account Michael Jaffé's extensive study on the progression of Rubens's work, nor his suggestion that Rubens's preparatory sketch (the Montpellier drawing) shows an oval outline in preparation for the icon, and the Grenoble altarpiece with pentiment reveals Rubens's experimentation with various openings to receive the icon; see M. Jaffé, "Peter Paul Rubens," 229 and tav. 13–16, 23, 24. Justus Müller Hofstede identified Rubens's *bozzetto* or preparatory sketch in satisfaction of the contract in "Rubens's first bozzetto for Sta. Maria in Vallicella, *Burlington Magazine*, 106 (October 1964) 442–450; see also idem, "Zu Rubens's zweitem Altarwerk für Sta. Maria in Vallicella," *Nederlands Kunsthistorisch Jaarboek* 17 (1966) 1–78. See also Martin Warnke's discussion of the *Einsatzbild*, or insert picture, in relation to Rubens's commission in "Italienische Bildtabernakel bis zum Frübarock," *Münchner Jahrbuch*, 3rd Ser., 19 (1968) 61–102.

⁵ For reproductions of the icon, see Hans Belting, *Likeness and Presence. A history of the image before the era of art* (Chicago: Univ. of Chicago Press, 1994) plate XI. See also Martin Warnke, "Italienische Bildtabernakel," fig. 20.

⁶ Umberto Gnoli states that *stufe* were introduced into Rome in the late fifteenth century by the Germans and that the first *stufe* were located near the German community church of S. Maria del Anima, not far from the area of the Pozzo Bianco. See "Stufe romane della Rinascenza," *Pan*, II/7 (Luglio, 1934) 402–408.

⁷ Elizabeth Cohen has informed me that there was a concentration of prostitutes at the Pozzo Bianco in the 1540s, but that the municipal authorities chased them from the area in 1549. See E. S. Cohen, "'Courtesans' and 'Whores': Words and Behavior in Roman Streets," *Women's Studies*, 19 (1991) 201–08. In 1566, Pope Pius V established the formal "ghetto" or serraglio for prostitutes, which enclosed them behind walls in the area of the Campo Marzio

between via di Ripetti, the Piazza Condopula and the Piazza Lombarda. This enclosure became known as the Ortaccio, or "Naughty Garden." See Umberto Gnoli, *Topografia e Toponomastica di Roma, Medioevale e moderna* (Roma: Edizioni dell'Arquata, 1984) 194–95. For fifteenth and sixteenth century prostitution in Rome, see Jean Delumeau, *Vie économique et sociale de Rome dans la seconde moitié du XVIe siècle*, 2 Vols. (Paris: E. de Boccard, 1957) 1:416–32; see also Pio Pecchiai, *Roma nel Cinquecento*, Cappelli: Bologna, 1948, 297–320; see also G. Alberti, "Le Cortigiane, le stufe e la lue nella Roma del primo Cinquecento," in *Vasari*, XII (1941) 64–73; U. Gnoli, "Cortigiane della Rinascenza," *Vasari*, XI (1940) 5–39, 66–84, 107–28 and XII (1941) 5–33 and idem, *Cortigiane Romane: note e bibliografia* (Arezzo, 1941), 13–14. See also A. Bertolotti, "Repressione straordinaria della prostituzione a Roma nel secolo XVI," *Rivista di discipline carcerarie*, XVI (1887), facs. 10–11.

[8] For a description of the miracle and date of 1535, see M. Dejonghe, *Roma Santuario Mariano*, 7, Roma Cristiana, (Bologna: Cappelli, 1965) 131–32. See also Maria Teresa Bonadonna Russo's description in "Il Contributo della Congregazione dell'Oratorio alla topografia Romana: Piazza della Chiesa Nuova," *Studi Romani*, 13 (1965) 21–43; esp. 26. See also idem, "Pozzo Bianco nella finzione letteraria e nella realtà," L'Urbe (Luglio, 1962) 21–24. For a fascinating discussion of cults based on miraculous images, see Michael P. Carroll, *Madonnas that Maim. Popular Catholicism in Italy Since the Fifteenth Century*, (Baltimore/London: Johns Hopkins Univ. Press, 1992).

[9] Eugénie Strong has indicated that in the old Vallicella, this was the Polidoro family chapel; E. Strong, *La Chiesa Nuova (Santa Maria in Vallicella)*, (Roma: Società editrice d'Arte Illustrata, 1923), 98–99.

[10] For the old basilica, see M. Teresa Bonadonna Russo, "Appunti sull'antica parrocchia Vallicelliana," Studi offerti a Giovanni Incisa della Rocchetta. *Miscellanea della Società Romana di Storia Patria*, 23, (1973): 89–115.

[11] The name Vallicella, or "little valley," came from a mild depression in the terrain. See the discussion of the Tarentum and *Dis Pater et Proserpina* in Samuel B. Platner and Thomas Ashby, *A Topographical Dictionary of Ancient Rome* (Rome: L'Erma di Bretschneider, 1965), 152 and 508–9. See also M. T. B. Russo, "Il contributo della Congregazione," 21–43, and idem, "Appunti," 89–115.

[12] When one wanted to exaggerate an infamous deed, one said "this could not have happened even at the Pozzo Bianco" because "the quarter ... was [infamous for] its public brothels": see M. T. B. Russo, "Il Contributo," 27. For sixteenth-century literature on the Pozzo Bianco see idem, "Pozzo Bianco"; 21–24. Russo has indicated that Pietro Aretino, *Dialogo dello Zoppino. De la vita e genealogia di tutte le cortigiane di Roma* (Milano, 1922) and Luca Contile *La Pescara* (Milano, 1550) wrote of the Pozzo Bianco.

[13] For courtesans and their association with Sant'Agostino, see Domenico Gnoli, *La roma de Leon X* (Milano: Ulrico Hoepli), 1938. See particularly 185 ff.

[14] See L. Ponnelle and L. Bordet, *St. Philip Neri and the Roman Society of His Times*, R. F. Kerr, trans. (London: Sheed & Ward, 1932), 68–165. See also Howard E. Smither, *A History of the Oratorio*, Vol. 1, *The Oratorio in the Baroque Era* (Chapel Hill: Univ. of North Carolina Press, 1977), 39ff.

[15] Carlo Gasbarri, *L'oratorio filippino (1552–1952)* (Rome: Instituto di Studi Romani, 1957), 17.

[16] H. Smither, *Oratorio*, 44. As a Florentine, Filippo Neri was undoubtedly aware of the Madonna dell'Impruneta, another powerful icon located in a small, nearby village. This Madonna was kept at a "safe" distance from the city, but on certain occasions was carried in procession to Florence. As Michael Carroll has demonstrated, the image was always taken back to its sanctuary, which served as a controlling element within the icon's cult; M. Carroll, *Madonnas That Maim*, 26. For the Madonna dell'Impruneta, see *Impruneta: una pieve, un paese. Cultura, parrocchia e società nella campagna toscana*, G. Cherubini, et al. (Firenze: Libreria Salimbeni, 1983). See also *Convegno di studi, L'Impruneta: una pieve, un santuario, un comune rurale*, David Herlihy and Richard C. Trexler, eds. (Firenze: F. Papafava, 1988).

[17] Ponnelle and Bordet, *St. Philip Neri*, 68–165.

[18] A July 15, 1575 document granted "the parish church of S. Maria in Vallicella, in the Rioni of Ponte and Parione," to the congregation; Vatican, *Secr. Brev.*, 82, *Bull. Gregory XIII, Lib.* II, 1575, fols. 161 seq. The original building was a simple basilica which had been in existence since 1145–53; see M. T. Russo, "Appunti sull'antica parrocchia vallicelliana," *Studi offerti a Giovanni Incisa della Rocchetta*, (Rome, 1973) 89–115.

[19] Ponnelle and Bordet, *St. Philip Neri*, 68–165. See also Jacob Hess, "Contributi alla storia della Chiesa Nuova (S. Maria in Vallicella)," *Scritti di storia dell'arte in onore di Mario Salmi*, II, (Rome, 1963) 215–38.

[20] Floor plan: Samantha Paige Francisco. Milton Lewine confirms that the scheme was in place between 1577 and c. 1584; M. Lewine, *The Roman Church Interior*, Ph.D. diss., UMI: Ann Arbor, MI, 1960; 406–12. The chapels are outlined by Eugénie Strong in *La Chiesa Nuova*, 68ff.

[21] Ponnelle and Bordet, *St. Philip Neri*, 415–16.

[22] One exception appears to be Sebastiano del Piombo's *Nativity of the Virgin* for the Chigi Chapel in S. Maria del Popolo, Rome. See John Shearman, "The Chigi Chapel in S. Maria del Popolo," *Journal of the Warburg and Courtauld Institutes*, 24 (1961) 129–60.

[23] The textual source of the Virgin's Life is the *Golden Legend of Jacobus da Voragine*, a thirteenth-century interpretation of the *Protoevangelium of James*. For the iconography of the Virgin's nativity, see Jacqueline LaFontaine-Dosogne, *Iconographie de l'enfance de la Vierge dans l'Empire byzantin et en Occident*, 2 Vols. (Brussels, 1964). See also Gertrude Schiller, *Ikonographie der christlichen Kunst*, Vol. 4.2 (Gütersloh: Gütersloher Verlagshaus, 1966).

[24] See the moment of Mary's humble acceptance of her fate, or the *ancilla Domini*, in Luke 1:38: "And Mary said, Behold the handmaid of the Lord; be it unto me according to thy word. And the angel departed from her."

[25] Additional evidence of Filippine emphasis on this virtue is found in St. Philip's chapel (see floor plan, fig. 2). Above the body of the saint is a copy of Guido Reni's portrait of Neri kneeling before an apparition of the Madonna and Child. The frame is inscribed *Exaltavit Humiles*, extolling the viewer to value humility above all else. See E. Strong, *La Chiesa Nuova*, 79ff.

[26] For the history of the Immaculate Conception, see E. D. O'Connor, *The Dogma of the Immaculate Conception* (Purdue: Univ. of Notre Dame Press, 1958).

[27] See Regina Stefaniak, "Amazing Grace: Parmigianino's 'Vision of Saint Jerome'," *Zeitschrift für Kunstgeschichte*, 58/1 (1995) 105–10.

[28] See *Origen, The Song of Songs: commentary and homilies*, R. P. Lawson, trans. and ann. (New York: Newman Press, 1957).

[29] See Maurice Vloberg, "The Iconography of the Immaculate Conception," in *Dogma of the Immaculate Conception*, E. D. O'Connor, ed., 463ff. See also Mirella Levi d'Ancona, *The Iconography of the Immaculate Conception in the Middle Ages and Early Renaissance* (New York: College Art Association/Art Bulletin, 1957).

[30] See H. J. Schroeder, *Canons and Decrees of the Council of Trent* (St. Louis, MO/London: B Herder, 1941). See also Hubert Jedin, *A History of the Council of Trent*, E. Graf, trans., 2 Vols. (New York: T. Nelson, 1957–1963).

[31] For example, Claudio Iaius and Alphonse Salmeron delivered sermons on the sacraments associating the militant, imperfect Church with Canticle 1:4 and Ephesians 5:27, and the triumphant, perfect Church with Canticle 4:7. See *Concilium Tridentinum: diariorum, actorum, epistularum, tractatuum nova collectio*, 13 Vols. (Freiburg Brisgoviae: Herder, 1966), 3:400.

[32] Canticle 3:1–2: "By night on my bed I sought him whom my soul loveth: I sought him, but I found him not. I will rise now, and go about the city in the streets, and in the broad ways I will seek him whom my soul loveth: I sought him, but I found him not." In 1566, Federico Zuccaro represented a triumphant Virgin in his *Coronation of the Virgin* for S. Lorenzo in Damaso, 1566. See my master's thesis, *The Zuccari 'Coronation of the Virgin': An interpretation of the high altarpiece of San Lorenzo in Damaso in Rome within its cultural context* (Univ. of California: Riverside, 1993). For the triumphalist rhetoric prevalent in Rome in 1575, see Frederick J. McGinniss, *Right Thinking and Sacred Oratory in Counter-Reformation Rome* (Princeton: Princeton Univ. Press, 1995). See idem, "The Rhetoric of Praise and the New Rome of the Counter Reformation," in *Rome in the Renaissance, the City and the Myth*, P. A. Ramsey, ed., Medieval & Renaissance Texts & Studies (Binghamton, NY: 1982), 355–70.

[33] The contradiction reveals Neri's own views on the Immaculate Conception and leaves room for future interpretation and research.

[34] Filippo Neri died in 1595, and was venerated and canonized in 1622; Ponnelle and Bordet, 13–17 and 212–19.

[35] As Jaffé pointed out, an entry in the Liber de Decreti dated July 29, 1606, indicates that the Filippini were trying to decide whether to move the icon to the high altar. *Archivio di Roma*, Liber IV de Decreti della Congregatione dell'Oratorio, 290; M. Jaffé, "Peter Paul Rubens," 211.

[36] The issue was taken up in the context of the sacrament of marriage; see H. J. Schroeder, *Canons and Decrees*, 180–82. The idea of celibacy had been discussed since the early beginning of the Church, but had never been ruled upon. For the history of celibacy, see H. Leclerq, *Dictionnaire d'Archélogie chrétienne et de Liturgie*, F. Cabrol, ed., 2.2 (Paris: Letouzey et Ane, 1907–1953), 2802–32; Roger Gryson, *Les origines du célibat ecclésiastique du premier au septieme siecle* (Gembloux: J. Duclot, 1970); *Priesthood and Celibacy*, A. M. Charue, et al. (Milano e Roma, 1972); Raniero Cantalamessa, *Etica sessuale e matrimonio nel cristianesimo delle origini* (Milano: Vita e pensiero, 1976); and Peter Brown, *The Body and Society. Men, Women and Sexual Renunciation in Early Christianity* (New York: Columbia Univ. Press, 1988).

[37] "Thou art beautiful, my love, and there is no stain in thee." The façade was completed in 1605 by Fausto Rughesi; see M. Lewine, *Roman Church Interior*, 410.

[38] A Nativity scene does, in fact, exist in the chapel of the Assumption of the Virgin where scenes from the Life of the Virgin are juxtaposed with scenes from the Old Testament in the vault and arches. It appears that the Nativity of the Virgin was, quite literally, pushed aside into the Assumption chapel, along with the remaining stories of the Virgin's life. See E. Strong, *La Chiesa Nuova*, 106–12 and tavole XIX–XXI.

[39] See Contract, note 2.

[40] Cristoforo Roncalli (il Pomarancio) had executed an altarpiece featuring SS. Domitilla, Nereus and Achilleus for Baronio's titular church of SS. Nereo ed and Achilleo; M. Jaffé, *Rubens and Italy*, 93. Baronio was instrumental in transferring the heads of the martyred eunuchs to the high altar of the Chiesa Nuova in 1604 and paid for the two silver reliquary heads; Archivio Chiesa Nuova, IV, de Decreti, entries for February 4 and September 9, 1604. The silver reliquary heads of the SS. Maurus and Papianus were already on the Chiesa Nuova altar in 1605. A 1602–1603 engraving by Francesco Villamena entitled *Cardinal Baronius in his Study*, reveals a small, framed reproduction of the Vallicella icon on his desk. For a reproduction of this image, see J. Müller Hofstede, "Rubens's first bozzetto for Sta. Maria in Vallicella, *Burlington Magazine*, 106 (October 1964) 442–50, fig.5. In fact, Baronio placed a copy of the Vallicella icon on the title page of his *Annales Ecclesiastici*, eight volumes published in 1590. For an illustration of this coverpiece, see H. G. Evers, *Peter Paul Rubens* (Munich: F. Bruckmann, 1942) 53. For a discussion of Baronio's intervention in

the Rubens's commission see Frances Huemer, *Rubens and the Roman Circle. Studies of the First Decade.* (New York/London: Garland, 1996), 87ff; see also Fernanda Castiglioni, " 'Non sono, dunque, si' mala cosa le immagine' " (C. Baronio). Stato degli studi considerazioni e ipotesi sui Rubens della Vallicella," *Annuario dell'Istituto di Storia dell'arte*, Vol. 2 (Roma: Bulzoni, 1982/83) 14–22. Caecilia Davis-Weyer, "Ein Berliner Bild des Rubens. Baronius und die Heiligen der Chiesa Nuova," *Festschrift für Martin Sperlich zum 60 Geburtstag* (Tübingen, 1980), 208–20.

[41] Baronio died June 30, 1607; M. Jaffé, "Peter Paul Rubens," 220. See Rubens's letter to Annibale Chieppio of February 2, 1608 explaining the rejection of the work due to a lighting problem in R. S. Magurn, ed., *The Letters of Peter Paul Rubens* (Cambridge, Mass.: Harvard Univ. Press, 1955), 42–43.

[42] See June 9, 1607 letter from Rubens in M. Jaffé, "Peter Paul Rubens," 218.

[43] See Contract, note 2.

[44] Photos: Art Resource. M. Jaffé, "Peter Paul Rubens," 230.

[45] M. Jaffé, "Peter Paul Rubens," 219.

[46] In fact, on two occasions, even after the icon was finally placed within Rubens's final panel, the Oratorians were still debating whether to move it back to its original location: M. Jaffé, "Peter Paul Rubens," 219.

JAMES BYRNES

Viewing Foucault Viewing Velásquez's Las Meniñas

MICHEL FOUCAULT'S DETACHED VIEW of the Subject in history finds its *locus classicus* in the "*Las Meniñas*" section of *Les Mots et les choses,* in which Foucault posits Velásquez's painting of 1656 as an emblem of classical representation, an historical period of representation in which the Subject eludes direct representation and is concealed from direct view. For Foucault, the Renaissance ends in a rupture of the governing principles underlying the internal connections within a system of thought and its overarching chronological limits. Foucault was working on the constitution of self in the medieval period at the time of his death. Regrettably, the last volume of the *History of Sexuality, Confessions of the Flesh,* was not completed at his death in 1984 and has yet to appear. It promises to shed light on Foucault's idiosyncratic choice of discursive criteria in delimiting historical periods, especially the Renaissance. This paper will undertake to sketch some issues related to the evidentiary use of Velásquez's *Las Meniñas* in Foucault's idiosyncratic delineation of what is proper to an historical period. By looking closely at Foucault's use of Las Meniñas one necessarily looks more closely at Foucault's understanding of power, meaning, historical totalization, change, systems of thought, reflection and determination. By questioning the interactions between knowledge and power, and the suppressions, displacements, repressions and reciprocal productions inherent in them, Foucault traces the exclusions and silences that create a non-static space, which in turn permits the emergence of subjects and their sudden disappearance.

Foucault had found the exemplar of the break between the Renaissance[1] episteme of "identity" and the classical episteme of "difference" in Spain in the most Spanish of texts, Cervantes's *Don Quixote.*

He asserts that the dramatic rupture between the two periods of pan-European systems of thought can be localized and viewed in conflict within that document or literary monument. The Subject as cognitive achievement and agency is subordinate to the ideal exteriority of the episteme; neither a Renaissance nor a classical episteme is ever fully justified or grounded by Foucault, although his assumption of this paradigmatic historical division has important consequences for the production of meaning in both epochs. Within the classical episteme (roughly the late sixteenth, early seventeenth century and the first half of the eighteenth century), the disciplines that claim as their field of knowledge life, labor, and language are constituted according to specific historical conditions, which diverge radically from those within other epistemes. Within the classical episteme, the Subject had no place in its own representation—man was a rational animal at the highest point of the great chain of being, but had no specific place inside the tables of orderly measure which described him. The tension that logically follows from this ontological and mimetic instability characterizes the specific painting of Velásquez, as well as the Cartesian perspective upon the Subject which is isomorphic to it, within the classical episteme. If Cervantes inaugurated the transformation to classical representation, classification, and exchange in literary discourse, it was Velásquez's new deployment of the pictorial sign that described the death of Renaissance representation in the European world. According to Foucault, Velásquez's work delimits the specific Classical configuration of representation:

> Perhaps there exists, in this painting by Velásquez, the representation as it were, of Classical representation, and the definition of the space it opens up to us. And, indeed, representation undertakes to represent itself here in all its elements, with its images, the eyes to which it is offered, the faces it makes visible, the gestures that call it into being. But there, in the midst of this dispersion which it is simultaneously grouping together and spreading out before us, indicated compellingly from every side, is an essential void: the necessary disappearance of that which is its foundation—of the person it resembles and the person in whose eyes it is only a resemblance. This very subject—which is the same—has been elided. And

representation, freed finally from the relation that was impeding it, can offer itself as representation in its pure form.[2]

The spectator, model, and painter in *Las Meniñas* remain surface concepts that function to occupy space but not to create or arbitrate an origin of meaning. They are limited and contextualized elements at different levels of the representation, but the central focus is the absence that governs it—that of the two sovereigns, Philip IV and Maria Ana of Spain. Foucault's analysis of this painting and the claims he makes for it have inspired much commentary by art critics, historians and philosophers alike. Three of the more recent commentators—Jean-Joseph Goux,[3] Svetlana Alpers,[4] and Carlos Fuentes[5]—reveal a great deal about Foucault's reasoning in the manner that they make use of it. Foucault uses the French translation of *Las Meniñas*—Les Suivantes—to indicate the title of the painting. This slight change indicates a change of meaning, which I will comment upon later when I take up the analyses of Goux and Alpers. Foucault is not interested in the possible narrative tales that might explain this painting; instead, he is interested in the external aspects of the painting as representation, not as a plausible support to traditional historical interpretation or analysis. The figures depicted in the painting, their historical contingencies and their narrative possibilities are ignored in order to focus on the Subject and its representation.[6]

The reading he presents of this painting is intended to recapitulate the structure of classical knowledge and that of the Age of Man, as well as the conditions of possibility that subtend those structures and organize them. Epistemes seem to function both as causal forces and coincidental structural points of convergence. The epistemes that he reveals give coherence to the many links between the thought of an age, its unthought preconditions, and its institutional and social environment as well as the concrete expression that represents that knowledge. The provisional linking of the diachronic to the synchronic purports to more than a formalization of a period but makes no claim of universal validity.

One of the primary organizing factors in classical thought was vision itself. Martin Jay has described the evolution of Foucault's (the decay from classical uses) and other French intellectuals' ambivalent consideration of sight in intellection within the triad of *voir, savoir,* and *pouvoir*:

> To detail the history of attitudes toward vision, including such anti-oracular moments as the Jewish prohibition of graven images, the iconoclastic controversy of the eighth century or the Protestant Reformation, is impossible here. Suffice it to say that the rise of modern science, the Gutenberg revolution in printing and the Albertian emphasis on perspective in painting, vision was given an especially powerful role in the modern era. In France in particular, the domination of visual experience and the discourse of sight seems to have been especially strong. Whether in the theatrical spectacle of Louis XIV's court, the emphasis on clear and distinct ideas in Cartesian philosophy, the enlightening project of the philosophes, or the visual phantasmagoria of the 'city of light', the oracularcentric character of French culture has been vividly apparent.... Not surprisingly, one of the most striking aspects of twentieth-century French thought is the almost obligatory consideration of painting on the part of a wide variety of thinkers, such as Merleau-Ponty, Sartre, Derrida, Lyotard, Kofman, Lefort, Marin, Deleuze, Starobinski and, of course, Foucault himself.[7]

Within the frame, Foucault notes, we are linked to the painting and positioned by the gaze of the painter who is himself at work on a painting which we, as spectators, cannot see since we occupy the space of the model as well as that of the spectator. What we can see is the reflection in the mirror, which reflects the two representing. The space of the sovereign is the space of the model and the spectator— any spectator. The subject is detached, exterior to its representation, deployed in a space which is ordered by its representation. The abstraction of the spectator reflects the historically situated articulation of a specifically classical *mathesis*, the universal science of measurement and order that is deployed in the painting. A transformation in the episteme is necessary before man, the unitary subject, can be represented in his organizing and differentiating function; a transformation that is revealed in the work of Kant and during the Enlightenment.

Svetlana Alpers's article, "Interpretation without Representation or the Viewing of *Las Meniñas*," builds upon the work of Foucault and is concerned with the historicity of representation in its discontinuity. Like the American revolutionaries who resisted taxation without representation, Alpers resists the interpretative tyranny which seeks to impose its narration upon the intentionally self-reflexive painting. Her work is premised by the work of Foucault which revealed the status of *Las Meniñas* as a great pictorial representation of representation in general. Like Foucault, she explores the representational aspect of the painting to the exclusion of its narrative aspect, which could hide the core representation under deforming interpretations. Alpers and Foucault disdain anecdotal history and find it necessary to ignore or exclude traditional art history and its concern with style and meaning. For both, it is no longer a question of explaining or describing, but of eliciting the salience of systems of representation in their continuity or discontinuity. It might be said that this is simply a search for meaning at a different level or in a different mode.

Alpers contends that Foucault, despite his interest in historically specific representation, was mistaken in positing the existence of hermetically autonomous, monolithic epistemes. She indicates that his reasoning, based on the necessary absence of the subject-spectator, misunderstands Velásquez's project of putting in one painting two conflicting modes of representation which evince profoundly differing, contradictory relationships between the spectator and the representation of his world. According to Alpers, *Las Meniñas* is not the product of a notion of representation based upon a solitary classical episteme, but rather it includes elements from two pictorial traditions. One functions as a window and assumes the priority of a spectator who is the measure of his world, the goal and foundation of its values; the other functions as an opaque surface which assumes a world which precedes man and presents itself as radically other to him. She reasons that the presentation of the self within the social order and its representation within the framework of art must be conceived together in order to reveal the conditions of possibility— aesthetic and social—of aesthetic representation. She finds that Velásquez shows this with genius but his commentators hide this by attempting to introduce domesticated, familiar meanings to a painting that strives for an effect of strangeness.

By putting the spectator and the art critic in the privileged site of the sovereign, *Las Meniñas* encourages a certain interpretative tyranny. This site itself has noxious effects, presenting the temptation of an absolute power of vision—a corrupting power of interpretation. Having occupied this sovereign site, Alpers attempts to render it uninhabitable by narrative glossers—a gesture different from that of Foucault who was indifferent to any supplementary meaning the painting might have. Her gesture is diametrically opposed to that of Carlos Fuentes who, being an irrecuperable tale-teller under the sway of language's narrative power, sings the praises of a painting that opens itself to any and all, that permits viewers, each in turn, to enter a place which is never their own place, or their own property, but which accommodates them and their "meaning." According to Michel Serres' reading this is also the position of the archaeologist:

> Son site n'est ni celui de l'émetteur, ni celui du récepteur, mais celui de l'intercepteur; c'est encore celui du spectateur ou du peintre des Ménines, entré là, par surprise, à la faveur d'un interstice paradoxal. L'historien, enraciné en un lieu, faisait l'oeuvre de réception, et ce faisant déterminait d'une manière l'émission, et son savoir s'approfondissait à mesure de cet échange pérenne en spirale; l'archéologue cherche à se mettre en situation d'interception universelle.[8]

According to the view of the universal interceptor, the archeologist, this site of sight belongs to no one; it is universal, it belongs to everyone, including the "n'importe qui"[9] of Jean-Joseph Goux.

The paradox of this place, according to Goux, is that it represents the perspective of a universal Cartesian rationality, a solitary and autocratic status of a *moi-soleil* or a *soi-soleil*, but at the same time is in harmony with an always possible democratic alternation: Royalty cannot be shared, but this site, whether violently opened-up or voluntarily surrendered, remains the ideal point of political and intellectual power:

> Dans cette tension paradoxale de la raison entre solitude de la monarchie et universalité virtuelle du sujet bourgeois se jouerait le site énigmatique à partir duquel le monde peut être mis en perspective.

> Mais alors se conçoit mieux une nécessité que Michel Foucault n'avait fait qu'entrevoir dans sa célèbre description des Meniñas de Velásquez, ce peintre strictement contemporain de Descartes. Il faut supposer, explique Foucault au terme de l'analyse de cette peinture (qu'il considère comme "la représentation de la représentation classique") une place en dehors du tableau qui est à la fois, en une alternance sans limite, celle du peintre, du souverain, et du spectateur. Trois fonctions regardantes qui se confondent en un même point extérieur au tableau', point idéal, virtuel, qui est le centre de perspective à partir duquel devient possible l'ensemble de la représentation.
>
> Or, à notre tour, nous retrouvons jusque chez Descartes la postulation implicite de ce triple regard, placé au bon point de vue. C'est celui du un seul qui, en droit, est à la fois non plus le peintre, le souverain et le spectateur, mais le philosophe, le monarque, et n'importe qui....[10]

This ambivalent site, that of the monarch and "anybody," belongs to no one but to the painting and its internal logic. Everyone can parasite it: Michel, Svetlana, Jean-Joseph, Carlos, Curly, Larry and Monet occupy it in a string of provisional occupations, on the condition that they leave it for the Suivantes—"celles qui suivent." The visual logic of the painting creates a space which attracts a chain of spectators whose sight cannot help but be conscious of its own subordination in the pictorial hierarchy, exactly as the Infanta is surrounded by her followers. The excess of the spectacle gives us a rare privileged spot which belongs to no one and thus gives us the possibility of the spectacle of excess which is the struggle for interpretative authority, for the center of the viewing structure, for the "*cogito dominant*" or the "*cogitamus democratique*"[11] for power. Further, this site is also under the sign of death according to Michel Serres:

> ... à hauteur de tête de Vélasquez, yeux pour yeux, bouche à bouche, se détache, parmi les taches de hasard et la grisaille vague, une tête de mort, bien centrée sur les parcours optiques, et à gauche—pour nous—de la faille... L'objet caché par la double représentation n'est autre que ce dont l'envers est la Mort. La Mort est bien" ce à partir de quoi le savoir est possible"... L'autre devenu sujet prononce maintenant la

mort objective du même; le non-moi devenu sujet amène le moi-sujet au non pur, le néant de la Mort.[12]

This position of viewing cannot be thought of without immediately bringing to mind the question of authority and the medical gaze of *The Birth of the Clinic* or the panopticon of *Discipline and Punish*. The chapter "The Visible Invisible" in *The Birth of the Clinic* most dramatically depicts the importance of the changing spatialization of knowledge:

> That which we know already: death as the absolute point of view over life and opening (in all senses of the term, even the most technical) on its truth. But death is also that against which life, in daily practice, comes up against; in it, the living being resolves itself naturally: and disease loses its old status as an accident, and takes on the internal, constant, mobile dimension of the relation between life and death ... beneath the chronological life/disease/death relation, another, earlier, deeper figure is traced: that which links life to death, and so frees, besides, the signs of disease ... In former times, doctors communicated with death by means of the great myth of immortality or at least of the gradually receding limits if existence. Now, these men who watch over men's lives communicate with their death in the fine, rigorous form of the gaze ... Death left its old tragic heaven and became the lyrical core of man: his invisible truth, his visible secret.[13]

Death, both as the "lyrical core of man" and his limit, was present in much of Foucault's work. Miller sees this as a determining obsession in Foucault:

> the crux of what is most original and challenging about Foucault's way of thinking, as I see it, is his unrelenting, deeply ambiguous and profoundly problematic preoccupation with death, which he explored not only in the esoteric form of his writing, but also, and I believe critically, in the esoteric form of sado-masochistic eroticism.[14]

Power saturates the spatialization of sight in all fields, disciplines, practices, and in all discourses, perhaps most saliently in the work of

Descartes, where scientific objectification and its founding subjectivity depend on a dualistic perspective. To know truth and not to just have evidentiary certainty depends upon the security of perspective at the level of premises—one must be situated, one must know where one is, one's place—madness and death must be limited and on the other side.

The Order of Things along with *Discipline and Punish* and *The Archeology of Knowledge* evinced the greatest similarity of Foucault's work with that of the other "Structuralists." The position of the Subject vis-à-vis language and its rigorously non-transhistorical character were in line with other synchronically-oriented structuralist work, but Foucault's unique privileging of discursive practice and of an undefined discourse, as opposed to language, set him (intentionally) clearly apart. The ambivalence of Foucault's relationship with synchronic structuralist thought is negligible compared to the extraordinary amount of dissonance and contradiction involved in his relationship with diachronic historical studies. Despite much theorizing by Barthes, amongst others, this dichotomy between synchrony and diachrony was never mutually exclusive in the *sciences humaines*. Although he had words of praise for historians who are accepted by other historians as orthodox, he was highly critical of the basic principles that ground the history of ideas:

> Dans ce qu'on appelle l'histoire des idées, on décrit en général le changement en se donnant deux facilités: 1) On utilise des concepts qui me paraissent un peu magiques comme l'influence, la crise, la prise de conscience, l'intérêt porté à un problème, etc. Tous utilitaires, ils ne paraissent pas opératoires; 2) Lorsqu'on rencontre une difficulté on passe du niveau d'analyse qui est celui des énoncés eux-mêmes à un autre, qui lui est extérieur. Ainsi devant un changement, une contradiction, une incohérence, on recourt à une explication par les conditions sociales, la mentalité, la vision du monde, etc.[15]

The Archeology of Knowledge, which can be read as either Foucault's *Discourse on Method* or his parody of a discourse on method, continues the multifold attack on the history of ideas in particular and non-Annales historiography in general. The guilty suspects, historiography, textuality, and authority are continually interrogated. He is vehement in his criticism of the reductionist fallacies of interpretation, although in truth Foucault's polemic is addressed against a flabby historiographical strawman of transparent weakness. He defends his approach as follows:

> The cry goes up that one is murdering history whenever in historical analysis—and especially if it is concerned with thought, ideas or knowledge—one is seen to be using in too obvious a way the categories of discontinuity and difference, the notions of threshold, rupture and transformation, the description of series and limits. One will be denounced for attacking the inalienable rights of history and the very foundations of any possible historicity. But one must not be deceived: what is being bewailed with such vehemence is not the disappearance of history, but the eclipse of that form of history that was secretly but entirely related to the synthetic activity of the subject ... what is being bewailed is the possibility of reanimating through the project, the work of meaning, or the movement of totalization, the interplay of material determinations, rules of practice, unconscious systems, rigorous but unreflected relations, correlations that elude all lived experience; what is being bewailed, is that ideological use of history by which one tries to restore to man everything that has unceasingly eluded him for over a hundred years. All the treasure of bygone days was crammed into the old citadel of this history; it was thought to be secure: it was sacralized.[16]

In order to uphold his *sui generis*, intellectually debt-free, status, he distances himself from any school or method (in particular structuralism), declaring:

> ... my aim is most decidedly not to use the categories of cultural totalities (whether world-views, ideal types, the particular spirit of an age) in order to impose on history, despite itself, the forms of structural analysis. The series described, the limits fixed, the comparisons and correlations made are based not on the old philosophies of history, but are intended to question teleologies and totalizations....[17]

His eccentric or idiosyncratic desire to keep his discourse, whether one considers it historical, philosophical or critical, free from the taint of an unexamined center or theme continues into his later work where, despite the sustained thematic analysis of the power-knowledge couplet, he keeps these concepts so undefined and labile (or profusely re-defined) that they remain clear of any historically determined use (i.e., they are used in a way no other historian has used them or could use them; they remain his own unlimited tools for attack). He frequently acknowledges the strong correlation between his work and that of Nietzsche, whom he accepts as a fraternal spirit. O'Hara has stressed these stylistic or methodological links as part of the radical "parody" that informs their ironic discourses and has been appropriated by other, more recent, critics.[18]

The danger of self-parody was avoided by Foucault in part because of his refusal to adopt a consistently hard concept of period, choosing instead to leave open the horizons of any historical moment by a readily adaptable and shifting synchrony that continually problematizes itself. The rigorous formalism of his analysis of *Las Meniñas* in *The Order of Things* was never developed into a strict method, but remained a stylistic trait that was deployed on a periodic basis. It was used in part to shore up his arguments for strict delimitations between eras of the historical Subject and disciplinary regimes. I concur with Anthony Close who relates that Foucault, despite himself, upholds "the value of traditional forms of interpretation by showing that though Foucault, like other decoders, casts radical doubts upon them in theory, he tends to negate those doubts by the implications of his practice."[19] Foucault's over-emphasis of historical ruptures is explicit in his viewing *Las Meniñas* as representative of a shifting level of expressive abstraction.

State University of New York at Buffalo

Notes

[1] For a glance at Foucault's historiographical failure see Maris-Rose Logan, "The Renaissance: Foucault's Lost Chance?" *After Foucault*, ed. Jonathan Arac (1988), 97–109.

[2] Michel Foucault, *The Order of Things: An Archaeology of the Human Sciences*, trans. *Les mots et les choses* (New York: Vintage Books, 1973), 16.

[3] Jean-Joseph Goux, "Descartes et la perspective," *Esprit Créateur* vol. XXV, No.1 (Spring 1985).

[4] Svetlana Alpers, "Interpretation without Representation, or, The Viewing of Las Meniñas," *Representations*, vol. I, No. 1 (February 1983).

[5] Carlos Fuentes, "Velasquez, Plato's Cave and Bette Davis," *New York Times* (Sunday, March 15, 1987. Section 2): 1.

[6] Carrol presents a reasoned analysis of this methodological dichotomy that results in the *mise en abyme* of historical representation: "Only well into his analysis does Foucault name the models being painted, Philip IV and his wife Maria Ana, who are absent from the scene except in this distant mirror. An "honest" representation, no matter how faint, evokes names and identities, and with them the representational dynamics of the scene appear to have a particular purpose and end outside themselves. Representation, no matter how circuitous its path, would thus appear to culminate in the models outside the scene (in their names and identities)—even if the painting being painted within the painting remains invisible. Here Foucault intervenes forcefully from offstage to assert that this is not the case; the support for such an assertion is not provided by the painting itself, but by a general principle: language and painting, because they come from totally different spheres, are irreducible to each other." David Carroll, *Paraesthetics: Foucault, Lyotard, Derrida* (New York: Methuen, 1987), 64.

[7] Martin Jay, "In the Empire of the Gaze: Foucault and the Denigration of Vision in Twentieth-Century French Thought," *Foucault: A Critical Reader*, ed., David Couzens Hoy (Oxford: Basil Blackwell, 1986), 177.

[8] Michel Serres, *Hermès I: La Communication* 200. "His site is not that of the sender, nor that of the receiver, but that of the interceptor; it is also that of the viewer or the painter of Las Meniñas, entering there, by surprise, thanks to a paradoxal interstice. The historian, rooted in place, doing the work of reception, and in so doing determining the manner of the emission, and his knowledge deepens with this perennial spiraling exchange; the archeologist seeks to put himself in the position of the universal interceptor." (My translation.)

[9] Jean-Joseph Goux, "Descartes et la perspective," 20.

[10] Jean-Joseph Goux, "Descartes et la perspective," 20. "The paradoxical tension that pulls reason between the solitude of monarchy and the virtual universality of the bourgeois subject plays itself out on the enigmatic site on which the world can be put in perspective." (My translation.)

[11] Jean-Joseph Goux, "Descartes et la perspective," 17.

[12] Michel Serres, *Hermès I: La Communication*, 192–94.

[13] Foucault, *The Birth of the Clinic*, 154, 166, 172.

[14] James Miller, *The Passion of Michel Foucault* (New York: Simon and Shuster, 1993), 7.

[15] Raymond Bellour, "Deuxième Entretien," *Les Lettres Françaises* (15 juin 1967), 6.

[16] Foucault, *The Archaeology of Knowledge*, trans. by A. M. Sheridan (New York: Pantheon, 1972), 96.

[17] Foucault, *The Archaeology of Knowledge*, 15–16.

[18] Daniel T. O'Hara, "What was Foucault?" *Radical Parody: American Culture and Critical Agency After Foucault* (New York: Columbia Univ. Press, 1992), 59.

[19] "Centering the De-Centerers: Foucault and Las Meniñas," Anthony Close, *Philosophy and Literature*, Volume 11, No. 1, April (1987), 21.

LOUIS MONTROSE

Form and Pressure: Shakespearean Drama and the Elizabethan State

I

IN THE YEAR 1600—at a time of great socioeconomic uncertainty and political ferment, when London's professional and commercial theaters were enjoying unprecedented popularity and success—the Elizabethan Privy Council sought strictly to limit the number and location of playhouses, the frequency and times of performances, and the number of companies that would be allowed to play. In setting forth these orders, the Privy Council summarized the complex attitude of the state toward the theater at the end of the century and at the close of the reign:

> Forasmuch as yt is manifestlie knowne and graunted that the multitude of the said houses and the misgovernment of them hath bin made and is dailie occasion of the idle riotous and dissolute livinge of great numbers of people, that leavinge all such honest and painefull Course of life, as they should followe, doe meete and assemble there, and of maine particuler abuses and disorders that doe there uppon ensue. And yet nevertheless yt is Considered that the use and exercise of such plaies, not beinge evill in yt self, may with a good order and moderacion be suffered in a well governed estate, and

---

This article is adapted from Chapters 5 and 6 of *The Purpose of Playing*, by Louis Montrose. Copyright © 1996 by Louis Adrian Montrose. Reprinted by permission of the author and the University of Chicago Press.

that, hir Majestie beinge pleased at some times to take delighte and recreacion in the sight and hearinge of them, some order is fitt to bee taken for the allowance and mainteinance of suche persons, as are thoughte meetest in that kinde to yeald hir Majestie recreacion and delight, & consequentlie of the howses that must serve for publique playenge to keepe them in exercise.... Bothe the greatest abuses of the plaies and plaienge houses maye be redressed, and the use and moderacon of them retained.[1]

The Privy Council's order reiterates the familiar claim that the professional players' public performances kept them in readiness to perform at court. However, the order's justification for the allowance of public playing goes well beyond consideration of the ruler's personal pleasures: It also justifies the allowance of a carefully limited and controlled public theater upon the ground that such a theater has its own legitimate place in a secure and flourishing commonwealth. The order fully acknowledges all of the massive social problems that were perennially blamed upon the theaters; nevertheless, it is unequivocal in its approach to correction in terms of more precise controls rather than total suppression. The official understanding made explicit here is that, although the performance of plays in the public theater might sometimes, *in practice*, be subject to abuses, the theater was not inherently corrupt or corrupting—that, indeed, with careful supervision, it could be made to serve the interests of the commonweal and the state. The Privy Council directed its attention to specific playhouses, where particular companies under the patronage of individual Privy Councilors performed. The perspective of the Council was situational, focusing upon particular dramatic repertoires and the particular circumstances of their performance and reception. Thus, the further implication of the Council's orders is that, although public dramatic performance might indeed have considerable representational power, the actual ethical and political intent and consequences of such power could only be determined in local instances.

Such an understanding as that implied in the Privy Council's orders of 1600 seems to me to conform with what we know of the part played by Shakespeare's company in the notorious Essex rebellion of 1601, and of the royal response to that performance. This singular conjunction of drama and sedition has been a basis for much generalizing about the political valence of the Elizabethan theater; for this reason, I would like to consider it briefly here.[2]

On the afternoon of Saturday, 7 February 1601, Shakespeare's company performed at the Globe a "play of the deposyng and kyllyng of Kyng Rychard the second" that was presumably—although not incontrovertibly—Shakespeare's *Tragedie of King Richard the Second*.[3] The first quarto of Shakespeare's play—"As it hath beene publikely acted by the right Honourable the Lorde Chamberlaine his Servants"—had been printed in 1597; two more quarto printings followed in 1598. Presumably, the book of the play had been allowed by the Master of the Revels when it began its life on the stage, circa 1595. The revival performed on 7 February 1601 had been commissioned a day or two earlier by several of the conspirators; eleven of them—but not the Earl himself—actually attended the performance. On the morning following, the Earl of Essex and his friends staged their own ill-conceived performance at Essex House and in the open streets of London. They failed to win over the populace, the conspiracy began to unravel almost immediately, and the attempted coup was crushed before the following day. Subsequently, in the course of investigating the conspiracy, the Privy Council questioned one of the Lord Chamberlain's players, Augustine Phillips, and took testimony from some of the conspirators regarding the Globe performance. As a consequence of the investigation, several of those who had arranged and attended that Globe performance as a prelude to their rebellion were tried and executed for treason. In at least one case, that of Sir Gelly Meyricke, Steward to the Earl of Essex, procurement of the performance at the Globe was among the acts that were used in evidence.

The Privy Council's orders of 1600 had stipulated that "there shall bee about the Cittie two howses and noe more allowed to serve for the use of the Common Stage plaies," and that one of these should be the Globe as occupied by "the Servantes of the L. Chamberlen" (Chambers, *Elizabethan Stage*, 4:330, 331). Given so recent and powerful a demonstration of the state's trust and favor, it may be thought that the implication of Shakespeare's company in the events of the Essex revolt would have proven professionally disastrous. However, the players' reputation and livelihood emerged from the crisis apparently unscathed. Indeed, the Lord Chamberlain's Men performed at

Court before the Queen just a few days later, on the night of Shrove Tuesday, 24 February. On the morning following, upon a scaffold in the Tower of London, and before an exclusive audience of lords, gentlemen, and divines, the Earl of Essex gave his own final command performance, which concluded with his beheading.[4] This conjunction of courtly entertainment and state execution may have been merely fortuitous, but it is tempting to see it as an intended royal response to the conjunction of tragic actions that had been devised by the conspirators a little more than a fortnight earlier: From this perspective, the extension of an invitation to the professional players of Shakespeare's company to perform again at court affirmed the continuity of royal favor toward The Lord Chamberlain's Men, and simultaneously confirmed the continuity of royal authority over the public theater; it was a symbolic assertion that the state was secure and that its subjects were loyal.

What was the motive of the Essex party in requesting and subsidizing that particular performance of *Richard II*? Like the Elizabethan Privy Council, many modern scholars and critics assume that the performance was intended to incite the playgoing public of London to insurrection—or, at least, to predispose them to sympathize with the Earl's claim that he had been victimized by the upstart caterpillars of the commonwealth who now controlled the sovereign, and that he was justified in rising to his own defense. There is a basis for this hypothesis in the events surrounding the 1599 publication and suppression of John Hayward's *The First Part of the Life and Raigne of King Henrie the IIII*. One of the reasons why Hayward's history of Henry IV was of concern to the Privy Council and of interest to the Essex faction was that it abandoned providentialist historiography for one that was indebted to the perspectives of Tacitus and Machiavelli. Hayward's book embraced an understanding of history and politics as processes shaped by the interaction of strumpet Fortune with the will and intellect of the individual human agent. There is considerable evidence to suggest that the identification of Essex with Bolingbroke was current, and had perhaps been surreptitiously encouraged by the Earl himself.[5] The hypothesis that the conspirators expected and desired the other spectators to identify Essex with Bolingbroke seems to assume that the Globe audience would have approved Bolingbroke unhesitatingly as the hero of the play. Such an assumption begs complex questions of intention, interpretation, and effect—questions for which the extant evidence offers few answers. The related but distinct hypothesis that the commissioned performance of *Richard II* was intended to catalyze a popular uprising must rely upon an assumption that the eleven conspirators who attended the performance in question did not have the capacious Globe to themselves; that they must have shared the dramatic experience with a reasonable number of ordinary playgoers, upon whom the play might have worked the desired seditious effect.[6]

There certainly existed at least an appearance of complicity by the Lord Chamberlain's men in a seditious action that was of the gravest possible national significance; nevertheless, the perpetually suspicious and vigilant Privy Council quickly exonerated them. Richard Dutton has suggested, "because they played the whole affair by the book— only performing an 'allowed' text and in their assigned playing-place—that, unlike Hayward, [the Chamberlain's Men] did not suffer severely for their indiscretion, wilful or otherwise."[7] But this benign official response to the players may also have been due in part to the refusal of the inhabitants of London to give active support to the Earl on the morning following the play's performance. To the Elizabethan government, the spectacular failure of Essex in his attempt to arouse the Queen's subjects in the streets of London may not have signified that the theater was politically ineffectual, but rather that the players' performance of their playwright's play was innocent of seditious intent. In other words, the Privy Council may have judged the players' intention by the citizens' response. Such an assumption implies, by negation, a fundamental conviction that the theater was powerful indeed.

Unlike the players and the populace, however, the conspirators shaped the import of the play to their own dangerous fantasies. Such is the implication of certain comments in the records of the revolt. There is, for example, the report of the trial of Sir Gelly Meyricke, at which Sir Edward Coke, the Attorney General, cited Meyricke's insistence to the players, during arrangements for the performance, that "they must needs have the play of *Henry IV*," in which there was "set forth the killing of the King upon a stage." Francis Bacon provides a vivid parallel description of Meyricke's theatrical enthusiasms: "So earnest hee was to satisfie his eyes with the sight of that tragedie which hee thought soone after his lord should bring from the stage to the state."⁸

In conjunction, these comments strongly suggest that one of the conspirators' primary motives in commissioning the performance was to rouse *themselves* to action. They wished to witness a vividly dramatic reenactment of that historical event which they hoped to emulate in deed almost immediately following the performance. It seems, in other words, that the Essex conspirators subscribed to the belief that drama has the capacity to imitate action and, by example, to impel its audience to action—an understanding that they shared with the theater's most vocal defenders and detractors. *Richard II*, as compellingly performed by the Lord Chamberlain's Men at the Globe, might well be thought to have stirred the conspirators to emulate Bolingbroke's successful precedent, to have emboldened and resolved them to execute their dangerous and doubtful designs. Such an effect is clearly what at least one of the conspirators sought in the performance, and what, in principle, both critics and defenders of the theater thought it to be capable of effecting. However, the subsequent exoneration of the players from any charge of complicity implies that neither in their play nor in their performance of it were they deemed by the authorities to be responsible for the constructions applied by the conspirators.

Shakespeare and his company were engaging a delicate topic when they originally produced *The Tragedy of Richard II* in the mid 1590s. Surely, they were knowingly treading upon dangerous ground when they agreed to a special public performance for the Essex faction in 1601. What, then, may have motivated them to agree to such a performance? Let us consider the official record of the sworn statement taken from Shakespeare's fellow sharer, Augustine Phillips, on 18 February 1601:

> He sayeth that ... Sr Charles Percy Sr Josclyne Percy and the L. Montegle with some thre more spak to some of the players in the presans of thys examinate to have the play of the deposyng and kyllyng of Kyng Richard the second to be played the Saterday next promysyng to gete them xls. more then their ordynary to play yt. Wher thys Examinate and hys fellowes were determyned to have played some other play,

holding that play of Kyng Richard to be so old & so long out of use as that they should have small or no Company at yt. But at their request this Examinate and his fellowes were Content to play yt the Saterday and had their xls. more then their ordynary for yt and so played yt accordyngly.[9]

The conspirators came to the players with a request for a special performance of a play on a controversial and potentially dangerous subject. Understandably, the players hesitated to comply. Nevertheless, the lords and gentlemen were insistent, and the players finally deferred to the wishes of their betters. After all, not only were the members of the delegation men of honor and substance in their own right, they were also the intimate friends and followers of the preeminent earls of Essex and Southampton, both of whom were generous benefactors of scholars and poets. Thus, one subtext of Phillips's deposition is the vulnerability of inferiors and clients to the pressures exerted by their superiors and patrons.

But there is also another subtext that is ideologically at variance with the first—one based not upon codes of social deference or political allegiance but upon market calculations and professional judgments. According to Phillips's testimony, the conspirators presented their request to the players wholly in terms of financial gain, "promysyng to gete them xls. more then their ordynary to play yt"; the players resisted on a mixture of commercial and professional grounds, "holding that play of Kyng Richard to be so old & so long out of use as that they should have small or no Company at yt." The players were finally persuaded by the conspirators, and their performance was rewarded according to the financially advantageous terms agreed upon: they "had their xls. more then their ordynary for yt and so played yt accordyngly." The players were to receive from the conspirators substantially more than their usual take from a public performance, and that profit would have been over and above whatever they took in from the ordinary paying customers who may also have attended. Although the topic was potentially inflammatory, it was also the case that *Richard II* had already been allowed for public performance and for subsequent printing by the licensing authorities—although not, perhaps, without prior censorship.[10]

As I have already noted, the title page of the first quarto (1597), claims to present the play "As it hath been publikely acted by the right Honourable the Lorde Chamberlaine his Servants." The printing of a second and then a third quarto in the next year, 1598, was unprecedented for a Shakespearean play at this date, and suggests an unusually strong reader interest.[11] This demand presumably came from the same politic readership that, a few months later, would be so eager to obtain copies of Hayward's *Life and Raigne of King Henrie IIII*.[12] Thus, we may have reason to suspect that Phillips was being somewhat disingenuous when he claimed, in 1601, that the play was "so old & so long out of use as that they should have small or no Company at yt."

The motivations of the players do not seem to have been *political*—if we construe that term narrowly, to mean actively promoting the agenda of a particular faction. The players' motives were, nevertheless, shaped by considerations of a distinctly *ideological* character. More precisely, in agreeing to perform the play in their public playhouse, The Lord Chamberlain's Men seem to have been motivated by a combination of social deference and commercial gain. The foundation and continued viability of the public, professional theaters, their players, and their plays depended upon a strategic alliance of noble patronage and entrepreneurial investment. This theater was sustained by a frequently advantageous but inherently unstable conjunction of two theoretically distinct modes of cultural production: one, hierarchical and deferential, based upon traditional relations of patronage and clientage; the other, fluid and competitive, based upon market relations. The acceptance of the conspirators' commission by the Lord Chamberlain's Men exemplifies this unstable conjunction and aptly manifests the ambiguous status of the professional players and their theater within the shifting socioeconomic and cognitive frameworks of late Elizabethan England.

2

In his *Chronicles of England, Scotland, and Ireland*, Holinshed reports that, in her response to a parliamentary petition for the execution of Mary, Queen of Scots in 1586, Queen Elizabeth told the joint delegation from the House of Lords and the House of Commons, "we princes ... are set on stages, in the sight and view of all the world dulie observed; the eies of manie behold our actions; a spot is soone spied in our garments; a blemish quicklie noted in our dooings."[13] The putative royal phrase, "we princes ... are set on stages, in the sight and view of all the world," has sometimes been invoked to epitomize what Stephen Greenblatt has called "the whole theatrical apparatus of royal power," and to make the point that "Elizabethan power ... depends upon its privileged visibility."[14] Indeed, Greenblatt goes so far as to suggest that, because "a poetics of Elizabethan power" is synonymous with "a poetics of the theater," the drama produced in the Elizabethan public theaters is always already co-opted by the state. He writes in *Shakespearean Negotiations* that, "It is precisely because of the English form of absolutist theatricality that Shakespeare's drama, written for a theater subject to state censorship, can be so relentlessly subversive: the form itself, as a primary expression of Renaissance power, helps to contain the radical doubts it continually provokes" (64, 65). Here, as elsewhere in my work, I take issue with arguments, like Stephen Greenblatt's, that bind the practices of the professional Elizabethan theater to the practices of the Elizabethan state, and that bind Elizabethan theatricality to political absolutism.

Without the benefit of having read Stephen Greenblatt, Queen Elizabeth failed to appreciate that the drama was so safely in hand. Consider, for example, the celebrated remark, "I am Richard II. know ye not that?" This pointed observation may suggest that she shared with members of the Essex circle a habit of reading history that found analogies and parallels between the shape of the past and the shape of the present. However, as the rest of her putative conversation with William Lambarde makes emphatically clear, the Queen found the ideological implications of Renaissance Tacitism to be not only seditious but sacrilegious:

> W. L. 'Such a wicked imagination was determined and attempted by a most unkind Gent. the most adorned creature that ever your Majestie made.'

Her Majestie. 'He that will forget God, will also forget his benefactors; this tragedy was played 40tie times in open streets and houses'.¹⁵

As David Kastan has pointed out, Lambarde's reference to Essex's "wicked imagination" has a legal force, since the Tudor law of treason defined it in part as the "imagining and compassing of the death of a king."¹⁶ Like the power of the imagination in Lambarde's usage, the power of the theater in Queen Elizabeth's usage may take on an instrumental force. The Queen's reference to "this tragedy ... played 40tie times in open streets and houses" has often been taken literally by literary historians, as referring to multiple performances of a tragic drama on the subject of Richard II, despite the implausible implications of such a reading. The attributed royal remark seems to me to make clearer sense when taken metaphorically, as an application of the *theatrum mundi* trope to the recurrent enactment of treason in a theater-state in which "princes ... are set on stages, in the sight and view of all the world." In this sense, the remark attributed to the Queen is cognate with Bacon's description of Sir Gelly Meyricke's "wicked imagination": "so earnest hee was to satisfie his eyes with the sight of that tragedie which hee thought soone after his lord should bring from the stage to the state."

Let me return to my initial quotation from Queen Elizabeth's reputed speech, which strongly suggests that what Greenblatt calls the "privileged visibility" of royal power also entails potential liabilities, that visibility implies vulnerability. The ironic tenor of the Queen's observation is that her privileged position exposes her to "the sight and view of all the world ... the eies of manie": It subjects her to the scrutiny of her own subjects, and solicits the approbation of her inferiors. As Queen Elizabeth herself seems ruefully to have understood, to set princes on public stages meant in practice that the state could not fully control the charismatic royal image. Thus, there was good reason why the state forbade explicit personations of the reigning monarch upon the stage, and sought to regulate strictly all iconic and verbal representations of the Queen. Greatness could be, and routinely was, appropriated for representation within an affective and commercial transaction between the players and their common audiences. A significant segment of the audiences for whom princes were set on stages was made up of what Sir Thomas Smith classified as "the fourth sort or classe amongest us." According to Smith, this sort included "marchantes or retailers which have no free lande, copiholders, and all artificers.... These have no voice nor authoritie in our common wealth, and no account is made of them but onelie to be ruled, not rule other."[17] Other significant segments of the public theater audiences—namely, women, servants, and apprentices—did not even rate a mention from Smith. Nevertheless, despite the exclusion of all these groups from what constituted the Elizabethan political nation, payment of a penny might entitle some of their members to observe and to judge the players' personations of princes.[18]

Sir Henry Wotton appreciated the dangers of demystification that attended the setting of princes on stages. The context is a letter in which he relates the accidental destruction of the Globe by fire during a performance of Shakespeare's *Henry VIII*:

> The Kings's players had a new play ... representing some principal pieces of the reign of Henry VIII, which was set forth with many extraordinary circumstances of pomp and majesty, even to the matting of the stage; the Knights of the order with their Georges and garters, the Guards with their embroidered coats, and the like: sufficient in truth within a while to make greatness very familiar, if not ridiculous.[19]

It is not without interest that Wotton's observation is provoked by the performance of a play on the subject of English dynastic history, one that concludes by celebrating the birth of the reigning King's immediate predecessor, Elizabeth Tudor. Nevertheless, the possibly subversive political content of this or any other particular play is not at issue here. Wotton remarks upon a potential challenge to the authority of the great that is specifically stylistic and formal. His concern is focused upon the inherent capacity of dramatic representation in the public theater—even when ostensibly celebratory in its text, and entrusted to "the King's players" for its performance—to appropriate and to demystify what Greenblatt calls the "absolutist theatricality" of the monarchy, and to do so by the very process of staging it.

Thus if, as Stephen Greenblatt proposes, "kingship always involves fictions, theatricalism, and the mystification of power" (Greenblatt, *Renaissance Self-Fashioning*, 167), then fiction and theatricalism may also be the very media through which royal power is demystified. The "poetics of the theater" is founded upon an opposition and dialogical interplay of characters, interests, and ideologies. Through various formal means, enacted drama creates a multiplicity of perspectives. However, within the context of an absolutist ideology, such multiplicity signified an inherent capacity to produce heterodoxy. A practical consequence of theatrical illusion was that it could provide some measure of protection against the censorship, suppression, and punishment that otherwise threatened a cultural practice that was *formally disposed* to destabilize absolute and univocal claims. Thus, *contra* Greenblatt, I would propose that "the English form of absolutist theatricality" that characterizes the ideology of Elizabethan-Jacobean monarchy is not reinforced, but rather destabilized when it is represented in the Shakespearean theater; and that this is so precisely because "a poetics of Elizabethan power" is *not* synonymous with "a poetics of the theater"—because "the form itself" predisposes the drama of the Elizabethan public, professional, and commercial theater to be anti-absolutist.

3

Writing in reaction against the now-dominant critical tendency to politicize Renaissance drama—whether as an instrument of subversion or of containment, Paul Yachnin has recently claimed that the Elizabethan-Jacobean theater was fundamentally irrelevant to issues of power, and that it cultivated its own irrelevance. He asserts that,

> as a result of both the vigor of Elizabethan government censorship and the compliance of the players with that censorship, the theater of the late Elizabethan and early Stuart period came to be viewed as powerless, unable to influence its audience in any purposeful or determinate way. The dramatic companies won from the government precisely what the government was most willing to give: a privileged, profitable, and powerless marginality.[20]

Such a conclusion goes against the massive evidence that many guardians of Elizabethan religious, social, and political orthodoxy thought that the theater was very powerful indeed, and that it was powerful in the worst possible way. Furthermore, the persistent concern of the state to regulate the drama, even while tolerating or supporting it, does not argue for the perception that it was a trivial and impotent cultural practice.

It has sometimes been claimed that the salient point about the role of the theater in the Essex conspiracy is that, in failing to catalyze a rebellion, it proved itself to be merely ineffectual and irrelevant. As an example of the players' paradoxical liberation into powerlessness, Yachnin cites Shakespeare's *Richard II* and its performance on the eve of the Essex revolt: "*Richard II* is able to represent political issues openly by producing a political message which is depoliticized (that is, incapable of exerting determinate political influence) by virtue of being bifurcated, or two-faced." Here Yachnin makes clear that what he intends by the sweeping and provocative claim that the theater was powerless is the hardly controversial point that it could not effectively shape and control the specific political opinions and behaviors of all those in its audience. By framing the issues in terms of drastic antinomies—between "determinate political influence" and "powerlessness," or between political "power" and the "freedom" of artistic disinterestedness—Yachnin forecloses upon an analysis of the more mediated, subtle, unintended, and/or unprogrammatic ways in which the Elizabethan theater appropriated, shaped, questioned, and publicly disseminated socially significant meanings, values, and beliefs.

According to Yachnin, "the overall meaning or point of view" of *Richard II* "is designed to be indeterminate, open to a range of interpretations arrayed along an axis between orthodoxy, providentialism, and hierarchy at one pole and subversion, Realpolitik, and revolution at the other (66)." It is a critical commonplace that this play takes a multiple perspective upon the historical events which it represents.[21] But this critical commonplace must, itself, be historicized. The multiplicity of perspective characteristic of Shakespeare's plays has been construed, according to the canons of modern literary criticism, as a hallmark of Shakespeare's ambivalence and complexity; it has been celebrated as the achievement of negative capability, aesthetic disinterestedness, intellectual inquisitiveness, the transcendence of ideology, and/or universal humanity. In an Elizabethan context, however, such characteristics may have had a more precise and consequential ideological valence. The providentialist ideology that provided the interpretive framework for a central strain of Tudor historiography was also the basis for both the political discourse that legitimated the Elizabethan state and the personality cult that exalted the Queen. As is made abundantly clear by so basic and widely disseminated a text as the official Homily on Willful Disobedience, the principles of "orthodoxy, providentialism, and hierarchy"—which formed the core of this dominant discourse on Elizabethan state power—made no allowance whatsoever for alternatives or for indeterminacy: In the resonant and familiar words of the official "Exhortacion concernyng Good Ordre and Obedience to Rulers and Magistrates,"

> Almightie God hath created and appointed all thinges in heaven, yearth and waters in a moste excellent and perfect ordre.... Every degre of people, in their vocacion, callyng and office, hath appoynted to them their duetie and ordre. ... Where there is no right ordre, there reigneth all abuse, carnall libertie, enormitie, syn and babilonicall confusion.[22]

Those who advocated or appeared to advocate "subversion, Realpolitik, and revolution"—whether in print or in action—were guilty of sedition, and were frequently deemed to be satanic agents or to be merely depraved; they were subject to whatever modes of control and punishment the regime could muster.

The tacitly anti-providentialist *realpolitik* that was of immediate relevance to Shakespeare's *Richard II* and to the scholars and courtiers in the Essex circle was based upon the *politique* reading and contemporary application of Tacitus's Roman history.[23] The historian Mervyn James has characterized Renaissance Tacitism as

> the "politic" art by means of which the historical actor, his will powered by passion and interest, attained his objectives, which were understood in terms of the pursuit and preservation of dominance.... History simply became a field for the play of the heroic energy of the autonomous political will, seeking to dominate events by its command of the politic arts. It was an approach which, by comparison with that of the providentialist historian, could be thought of as "atheist"; for the historical actors it presented were seen as released from

the sanctions and controls imposed by morality and law, and underwritten by religion.[24]

Hayward's Tacitean perspective on the downfall of Richard II was fundamentally secular, pragmatic, and relativist. The Elizabethan government might have regarded such a perspective as dangerously heterodox under any circumstances; it was certain to regard it as seditious when the context was English rather than Roman history; when the pivotal event was the deposition of an anointed king; and when the consequence of usurpation was the establishment of the Lancastrian dynasty, through which the Tudors tenuously traced their own hereditary claim to the throne.

Shakespeare's *Richard II* does not explicitly *advocate* a Tacitean understanding of history and government, any more than it advocates the acts of "subversion, Realpolitik, and revolution" that it also represents. Instead, the play incorporates both providentialist and *politique* paradigms as opposing structures of meaning through which particular characters apprehend the shape of history; it mobilizes these paradigms as the conflicting terms in which characters enact and interpret the events in which they are enmeshed. As Joel Altman has convincingly demonstrated, there is a rhetorical basis for Elizabethan dramatic form in the intellectual interplay of academic debating positions; the plays of the professional theater motivate ideas in terms of conflicts existing among, and within, human characters, and they incarnate these characters-in-conflict in professional players who interact upon a stage.[25]

Andrew Gurr has pointed out that the art of characterization seems to have undergone a dramatic change of its own by the end of the sixteenth century, a change that may be apprehended in a significant terminological shift. He points out that,

> What the players were presenting on stage by the beginning of the [seventeenth] century was distinctive enough to require a whole new term to describe it. This term, the noun "personation," is suggestive of a relatively new art of individual characterisation, an art distinct from the orator's display of passions or the academic actor's portrayal of the character-types.... The first use of the term "personation" is recorded ... in 1599–1600.... The term was called into being by the same

developments—in the kinds of parts given the actors to play and their own skill in their parts—that made ... tragedians succeed the extemporising clowns on the pinnacle of theatrical fame. By 1600 characterisation was the chief requisite of the successful player.[26]

In the culture of early modern England, the development of the theatrical profession and the conceptual and practical establishment of dramatic personation were consonant with other material and ideological developments—capital accumulation, market calculation, contractual relations, and "possessive individualism"—that manifested the emergence of what we now characterize as merchant capitalism and bourgeois subjectivity.[27]

More immediately and particularly, these theatrical developments coincided with the keen interest of the late Elizabethan sociopolitical and intellectual elites in the employment of Tacitean/Machiavellian paradigms in order to speculate upon the acquisition of power and the legitimation of authority; upon the relationship of agency and history, subjects and the state. Such an interest represented a conceptual challenge and a perceived political threat to the absolutist pretensions of the sovereign. In comparison with the medieval religious civic drama, the professional drama of the Elizabethan commercial theaters marks a decisive shift in the coordination of playing dimensions: a reorientation of the dramaturgical axis from the vertical plane, which related earthly events to a divinely ordained master narrative, to the horizontal plane, upon which human characters interact within an imagined social space. This shift of emphasis from a metaphysical to a social dialectic implied that the temporal and mutable human realm of second causes had become the locus of dramatic action. And the increasing concern of players and dramatists with individual characterization in the motivation of dramatic action suggests that this mode of drama was especially congenial to Tacitean/Machiavellian views of historical process. In English history plays and tragedies of state—genres which were central to the late Elizabethan theatrical repertoire—the creation and motivation of characters was thus a cultural development of considerable philosophical and political import. Whether or not Queen Elizabeth actually said that "we princes ... are set on stages, in the sight and view of all the world dulie observed," the player-playwright who was her subject was likely to have read in Holinshed that she had. In any case, when he came to write his second tetralogy of English history plays, Shakespeare dramatized the theatricality of power as a recurrent contest among historical actors to control the *personation* of the King.[28]

The performance of plays in the Elizabethan public theater puts into action a dialectic among characters within the playworld; a dialectic between the fictional world of the characters and the experiential world of the audience; and a dialectic between the professional players and those who pay to see them play. Through this multidimensional theatrical dialectic of identification and estrangement, the Elizabethan drama produces that "objectivity" which modern criticism has come to see as its formal and conceptual hallmark. However, to historicize this objectivity-effect is to clarify that the "objectivity" required to represent the dominant as merely one among a range of possible positions is itself a perspective with profound political implications. Within the specific constraints of the dominant Elizabethan ideology, freedom of interpretation and indeterminacy of meaning were inherently dangerous and potentially subversive notions.[29] It is precisely by appropriating the authoritative Elizabethan principles of "orthodoxy, providentialism, and hierarchy," and then (in Yachnin's phrase) arraying them indeterminately along an axis of interpretive positions, that Shakespeare's history plays *decenter* those principles and demystify their claim to the status of divine and immutable truth.

4

While Shakespeare's plays reproduce the legitimating structures of the dominant Elizabethan ideology, they also produce challenges to their legitimacy. Within the course of a given dramatic action, representatives of opposition and difference are usually defeated, banished, converted, or otherwise apparently contained by the play's ideologically dominant forces and forms. Nevertheless, in the very representation of alternatives and resistances, the plays articulate and disseminate fragments of those socially active heterodox discourses that the politically dominant discourse seeks, with only limited success, to appropriate, repudiate, or suppress. The plays may try to impose symbolic closure upon the heterodoxy to which they also give voice, but that closure can be neither total nor final. And such ideological instability or permeability in the drama may be a consequence not only of its performance but also of its inscription. It is obvious that theatrical productions and critical readings originating from beyond the cultural time and place of the text's origin may work against the grain to achieve radically heterodox meanings and effects. But it may also be the case that the appropriative potential of such subsequent acts of interpretation is enabled by Elizabethan cultural variations and contradictions that have been sedimented in the text and scenario of the play at its originary moment of production.

By representing particular cultural forms and human actions within fictional frames, Shakespeare's theater invited its audience to reflect upon those forms and actions. But the theater also reached out to frame and to elucidate the world of the audience by means of its own cultural form—a dramatistic paradigm of social life, based upon the interaction of protean players. The heterodoxy enacted in the plays performed at the Globe is the logical consequence of the Elizabethan theater's claim to hold the mirror up to nature. And this theater holds the mirror up to nature precisely by reflecting upon its own artifice, for not only does it exemplify the contradictions and conflicts of Elizabethan society and culture, but it also makes such contradictions and conflicts the very subject of its plays. The professional players, playwrights, and playhouses of Elizabethan London were abominations. They represented a profound challenge to traditional modes of thinking—not only to particular orthodox beliefs and opinions but also to the dominant paradigm of agency and authority—both because they failed to fit conveniently into existing cultural frameworks and because they presented an alternative framework, a dramatistic or theatrical world picture.[30]

When the Lord Chamberlain's Men performed Shakespeare's *As You Like It* at the newly opened Globe at the end of the 1590's, Queen Elizabeth's subjects heard the compelling assertion that "All the world's a stage,/And all the men and women merely players" (2.7.138–39). This declaration was both materially and symbolically affirmed in the very name, shape, and motto of the playhouse in which the play was being performed.[31] The metatheatricality of the Elizabethan drama did not necessarily obscure what Stephen Greenblatt has called the "privileged visibility" of the royal actor. Indeed, as I have argued above, when the public theater staged greatness—"in the sight and view of all the world dulie observed"—the equivocal privilege of this visibility was to be exposed to the subjects of its own authority. When the "absolutist theatricality" of the state was played in the public and professional playhouse, it became vulnerable to destabilization and available for appropriation. At the same time, in the process of asserting theatricality as a universal condition of social life, the professional players asserted their own privileged visibility within their circumscribed domain; they manifested that the symbolic social space of the professional theater was the locus of a power distinct from the "absolutist theatricality" of the Queen. Within the playhouse, as upon its stage, *all* the men and women were merely players.

The concerted efforts of the Elizabethan Privy Council simultaneously to patronize and to regulate the drama exemplifies the process of state formation through the expansion of ideological state apparatuses.[32] The Privy Council attempted to restrict the number of professional acting companies and the number and location of playhouses; all plays for public playing were made subject to censorship, licensing, and the payment of fees to the Master of the Revels. By such means as these, the royal government at once enjoyed and protected but also sought to limit, control, and profit from the professional theater. Perhaps the general point to be made here concerning the attitude of the Elizabethan state toward the Elizabethan theater is that it was complex and equivocal; that it was not constant but was subject to numerous shifts, variations, and inconsistencies; and that some of these were consequences of fundamental anomalies and contradictions, while others resulted from merely local or temporary exigencies. And what of the attitude of the Elizabethan theater toward the Elizabethan state? The extant evidence concerning the ideological positioning of the professional playhouses and their plays, both from the plays themselves and from other sources, is—unsurprisingly—ambiguous, diverse, contradictory. This suggests that, in practice, the Elizabethan theater must have proved a rather unreliable ideological apparatus in the service of the Elizabethan state. On the other hand, as the circumstances of the Essex revolt suggest, it was at least equally difficult to enlist the professional Elizabethan theater as a vehicle for concerted seditious action.

The Lord Chamberlain's Men gave a metatheatrical demonstration of the equivocal place of the stage, the cross-purposes of playing, when they performed *Hamlet* at the Globe. Within Shakespeare's play, "the tragedians of the city" have come "to offer ... service" to the Prince. Although "their residence, both in reputation and profit, was better both ways," they are now compelled to leave their public playhouse, temporarily reverting to itinerant status and seeking royal patronage because keen competition in the city's entertainment industry has hurt their profits.[33] The melancholy Hamlet is excited by the prospect of the players' visit, and in this unwonted enthusiasm, the King seeks occasion to mollify his "chiefest courtier ... and [his] son" (1.2.117), and to divert him from his malcontented brooding:

> It doth much content me
> To hear him so inclined.
> Good gentlemen, give him a further edge
> And drive his purpose into these delights.   (3.1.24–27)

Claudius hopes that Hamlet's purpose will be vitiated in playing. However, he unwisely entrusts the office of Master of the Revels, and its censoring authority, to Hamlet himself:

> *King.* Have you heard the argument? is there no offense in't?
> *Ham.* No, no, they do but jest, poison in jest—no offense i'th' world.   (3.2.230–33).

The antically disposed Prince mocks the King's conviction that the drama is an innocuous pastime; he has a rather different notion of what it would mean to "drive his purpose into these delights." Hamlet's sententious speech on "the purpose of playing" (3.2.1–45) is spoken in the context of his own particular purposes: "The play's the thing/Wherein I'll catch the conscience of the king" (2.2.604–05).[34] The princely patron of the city's professional players will employ a courtly command performance as an ethical instrument for the determination of political action; Hamlet will place a dramatic performance at the center of his design to delegitimize the monarch.

Immediately upon the arrival of the players, Hamlet requests that the company's leading player recite "a passionate speech" (2.2.431–32) describing the murder of Priam, and then, that these "tragedians of the city" (2.2.329) "play something like the murder of [his] father/

Before [his] uncle" (2.2.596–97). Shakespeare's Hamlet subscribes to a belief in the doubly mimetic capacity of drama—its status as a representation of, and provocation to, action. By employing the theater's powerful capacity to move its audience by a mixture of language and gesture, he seeks to confirm the King's occulted guilt and, simultaneously, to galvanize his own revenge, to rouse himself to regicide:

> I'll observe his looks;
> I'll tent him to the quick. If 'a do blench,
> I know my course.   (2.2.597–99)

In the very process of catching the king in his metatheatrical mousetrap, however, Hamlet himself becomes so affected by the power of theatrical mimesis that he exposes his own suspicions and intentions to the king. Serving as Chorus to the play-within-the-play as well as Master of the Revels, Hamlet identifies the regicide as a lively image not only of his uncle's consummated crime, but of his own prospective revenge: "This is one Lucianus, nephew to the King.... Begin, murderer.... Come, the croaking raven doth bellow for revenge" (3.2.242, 250–52). As repeatedly happens in *Hamlet*, the playwright's ironic designs defeat the characters' purposes and puzzle their wills. The strategies of Claudius and Hamlet enact opposed and complementary courtly attitudes toward the theater: At the same time that the monarch construes it as a means of diversion, his chiefest courtier construes it as a means of subversion. Regardless of the opposed intentions and expectations of the Prince and the King, however, Hamlet's "mousetrap" has an ambiguous and unpredictable effectivity within the world of Shakespeare's play.

As for the traveling company of professional players, their materially self-interested motives are evidently to maintain their livelihood and to insure the continuance of princely patronage. They are hardly in a position to refuse either Hamlet's choice of repertory—"Dost thou hear me, old friend? Can you play *The Murder of Gonzago?*"—or his request that they include in their performance, "a speech of some dozen or sixteen lines which [he] would set down and insert in't" (2.2.537–38, 541–42). The Lord Chamberlain's Men probably first performed *Hamlet* at the Globe not long before their infamous performance of *Richard II. Hamlet* is a metatheatrical tragedy of state; it internalizes the relationship of the public, professional, and commercial theater to the court, thereby foregrounding the cultural politics of that relationship. Thus, it gives imaginative form to some of the same ideas and interests that came into play when the Earl of Essex's friends propositioned the players. In its demonstration of a complex and contingent interaction of diverse interests, the meta-production of *The Murder of Gonzago* is emblematic of the real but limited, diffuse, and unstable power of the professional theater within late Elizabethan society.

The inconclusive conclusions I offer here cannot rival, for sheer excitement, the bold assertions that have become commonplace in the critical literature on the Elizabethan theater. However, from my perspective, any general characterization of the relationship between the Elizabethan theater and the Elizabethan state in terms of an either/or choice between *subversion* and *containment*, between *resistance* and *complicity*, or between *power* and *freedom*, appears to be hopelessly reductive. Certainly, the Elizabethan state did attempt to contain the Elizabethan theater. In practice, however, this attempt was inconsistent and haphazard, and was never uniformly and unequivocally effective. I suggest, furthermore, that it was wholly beyond the capacity of the Elizabethan state to achieve the uniform and absolute containment of alternative and oppositional discourses. Indeed, it could be argued that such total control is (as yet) beyond the power of any state.[35]

In my view, the professional, public, and commercial theater of Elizabethan London did have a subtle and diffuse power of its own, but the direction and effectiveness of that power were uncertain and intermittent. This theatrical power lay precisely in the combination of representational resources that enabled it to enact and to epitomize the *theatrum mundi* metaphor—resources that gave to it its specificity as a cultural institution, form, and practice. My point is that the source of this theater's power was in its very *theatricality*, and in the implications of theatricality for the construction and manipulation of social rules and interpersonal relations—implications touching fundamental epistemological and sociopolitical issues of causality and legitimacy, identity and agency. Even if, in the texts and scenarios of particular plays, such implications were not in the foreground—indeed, even if they were contained or suppressed—this power might nevertheless make itself felt in the process of performance, in which both the players and their audience participated actively in the making of meaning.[36] The theatrical power that I am seeking to describe did not lie in the explicit advocacy of specific political positions, but rather in the implicit but pervasive suggestion—inherent in the basic modalities of theatrical representation and dramatic conflict—that all such positions are relationally located and circumstantially shaped, and that they are motivated by the passions and interests of their advocates. In this precise and limited sense, Shakespearean drama as enacted in the Elizabethan theater *formally* contested the dominant ideological assertions of the Elizabethan state.

Notes

[1] "An order sett downe by the lordes and others of hir Majesties privye Councell the 22 of June 1600 to restrain the excessive number of Plaie howses & the imoderate use of Stage plaies in & about the Cittye"; rpt. in E. K. Chambers, *The Elizabethan Stage*, 4 vols. (Oxford: Clarendon Press, 1923), 4:329–31; quotation from 330. Also see the discussion in Glynne Wickham, *Early English Stages 1300–1660*, 3 vols. in 4 parts (London: Routledge & Kegan Paul, 1959–81), 2:2:9–29. Wickham construes the document in the context of a crisis between 1597 and 1603 concerning the fate of the public theaters. The resolution by the Crown in support of the theaters prepared the way for the more authoritarian control of the stage during the Jacobean reign; furthermore, by aligning itself unmistakably with the theater, "the monarchy . . . prompted all those who were [the theater's] enemies to align themselves against the monarchy" (26). Although obviously attractive to literary critics and theater historians, this argument may grant the theater unwarranted political importance as a precipitating cause of the English Civil War. If we were to continue arguing in a cause-and-effect mode, we might maintain with equal validity that, by aligning itself with the monarchy, the theater prompted enemies of the crown to align themselves against the stage. However, my own impulse would be to seek a more dialectical mode of interpretation.

[2] The topical connections were first fully set out in Evelyn May Albright, "Shakespeare's *Richard II* and the Essex Conspiracy," *PMLA* 42 (1927), 686–720; were contested in Ray Heffner, "Shakespeare, Hayward and Essex," *PMLA* 45 (1930), 754–80; and were defended and elaborated in Albright, "Shakespeare's *Richard II*, Hayward's History of Henry IV, and the Essex Conspiracy," *PMLA* 46 (1931), 694–719.

A number of recent critics (myself included) have cited the special performance of *Richard II* to exemplify the involvement of the Elizabethan theater in Elizabethan politics: See, for example, Louis Montrose, "Celebration and

Insinuation: Sir Philip Sidney and the Motives of Elizabethan Courtship," *Renaissance Drama*, new series, 8 (1977), 3–35, repr. in *Renaissance Drama as Cultural History: Essays from* Renaissance Drama *1977–1987*, ed. Mary Beth Rose (Evanston: Northwestern Univ. Press and The Newberry Library Center for Renaissance Studies, 1990), 367–99; Stephen Greenblatt, "Introduction," in *The Forms of Power and the Power of Forms in the Renaissance*, 3–5; Stephen Orgel, "Making Greatness Familiar," ibid., 45; Jonathan Dollimore, "Introduction: Shakespeare, Cultural Materialism and the New Historicism," in *Political Shakespeare*, ed. Jonathan Dollimore and Alan Sinfield (Ithaca: Cornell Univ. Press, 1985), 8–9; Leonard Tennenhouse, *Power on Display: The Politics of Shakespeare's Genres* (New York: Methuen, 1986), 88.

For a valuable analysis of the relevant historical materials, and a critique of some recent anecdotal uses of the Essex episode in Shakespeare studies, see Leeds Barroll, "A New History for Shakespeare and His Time," *Shakespeare Quarterly* 39 (1988), 441–64. For an illuminating interpretation of the conspiracy in the context of the late Elizabethan politics of honor, see "At the crossroads of the political culture: the Essex revolt, 1601," in Mervyn James, *Society, Politics and Culture: Studies in Early Modern England*, (Cambridge: Cambridge Univ. Press, 1986), 416–65.

[3] The play performed on 7 February 1601 is so identified in the deposition by Augustine Phillips (18 February 1601), Shakespeare's fellow sharer in the Lord Chamberlain's company. The text of the deposition is printed in E. K. Chambers, *William Shakespeare: A Study of Facts and Problems*, 2 vols. (Oxford: Clarendon Press, 1930), 2:325.

[4] See, for example, the "Account of the execution of the Earl of Essex" in *Calendar of State Papers Domestic*, 1598–1601, vol. 278, art. 112, 592–94.

[5] For a critical edition of the text and a detailed account of the controversy surrounding its printing and suppression, see *The First and Second Parts of John Hayward's The Life and Raigne of King Henrie IIII*, ed. John J. Manning, Camden Fourth Series, vol. 42 (London: Royal Historical Society, 1992). Quotations are from this edition. Also see Margaret Dowling, "Sir John Hayward's Troubles Over His *Life of Henry IV*," *The Library*, 4th series, 11 (1931), 212–24, which prints excerpts from the Attorney General's notes on his interrogations of Hayward. Hayward's text was first printed with a Latin dedicatory epistle to the Earl of Essex, followed by a preface, "A. P. to the Reader," extolling histories for setting forth "not onely precepts, but lively patterns, both for private directions and for affayres of state" (62). Within a few days of publication, the Earl of Essex complained to the Archbishop of Canterbury, who ordered that the Epistle be removed; an attempted second edition, with a new Epistle Apologetical by Hayward, was confiscated and burned on the Archbishop's orders. It was widely rumored that the Earl delayed his complaint until after the book had been widely circulated. This was also part of the official story, as

incorporated into the government's "Directions for the preachers," intended for dissemination from the pulpit in the wake of the Earl's revolt:

> Two years since, a history of Henry IV. was printed and published, wherein all the complaints and slanders which have been given out by seditious traitors against the Government, both in England and Ireland, are set down, and falsely attributed to those times, thereby cunningly insinuating that the same abuses being now in this realm that were in the days of Richard II, the like course might be taken for redress. This book was no sooner published but that the Earl, knowing hundreds of them to be dispersed, would needs seem the first that disliked it, whereas he had confessed that he had the written copy with him to peruse 14 days, plotting how he night become another Henry IV. (*Calendar of State Papers Domestic*, 1598–1601, vol. 278, art. 63, 567)

[6] Filled to capacity, the Globe would likely have held about three thousand customers (see Andrew Gurr, *Playgoing in Shakespeare's London*, [Cambridge: Cambridge Univ. Press, 1987], 18–22). Its audience for a successful play on a topical and controversial subject, performed on a Saturday afternoon, is likely to have numbered more than eleven. Of course, it is possible, although highly unlikely, that the conspirators really did have the Globe almost to themselves, and that they were content to have it so. In that case, however, we might then want to ask why they had not rather requested a private performance at Essex House.

[7] Richard Dutton, *Mastering the Revels: The Regulation and Censorship of English Renaissance Drama* (Iowa City: Univ. of Iowa Press, 1991), 124.

[8] The relevant excerpts from the report of the Trial and from Francis Bacon's *Declaration of the Practises and Treasons . . . by Robert late Earle of Essex* (both 1601), are reprinted in Chambers, *William Shakespeare*, 2:325–26. In his own examination, Meyricke attempted to portray himself as merely a casual spectator: "He can not tell who procured that play to be played at that tyme except yt were Sr Charles Percye, but as he thyncketh yt was Sr Charles Percye. Thenne he was at the same play and Cam in somwhat after yt was begon, and the play was of Kyng Harry the iiijth, and of the kyllyng of Kyng Richard the second played by the L. Chamberlen's players" (ibid., 324).

[9] Printed in E. K. Chambers, *William Shakespeare: A Study of Facts and Problems*, 2 vols. (Oxford: Clarendon Press, 1930), 2:325.

[10] Some 160 lines of the so-called "deposition scene" of *Richard II* (4.1) appear for the first time in print in the 1608 quarto, which on the title page advertises the additional material and the play's recent staging: "With new additions of the Parliament Sceane, and the deposing of King Richard. As it hath been lately acted by the Kinges Majesties Servantes, at the Globe." It is

usually assumed that the additions in the 1608 text were part of the original version and were performed during the reign of Elizabeth, but that the scene was censored in the Elizabethan printed editions. For a justifiably skeptical view of these assumptions, see Barroll, "A New History for Shakespeare and His Time," 448–49. For a recent critical review of the issues, see Janet Clare, *"Art made tongue-tied by authority": Elizabethan and Jacobean Dramatic Censorship* (Manchester: Manchester Univ. Press, 1990), 47–51; Dutton, *Mastering the Revels*, 124–27.

[11] Whatever the bases of reader demand—whether entertainment, edification, or conspiracy—the motives of The Lord Chamberlain's Men in allowing their precious playscript to be printed were presumably financial. This was a critical juncture in the company's history and fortunes: The Burbages' lease on the Theater property ran out in April 1597 and could not be renewed; at the same time, the company was being prevented from performing in the Blackfriars property that James Burbage had purchased and refurbished for their use. As Andrew Gurr has pointed out (7), the players shared the

> problem of their financier's lack of cash. The release of several Shakespeare playbooks, *Richard III, Richard II, I Henry IV* and *Love's Labours Lost*, amongst the most popular plays in their repertoire, to the publisher Andrew Wise in 1597 and 1598 was a cash-raising device they had never used before and never used again. The shortage of cash and the lack of a playhouse were the crisis out of which the Globe was born. ("Money or Audiences: The Impact of Shakespeare's Globe," *Theatre Notebook* 42 [1988], 3–14.)

The convergence of artistic, commercial, and political forces that is evident in the printing of *Richard II* aptly illustrates that, within the society of Elizabethan England, the status of the theaters and their plays, as well as the status of the players and their dramatists, was at once contingent and over-determined.

[12] Evidence for a strong reader demand derives from the testimony of John Wolfe, the printer of Hayward's history, when he was examined by Attorney General Coke on 13 July 1600. Wolfe testified that "500 or 600 copies were sold before" the Bishop's order was received, "as no book ever sold better. After receiving such order, cut out the epistle and the residue, being 500 or 600, sold shortly after." A few weeks later, a second, revised edition of 1500 copies, prefaced by an "epistle apologetical," was readied for sale, "the people calling for it exceedingly," but it was confiscated and burned by the authorities. See *Calendar of State Papers Domestic*, 1598–1601, vol. 278, art. 28, 450–51.

[13] "A Report of Hir Majesties most gratious answer, delivered by hir selfe verballie ... in hir chamber of presence at Richmond, the twelfe daie of November 1586," in *Holinshed's Chronicles of England, Scotland, and Ireland*, 6 vols. (1808; repr., New York: AMS Press, 1965), 4:934.

[14] For the first quotation, see Stephen Greenblatt, *Renaissance Self-Fashioning* (Chicago: Univ. of Chicago Press, 1980), 167; for the second, Stephen Greenblatt, *Shakespearean Negotiations* (Berkeley: Univ. of California Press, 1988), 64. The Queen's speech is invoked in each instance. The latter citation occurs near the end of a chapter focused on the second tetralogy of Shakespeare's English histories ("Invisible Bullets," *Shakespearean Negotiations*, 21–65).

[15] That which passed from the "Excellent Majestie of Queen Elizabeth, in her Privie Chamber at East Greenwich, 4 Augusti 1601, 43 Reg. sui, towards William Lambarde," printed in Chambers, *William Shakespeare*, 2:326–27.

[16] See David Scott Kastan, "Proud Majesty Made a Subject: Shakespeare and the Spectacle of Rule," *Shakespeare Quarterly* 37 (1986), 459–75; quotation from 473. Also see John Bellamy, *The Tudor Law of Treason* (London: Routledge & Kegan Paul, 1979), 9–82, passim. As Kastan remarks, "Certainly both Essex and Elizabeth understood the playing of *Richard II* on the eve of the rebellion as part of the treasonous imagining, as an invitation to the populace to participate—either in the fiction or in fact—in the deposition of an anointed king" (472).

[17] Thomas Smith, *De Republica Anglorum* (1583), ed. L. Alston (1906; repr., Shannon: Irish Univ. Press, 1972), 46.

[18] For a recent, judicious, and comprehensive discussion of the social composition, personal comportment, and dramatic tastes of the Elizabethan playgoing public, see Gurr, *Playgoing in Shakespeare's London*. In his discussion of women playgoers (55–63), Gurr notes that they formed a "high proportion" of the audiences, and that "women from every section of society went to plays" (55, 57). On the presence of women in large numbers in the paying audiences of the public theaters, and its possible ideological and material consequences for the players and their repertories, see Jean E. Howard, "Scripts and/versus Playhouses: Ideological Production and the Renaissance Public Stage," *Renaissance Drama*, new series, 20 (1989), 31–49; repr. in *The Matter of Difference: Materialist Feminist Criticism of Shakespeare*, ed. Valerie Wayne (Ithaca: Cornell Univ. Press, 1991), 221–36; and now republished in revised form in Howard, *The Stage and Social Struggle in Early Modern England* (London and New York: Routledge, 1994), 73–92. Also see Richard Levin, "Women in the Renaissance Theatre Audience," *Shakespeare Quarterly* 40 (1989), 165–74.

[19] Letter to Sir Edmund Bacon, 2 July 1613, in Logan Pearsall Smith, *The Life and Letters of Sir Henry Wotton*, 2 vols. (Oxford: Clarendon Press, 1907), 2:32–33. Also see Stephen Orgel, "Making Greatness Familiar," in *The Forms of Power and the Power of Forms in the Renaissance*, ed. Stephen Greenblatt (*Genre* Special Topics: 7 [1982]), 41–48; and Kastan, "Proud Majesty Made a Subject: Shakespeare and the Spectacle of Rule."

[20] Paul Yachnin, "The Powerless Theater," *English Literary Renaissance* 21 (1991), 49–74; quotation from 50. This essay is both thoughtful and provocative, and I have benefited from finding so much in it with which to disagree.

[21] For a classic statement stressing the "morality" of Shakespeare's "political agnosticism," see Wilbur Sanders's provocative and underappreciated study, *The Dramatist and the Received Idea: Studies in the Plays of Marlowe & Shakespeare* (Cambridge: Cambridge Univ. Press, 1968), 143–93; for a recent discussion, stressing the contradictions among the ideologies available to Shakespeare, see the chapter on "Ideological Conflict, Alternative Plots, and the Problem of Historical Causation," in Phyllis Rackin, *Stages of History: Shakespeare's English Chronicles* (Ithaca: Cornell Univ. Press, 1990), 40–85.

[22] *Certain Sermons or Homilies (1547) and A Homily against Disobedience and Wilful Rebellion (1570): A Critical Edition*, ed. Ronald B. Bond (Toronto: Univ. of Toronto Press, 1987), 161. A second edition of the 1547 text appeared in 1559, almost immediately after the accession of Queen Elizabeth, and this was reprinted frequently during the reign.

[23] A foundational text was provided by Sir Henry Savile's 1591 translation of Tacitus's *Agricola* and the first four books of the *Historiae*, with a commentary, an original essay on the Roman art of war, and a prefatory narrative history, "The Ende of Nero and Beginning of Galba," meant to account for events between the end of Tacitus's *Annales* and the beginning of his *Historiae*. It was in his original narrative of the revolt against Nero that Savile formulated a heterodox position on resistance to monarchs. See the important article by David Womersley, "Sir Henry Savile's Translation of Tacitus and the Political Interpretation of Elizabethan Texts," *Review of English Studies*, new series, 42 (1991), 313–42. Womersley writes that Savile

> seeks to rescue the act of resistance to a monarch from the status of a hideous irruption of chaos, and instead to present it, in the manner of the Huguenot political thinkers, as a political and legal act like any other which does not necessarily involve any rending of the fabric of national political life. It would be difficult to overstate the vigour and abruptness with which this challenges the prevailing political orthodoxies of late sixteenth-century England. (329)

Saville, the Warden of Merton College, Oxford, had connections to Essex's secretary, Henry Cuffe, whom the Earl subsequently accused of leading him into sedition; and also with Essex himself, who had extended his patronage and (according to Ben Jonson in his *Conversations*) had authored the prefatory "A. B. to the Reader" for Savile's edition of Tacitus. Following the Earl's revolt, Savile was put under restraint by order of the Privy Council.

[24] James, *Society, Politics and Culture*, 421.

[25] On the homology between Elizabethan dramatic structure and rhetorical traditions of inquiry in Humanist education, see Joel Altman, *The Tudor Play of Mind: Rhetorical Inquiry and the Development of Elizabethan Drama* (Berkeley: Univ. of California Press, 1978).

[26] Andrew Gurr, *The Shakespearean Stage 1574-1642*, 3rd ed. (Cambridge: Cambridge Univ. Press, 1992), 99-100.

[27] On the ideological changes, focused upon the understanding of human nature, that heralded the emergence of capitalism and modernity in England, see C. B. Macpherson, *The Political Theory of Possessive Individualism, Hobbes to Locke* (Oxford: Oxford Univ. Press, 1964); and Albert O. Hirschman, *The Passions and the Interests: Political Arguments for Capitalism Before Its Triumph* (Princeton: Princeton Univ. Press, 1978). On the complex relationship between these developments and the Renaissance theater, see the important discussions in Don E. Wayne, "Drama and Society in the Age of Jonson: Shifting Grounds of Authority and Judgment in Three Major Comedies," *Renaissance Drama* 13 (1982), repr. in *Renaissance Drama as Cultural History: Essays from* Renaissance Drama *1977-1987*, ed. Mary Beth Rose, 3-29, and Jean-Christoph Agnew, *Worlds Apart: The Market and the Theater in Anglo-American Thought, 1550-1750* (Cambridge: Cambridge Univ. Press, 1986), 101-48.

[28] See James L. Calderwood, *Metadrama in Shakespeare's Henriad: Richard II to Henry V* (Berkeley: Univ. of California Press, 1979), for a pioneering study of the metatheatrical dimension of Shakespeare's second tetralogy. As Calderwood declares, his approach is "devoted to the self-reflexive aspects of the plays.... Instead of regarding language as a means toward political ends, I would find Shakespeare solving problems of language by means of politics. Political affairs, in other words, become metaphors for art" (4). I first advanced an historicized account of the metatheatricality of the Elizabethan drama and the protean powers of the Elizabethan players in "The Purpose of Playing: Reflections on a Shakespearean Anthropology," *Helios*, new series, 7 (1980), 51-74. In large part, I was reacting against the aesthetic impetus of Calderwood's frequently acute and suggestive work when I wrote, in 1980, that the plays'

> artistic reflexivity needs to be seen in historical perspective, in the context of a dialectic between Shakespeare's profession and his society. The remarkably pervasive and sophisticated reflexivity of Shakespearean drama is not a symptom of aestheticism but the articulation of a dramatistic conception of human life, rooted in the historical circumstances of personal experience. ("The Purpose of Playing," 53)

The perspective adumbrated in that early work has been developed, in regard to Shakespeare's English histories, in two valuable essays by David Kastan: "Proud Majesty Made a Subject: Shakespeare and the Spectacle of Rule," and " 'The Kings Hath Many Marching in His Coats', or "What Did You Do During the War, Daddy?" in *Shakespeare Left and Right*, ed. Ivo Kamps (New York and London: Routledge, 1991), 241-58. My perspective is also in accord with the chapter on "King and Pretenders: Monarchical theatricality in the Shakespearean history play," in Jean E. Howard, *The Stage and Social Struggle in Early Modern England*, 129–53. The central argument of this fine study, which was published after my own had reached final form, is that

> there is a considerable difference between how theatricality is represented as a threat to identity and social stability in the three plays dealing with the reign of Henry VI and in the plays dealing primarily with Bolingbroke and his son. The difference ... has centrally to do with whether or not theatrical practice is represented as an external threat *to* monarchy or as constitutive *of* monarchy.... It is the plays dealing with Bolingbroke and his son ... that most insistently mark their modernity by demonstrating the inseparability of theatricality from social being. (130)

[29] For an overview of the legal and institutional aspects of Elizabethan censorship, see D. M. Loades, "The Theory and Practice of Censorship in Sixteenth-Century England," *Transactions of the Royal Historical Society*, 5th ser., 24 (1974), 141–57; on the interacting practices of censorship and interpretation in Elizabethan literary culture, see Annabel Patterson, *Censorship and Interpretation: The Conditions of Writing and Reading in Early Modern England* (1984; repr., with a new Introduction, Madison: Univ. of Wisconsin Press, 1990). On dramatic censorship, see Gerald Eades Bentley, *The Profession of Dramatist in Shakespeare's Time 1590–1642* (1971; repr., Princeton: Princeton Univ. Press, 1986), 145–96; Clare, *'Art made tongue-tied by authority'*; Dutton, *Mastering the Revels*.

[30] In the Introduction to the English language edition of his *Shakespeare and the Popular Tradition in the Theater: Studies in the Social Dimension of Dramatic Form and Function*, ed. Robert Schwartz (Baltimore: Johns Hopkins Univ. Press, 1978), Robert Weimann writes that

> Shakespeare's theater and his society were interrelated in the sense that the Elizabethan stage, even when it reflected the tensions and compromises of sixteenth-century England, was also a potent force that helped to create the specific character and transitional nature of that society.... The sensibilities and receptivity of the audience and the consciousness and artistry of the drama were so mutually influential that a new historical synthesis seems conceivable only through an increased awareness of the dialectics of this interdependence. (xii)

Dialectical, historicist, and materialist work has become central to the study of Shakespeare in the U.S. and Britain since the publication of *Shakespeare and the Popular Tradition in the Theater*; and such work—including mine—has been enabled by the critical perspective announced and exemplified in Weimann's landmark book.

[31] The many-sided first Globe playhouse had as its sign the figure of Her-

cules carrying the globe; and as its motto, *Totus mundus agit histrionem*. For a learned discussion of the circumstantial evidence for the sign and motto, see Richard Dutton, "Hamlet, An Apology for Actors, and the Sign of the Globe," *Shakespeare Survey* 41 (1988), 35–43.

[32] For a general reading of Elizabethan policy from such a perspective, see Corrigan and Sayer, *The Great Arch*, 55–71. For the concept of "ideological state apparatuses" (which is not used by Corrigan and Sayer), see "Ideology and Ideological State Apparatuses (Notes towards an Investigation)," in Louis Althusser, *Lenin and Philosophy and Other Essays*, trans. Ben Brewster (New York: Monthly Review Press, 1971), 127–86. In *Drama of a Nation: Public Theater in Renaissance England and Spain* (Ithaca: Cornell Univ. Press, 1985), Walter Cohen, working within Marxian categories, "pursues a single and simple hypothesis: that the absolutist state, by its inherent dynamism and contradictions, first fostered and then undermined the public theater" (19–20).

[33] See *Hamlet*, 2.2.316–62. I use the text in *The Complete Works of Shakespeare*, ed. David Bevington, 4th ed. (New York: Harper Collins, 1992).

[34] In *An Apology for Actors (1612)*, Heywood recounts some sensational case histories (G1v–G2v), in which guilty creatures sitting at a play are so moved by the feigned action that they spontaneously confess their hidden crimes.

[35] I discuss the bases for this argument in the Prologue to this book, and at greater length in Louis Montrose, "New Historicisms," in *Redrawing the Boundaries: the Transformation of English and American Literary Studies*, ed. Stephen Greenblatt and Gills Gunn (New York: Modern Language Association, 1992), 392–418.

[36] The importance of staging, performance, and actor-audience interaction to the collective creation of meaning in Elizabethan drama has been brilliantly explored by Robert Weimann. See *Shakespeare and the Popular Tradition in the Theater*, esp. 208–60; and, among several subsequent studies: "History and the Issue of Authority in Representation: The Elizabethan Theater and the Reformation," *New Literary History* 17 (1985–86), 449–76, and "Bifold Authority in Shakespeare's Theatre," *Shakespeare Quarterly* 39 (1988), 401–17. In a characteristic formulation, Weimann writes that, "in appropriating the author's function and self-authorized performative in the world of the Elizabethan theater, the common actors (articulating and gesticulating the representing language) might utterly and on every level contradict the matter political and ideological which was represented" ("History and the Issue of Authority in Representation," 474).

DAVID KINAHAN

Embodying Origins:
An Anatomy of a Yeoman's Daughter, Spenser's Argante, and Elizabeth I

THE HUMAN EMBRYO, ACCORDING TO AMBROISE PARÉ, is "ready like soft wax to receive any form."[1] For thirty to forty-two days after conception, the embryo lies vulnerable to the impressive power of the mother's imagination. However, the embryo's primary (and secondary) threat, to which no statute of limitations applies, is the formative judgement of God. A monstrous birth, then, might be taken to indicate, among other causes, the mother's failure to shelter herself from imaginative influence and/or the judgement of God on a disorderly originary coupling.[2] Poets too, Philip Sidney attests, "bringeth things forth," "delivering"[3] to the world the impressions of their imaginations and their judgements as makers. Both Paré and Sidney imply that monstrous bodies, whether they be actual or textual, set into motion interpretative work—the search for the fore-conceit of the maker that will endow the body with meaning.

In what follows, I will examine two monstrous bodies, both of which are connected to narratives of incest and both of which have a relatively marginal textual status. But, like Peter Stallybrass and Allon White, I am interested in the ways in which the culturally peripheral may be symbolically central.[4] The first of these bodies, an unnamed child of "wonderfull deformities,"[5] is described by an unnamed pamphleteer, and the second is Spenser's figure of Argante, who appears like a "furious spark"[6] by which one might momentarily glimpse a far more central body, Elizabeth I.

1

In 1600, Richard Jones published "A Most Straunge, and true discourse, of the wonderfull *iudgement of God*. OF A MONSTROVS, DEFORmed Infant, begotten by incestuous co*pulation, between the brothers sonne and the* sisters daughter, being both vnmarried *persons*." The pamphlet takes as its subject the birth of a deformed child to a "young maiden" (2), a yeoman's daughter, who is alleged in the pamphlet to have had sexual relations with (at least) one of her cousins. (See note 5 for explanation of pamphlet citations in parentheses.) The writer suggests he feels a moral compulsion to "do my countrie good" (Sig.A3ʳ) and employ his "poore talent" (Sig.A3ᵛ) against what he argues is the current abundance "these dayes" in the "sinnes of Incest, Onanisme, Whoredom, Adulterie & Fornication, with other Sodomiticall sinnes of vncleanesse & pollutions" (Sig.A3ʳ).[7] This monstrous (infant) body, reproduced in narrative, is explicitly made to serve an ethical and didactic purpose, the "restrainte of fleshly lustes" (Sig.A3ᵛ). It is also the example through which the author fashions his absolutes of (female) sexual behaviour. He alludes to the "wise and graue histories" of monstrous births, "our neglect" of which, he argues, has caused a contemporary excess of sexual incontinence (9). His narrative, then, takes its place among those "wise and graue histories" to which he gestures as reformative, to "make us tremble and quake, when we shall but reade and heare of them" (9).

After itemizing the deformities of "this monster," the author asserts that "It resteth now, that we make vse of it" (7). The monstrous birth here becomes a spectacle employed for its "positive and useful effects"[8] in generating social truth. Publishing makes public a birth that is constructed as a punishment, and like the public punishment of the period, it is staged to achieve social work; the young woman's narrative is coopted to serve a conservative agenda of sexual fashioning.[9]

Incest is only one of the woman's alleged transgressions. She is also indicted for her failure to conform to community standards and assume her expected social role as a wife. The author attests that, despite "conuenient offers of marriages, fit for her estate" (2), she refused to accept a husband. The community pressure is evident in the pamphlet as the author describes one instance, "among all the rest," where the woman did involve herself in a contract of marriage. He suggests that the man was of "competent wealth, and of good name, and fame in the place where he dwelt" (2) and "all the people of those parts thought for truth, that a full match in marriage, *should* shortly haue been solemnized" (2, emphasis mine). The imperative aspect of the phrase situates the woman as the subject of an evaluative and expectant society that has codified normative behaviour.

The woman's failure to live up to these expectations and demands is accounted for by two divergent notions: she is the victim of Satan, who "worked her mind against" the man; or, her behaviour is in accord with the "lightnesse and inconstancy of a great number of this sexe" (2). The agency of the woman's action is on the one hand external and demonized, yet the authorial gesture to the "great number of this sexe" is a suggestion that the action can also find its origin in the "nature" of women as the author understands it. This "proud ... wench" (4), he argues, must be punished, and it seems clear that her punishment has as much to do with her withholding of her body from the socially perpetuating institution of marriage as it does her subsequent incestuous relationship:

> God in his iust punishment (to shew his displeasure against mockerie with his holy institution of marriage, and his hatred of the sinnes of whoredom, adulterie, fornication, inceste, and all other vncleanesse) made this proud, this scornefull & vnconstant wench, the mother of a monster. (3-4)

The monstrous birth, then, is tied not only to an incestuous coupling, but to the unwillingness of the woman to form exogamous social relationships.

The deformed body of the infant is graphically and spectacularly described,[10] and the narrative of its literal and metaphysical origins grounds the anatomy of the infant in social ideology. The measurable physical distance between this child and "other children" (5), evident in size, sexual characteristics, and facial features, permits its classification as monstrous, and the constructed causal link between these physical differences and socially proscribed sexual activities suggests the behaviour itself is formative. The mother's sexual practices are made analogous to their productive result, and the baby is represented as "God['s] ... iust punishment." God behaves in this representation much as the monarchical state penal apparatus that Foucault analyzes in *Discipline and Punish*, creating a spectacular body on which can be read the signs of the crime of its origin. But, of course, God only makes the word flesh; it is up to the exegete to bring it back to the word.[11]

Finally, the gestures in the pamphlet to contemporary conditions add the possibility of another dimension to the social critique focused upon the "mother of this monster" (11). The pamphlet is written to dissuade others from falling into "the sinnes of Incest, Onanisme, Whoredom, Adulterie & Fornication, with other Sodomiticall sinnes of vncleannesse & pollution, [that] do so outragiously raign" (Sig.A3^r). The author says these sins have become particularly prevalent "these days" (Sig.A3^r) and "of late yeares"(Sig.A3^v). He then subtly suggests a connection between the sins that "outragiously raign" and the reigning monarch: with reference to the abundance of these practices, "the Queenes maiestie and her gouernement, the preachers of the Gospell and their teaching, are slaundered and euill spoken of by Papists, Brownists, and others, both abroade and at home" (Sig.A4^r). This statement suggests that the enumerated sins of English society provide rhetorical ammunition to those who have an interest in undermining the contemporary political and religious structures. Detractors can, he allows, connect the prevalence of "sin" with those ostensibly responsible for the conduct of the people. Elizabeth I is indicated as the primary target of this "slander." Using the same processes as the narrator, potential detractors perform an exegetic anatomy of the body politic and read it against its head. The author tries to contain the critique by suggesting that such readings are slanderous and "contrarie to the truth," that it is "the multitude of people [who] breedeth sinne" (sig.A4^r), but his protestations draw attention, particularly given the deployment of the discourse of maternity, to the availablity of a reading constructing Elizabeth as the maternal site of what the author understands to be monstrous sins. Just as he connects the yeoman's daughter's sexual practices to her monstrous offspring, so do "others" argue a linkage between the female monarch and the monstrous body politic.

That such a linkage was not only possible but circulating is borne out by John Knox. In *The First Blast of the Trumpet Against the Mon-*

strous Regiment of Women[12] (1558) Knox asserts that "Woman's authoritie *bringeth furth* monstres."[13] The commonwealth, at the mercy of Knox's monstrous female ruler, becomes monstrous, and Knox deploys the familiar metaphor of the body politic to describe the product of such rule:

> who would not judge that bodie to be a monstre, where there was no head eminent above the rest, but that the eyes were in the handes, the tonge and mouth beneath the bellye, and the eares in the feete? ... And no lesse monstruous is the bodie of that Common welth where a woman *beareth* empire.[14]

The monstrous body politic is, with Knox's terminology, a product of the female monarchical body's generative process—she "beareth" or "bringeth furth" such disorder. Like the woman in the Jones pamphlet who, because of her "proud" desire toward self-determination, delivers a deformed child, the female ruler's authority, "the uttermoste of [God's] plagues,"[15] is punishment in itself and the origin of social deformation.

But the Jones pamphlet and the literature condemning female rule[16] share another aspect; the women they represent are connected to monstrosity by way of incest. Knox concentrates his condemnation of "the Authoritie of all Women"[17] by paying particular notice to Mary Tudor, whom he calls "a traiteiresse and bastard."[18] To be accurate, in calling Mary a bastard was to judge the marriage between Henry VIII and Catherine of Aragon illegitimate. Incest was the only (legal) factor justifying the dissolution. In *Monarchy and Incest in Renaissance England*, Bruce Boehrer describes the way in which medieval canon law derived notions of affinity from prohibitions in *Leviticus*.[19] Henrican divorce tracts exploited these biblical passages to facilitate Henry's separation from Catherine and subsequent marriage to Anne Boleyn.[20] Knox's charge of bastardy reaffirms the overturned succession act of 1534 and constructs Mary as the illegitimate issue of an incestuous coupling between brother and sister-in-law. Both Knox and the pamphleteer, in variations on a theme, connect incest and monstrous birth, and each writer suggests that culpability may be located in the ruling female monarch.

The timing of the publication of *The First Blast* was perhaps not as fortunate as Knox might have hoped. The indictment that found much of its purpose in the anti-Catholic antagonism to Mary became available only seven or eight months before her death,[21] and the Protestant Elizabeth may not have necessitated the same kind of resistance for Knox. In a letter written in July, 1559, addressed to "Elizabeth, by the Grace of God, Quen of England," Knox tried to deny that *The First Blast* in any way touched her "person in especiall."[22] But Elizabeth was not persuaded by these denials; she recognized that even though Knox had not mentioned her name, his tirade against "the Authoritie of all Women" could easily be applied to her. And his inclusion of the detail of bastardy was as applicable to Elizabeth as it had been to Mary.

By 1536, Anne Boleyn had suffered a number of miscarriages, and Henry gave out word that God was expressing his condemnation of the match through its productive (or unproductive) result. "Within a short time," argues Henry Kelly, "Cromwell had gathered together evidence of some rather unlikely adulteries between Anne and a few of her intimates and crowned the whole case with a charge of incest between her and her brother."[23] As a result, Elizabeth, like her half-sister before her, was subjected, through the deployment of a narrative of incest, to a legislated bastarding that would disquiet her reign.

On Mary's death in 1558, Elizabeth attempted to re-establish her own legitimacy. 1 Elizabeth Cap. 3, "For recognition of the Queen's Highness' title to the imperial crown of this realm," the first statutory action of the new reign, proclaimed that "your Highness is rightly, lineally and lawfully descended and come of the blood royal of this realm of England," and referred to her "body lawfully begotten."[24] Elizabeth also issued numerous proclamations against "seditious words and rumours" (e.g., 23 Elizabeth Cap. 2), yet, throughout her lengthy reign, rumours of bastardy and incest reissued from the mouths and pens of her detractors. Bruce Boehrer cites the French *Martyre de la Royne d'Escosse* (1589) and a collection of French and Latin poems called *De Iezabelis Angliae Parricidio* (1587), both of which use incest to undermine the authority and legitimacy of Elizabethan rule.[25] Elizabeth, like the woman in the Jones pamphlet, was unmarried, self-determined, and involved in narratives of incest, and, also like the woman in the pamphlet, this left her vulnerable to associations with monstrous birth.

2

In Book 2 of *The Faerie Queene*, the poet-narrator makes explicit his text's relationship to his Sovereign: "And thou, O fairest Princess vnder sky, / In this faire mirrhour maist behold thy face" (2 Proem, 4). A. C. Hamilton suggests that this refers to this particular book's canto three appearance of Belphoebe (2, Proem, 4, n. 6–9). But, to my mind, this is an unnecessary and, to some extent, unwarranted narrowing of the text's potential mirroring of Elizabeth. Spenser's letter to Ralegh asserts that, in the representation of the Faery Queene, Spenser's particular meaning is "the moste excellent and glorious person of our Soueraine the Queene."[26] But he also suggests that "in some places els, I doe otherwise shadow her."[27] He seems to attempt to stabilize this openness with reference to the representation of Belphoebe: "This latter part," Elizabeth's virtue and beauty, "in some places I doe expresse in Belphoebe."[28] The gesture may be taken in at least two ways: Spenser is suggesting that he represents Elizabeth's virtue and beauty through Belphoebe's appearance in different textual situations; or, that only "some places" use Belphoebe to represent Elizabeth, and that she may still be "in some places els" shadowed. I am intrigued by the unbounded potential of this "shadowing," and, in the space remaining, I want to consider Spenser's figure of Argante to evaluate the extent to which, when incest is represented in *The Faerie Queene*, Spenser is "recoursing to the things forepast."[29]

The giant Argante enters the poem in canto seven of Book Three. Chased by Satyrane, she carries into the poem the Squire of Dames and his narratives of unchastity. The first of these narratives begins as the Squire of Dames describes the origins of Argante herself:

> Her sire *Typhoeus* was, who mad through merth,
> And Drunke with bloud of men, slaine by his might,
> Through incest, her of his owne mother Earth
> Whilome begot. (3.7.47)

Appearing in this genealogy is part of what was repressed in canto three's more explicitly Elizabethan genealogy. There, avoiding the War of the Roses, Henry VIII's six marriages, and Edwardian and Marian rule, Merlin's history of the Tudor monarchy follows a clean line from Henry of Richmond (Henry VII), born on Mona, to the "royall virgin raine" (3.3.48–49) of Elizabeth. Also silenced is the involvement of the line in incest. Yet, rather than being avoided entirely, it is instead displaced to the Argante episode, and this displacement registers in echoes that bring the two genealogies together. In Merlin's narrative, Henry VII takes his origin from a "freshly kindled" "sparke of fire" (3.3.48) that reappears in Argante's "firie eyes" that stare with "furious sparkes" (3.7.39). The inflammatory potential of incest locates itself in the Elizabethan line, only one generation removed. Canto seven, then, presents an alternate genealogy to the one suggested in canto three, and instead of ending with the royal virgin, it ends with the sexually aggressive (and endogamous) Argante. Argante becomes a (per)version of Elizabeth—of incestuous origin, unmarried, and refusing to participate in the socially (and, in her case, politically) perpetuating institution of marriage, Elizabeth is rendered monstrous.

One of the strongest indications that Spenser is working very close to his sovereign in the Argante episode is the fact that the name Argante itself is the name of the Fairy Queen in a thirteenth-century Arthurian romance. Judith Anderson finds that Argante is Arthur's final destination in Lawman's *Brut* (cf. lines 14277–14282).[30] Lawman's Argante, "the fairest of the elf-folke"[31] and the Queen of the fairies, will heal Arthur's wounds and be with him on Avalon until he is ready to return to his kingdom.[32] Spenser's letter to Ralegh asserts that his fairy queen is conceived, "in my particular," to represent Queen Elizabeth, yet, with Argante, he deploys the name of another literary fairy queen in a less than regal context. This connection, taken with what we know of the Tudor genealogical history and the narratives of incest surrounding Anne Boleyn (as either Henry's natural daughter, or her brother's lover), suggests that in Argante we have a very powerful and dangerous confrontation with the body of the sovereign.

The body of Elizabeth was of particular interest to her subjects, who felt themselves vulnerable to its actions and choices. A large factor in the monstering of Mary Tudor was her obstinate decision to marry Philip of Spain. Significantly, William Camden records that Elizabeth had the opportunity to wed Philip after Mary's death— Elizabeth, however, was careful to avoid an action that not only would have alienated her subjects as her sister had, but would have been a repetition of the original action that involved the Tudors in the controversy of incest. Camden suggests that certain courtiers convinced Elizabeth that to acknowledge the authority of the papal dispensation allowing her to marry her brother-in-law was to validate the authority that "has pronounced her Mother to have been unlawfully married to Henry the Eighth" and would in turn give support to the claim of Mary, Queen of Scots.[33] But Elizabethans did want Elizabeth to marry. Louis Montrose asserts that "In the 1560s and 1570s, Elizabeth witnessed allegorical entertainments boldly criticizing her attachment to a life of 'single blessedness,'[34] and Carole Levin suggests that this period of intense attention to Elizabeth's sexual behaviour continued into "the last two decades of her reign."[35]

The Jones pamphlet describes a woman pressured by community expectations and standards, and, when she fails to live up to those expectations and operate by those standards, the result is monstrous. Elizabeth too was under this pressure: though she might have had the heart and stomach of a king, the rest of her anatomy was constrained by the same cultural expectations that were imposed on other women, and that England would experience a crisis of succession if she failed to fulfil this role, served only to intensify her subjects' anxiety concerning her lack of conformity to the gendered order of things. There is an implicit critique of the actions (or inactions) of the Queen in Spenser's poetic division of her into Gloriana and Belphoebe. This fragmentation asserts that female rule and virginal chastity are incompatible. If Belphoebe remains an unattainable virgin, the Faery realm is not jeopardized because she exists in all female society and disdains courtly business, but if Gloriana assumes a similar form of chastity, and refuses the marriage that gives Arthur narrative direction, then that unbroken line of over "seuen hundred Princes, which maintaynd/With mightie deeds their sundry gouernments" (2.10.74) would experience rupture.

Incest, embodied in Argante, is deployed by Spenser as a refracted way of considering Elizabeth's unproductive sexuality. Lois Bueler suggests that incest is an apt device "for probing the moral relationship between individual passions and social well-being."[36] Society's prohibition on incest, often naturalized as Levitical "divine law," is constructed as necessary because it is through exogamous relationships that society is established. Endogamy is the denial of society because it closes off a family rather than involving it in a network of social relationships. "The argument against incest," asserts Bueler, "is the argument for the necessity of marital exchanges that create and cement social relationships."[37] Incest, then, as the refusal of an exogamy that ostensibly provides such social stability, is the anti-type to Spenser's narrative subject of chastity, and its representation will bear the weight of narrative condemnation. Though Elizabeth may not have participated in incestuous relationships, the charge resonates in her history, and her refusal of marriage and the procreative role has the same social effect as endogamy—the Tudor line consumes itself.

Argante's desire to "deuore / Her natiue flesh" (3.7.49) is expressive of the way in which incest is constructed as self-consuming.[38] Incestuous sex becomes a selfish feeding that ingests not only the brother of her nativity, but also her "natiue" flesh in its national sense—Argante "feed[s] her fancy" "ouer all the countrey" (3.7.50). This sense of Argante's sexuality as a national threat is in accordance with the anxiety of Elizabethans over the security of their nation should Elizabeth die without a clear successor.[39] Shakespeare's famous admonitions to the young man to procreate suggest quite clearly that the production of an heir is a social responsibility, the opposite of which is cannibalistic. The young man is advised to "Pitty the world, or else this glutton be,/To eate the worlds due, by the graue and thee."[40] The unproductive body becomes the grave of itself and its potential offspring. Elizabeth, as a ruler and as a woman, was expected to provide for her country's future, and Argante represents the way in which this future was being consumed.

The cannibalistic sexual feeding of Argante prefigures Book five's monster, the terror of Belge's kingdom. Gerioneo's monster, gendered female,[41] represents a perversion of maternity. Instead of producing offspring, the monster's genitalia serve as the conduit from which blasphemies arise—Argante is also described as uttering "blasphemous bannes" (3.7.39). Gerioneo's monster is a consumer rather than a producer—instead of bringing forth life, "she" takes in and is sustained by death. The death that sustains her is the life that should have sustained the kingdom. Belge accuses Gerioneo of having sacrificed twelve of her seventeen sons to this monster (5.10.7–8). Arthur's sword, thrust under the womb of the monster, stops up her blasphemies and facilitates her procreativity as she "issue[s] forth" the "loathly matter" that she had "damb[ed]" up (5.11.31). This monstrous body, then, mastered by the phallic sword, is rendered harmless, and the way is cleared for the succession of the male heirs left unconsumed by this monstrous female body. The connections between Elizabeth and Argante, and Argante and Gerioneo's monster, suggest a representation of Elizabeth in which she, through her form of sexuality (be it virginal, or premarital and unproductive), is consuming her own productivity, a productivity that could mean the smooth transition of power.

In a patriarchal system such as Renaissance England, the untroubled transfer of power and property depended on the maintenance of the blood line. Though Spenser suggests in his rather equivocal proems that he is celebrating Elizabeth, the celebratory focus of Book three is fruitful chastity. Argante is the anti-hero in a book profoundly concerned with the establishment of dynastic security and legitimacy in order to secure national stability. Her adversary, Britomart, must actively defend and represent chastity while she seeks to fulfil her destiny in marriage, a personal destiny that is inextricably linked to national destiny, ontogeny to phylogeny. Britomart's position in Book 3 is constructed as a kind of container of history; she is the embodiment of her ancestors, and she also embodies the future of which Elizabeth is part—she is, then, pregnant with her own future. The importance of this great expectation is signaled by the high profile in *The Faerie Queene* of royal genealogies (and Elizabeth is figured in all of them). Boehrer argues that this figurative involvement can be understood as Spenser's participation in "a series of compensatory gestures in Elizabethan literature."[42] Boehrer suggests that Spenser's apostrophe to Elizabeth in the proem to Book three casts her as poetic model, and that the figures she generates in Book three compensate for her lack of actual maternal productivity:

> The queen becomes at once the product of and the incomparable model for Spenser's work, generating her own ancestry through a species of textual proliferation that allows the poet to enter her and to expose the qualities 'shrined' within her 'brest.' She becomes, that is, the poetic mother of her poetic (fore)mother.[43]

Britomart's body contains the future, and Elizabeth is part of that future, but only in potential—it is the union of her body and Artegall's that is made the imperative of Books three and four.

The genealogies in *The Faerie Queene*, rather than displacing Elizabeth's "unfortunate resemblance to the childless, incestuous Argante,"[44] draw attention to the potential for disruption in the body politic should the monarchy fail to reproduce itself. The royal history, *Briton moniments* (2.10), is clear about the function and success of female rule. Three women are mentioned in that catalogue: Guendolene, Cordelia, and Bunduca. Of these three, Cordelia and Bunduca end in suicide and, childless, cause a rupture in the history—only Guendolene, who "first taught men a woman to obay" (2.10.20), is successful, and her success lies partly in the fact that she "surrendered" (2.10.20), her rule to her son when he came of age. Complicating this further is a male ruler, Lucius, who "without issew dide, / Whereof great trouble in the kingdome grew" (2.10.54). The cumulative effect of these genealogies and histories is to suggest that, for the monarchy, reproduction was a point of duty. While Elizabeth may be generative of poetic figures and (pre)-figurations, Britomart's genealogical future ends ("but yet the end is not" [3.3.50]) in nought; that is, Merlin says nothing. His narration stops and one of the reasons the poet-narrator offers for its lack of closure is that following Elizabeth's "royall virgin raine" (3.3.49) is a "ghastly spectacle" (3.3.50). In *The Faerie Queene*, Spenser typically reserves the term "spectacle" for embodied moments of moral exemplarity. The Spenserian spectacle is presented to be read by the reader or characters, and, by it, they infer the consequences of certain behavior. But the "ghastly spectacle" that the narrator speculates might have dismayed Merlin, goes unseen. Instead of providing the origin of reading, it is the end of all origins, and the rupture, rather than providing another exemplary body, registers the anxiety experienced in the historical absence of that body. The woman in the Jones pamphlet produces a monstrous body because she withholds herself from socially sanctioned expressions of sexuality. In Spenser's representation, Elizabeth's virgin reign produces a "ghastly spectacle" of absence, but it is an absence that is in some sense filled four cantos later when Spenser fashions an anxious expression of the monstrous potential of Elizabeth's withholding, namely the body of the childless product and practitioner of incest, Argante.

Argante's monstrosity is constructed to reflect both the transgressive aspect of her sexual desire and the moral charge on her originary conception. The origin of the "mighty Giauntesse" (3.7:37) is described by the Squire of Dames, whose narration of the events of her conception and birth is at least second-hand:

> These twinnes, *men say*, (a thing far passing thought)
> Whiles in their mothers wombe enclose they were,
> Ere they into the lightsome world were brought,
> In fleshly lust were mingled both yfere,
> And in that *monstrous* wise did *to the world appere*.
>
> (3.7.48, emphasis mine)

Monstrosity, then, is explicitly rendered as the evaluative label affixed by a gazing and speaking community ("world" of "men"). Female sexual desire is being fashioned in this text: chastity, the virtue that best serves the security (and calms the insecurities) of a patriarchal order, is reinforced through the monstering of the sexually aggressive female body. Though Britomart is also aggressive, her aggression is contained within a system that restricts the expression of her sexual desire. Argante has broken free of system and fulfils her desire through this liberation. That this behaviour should incur the censure of male voices, for it is "men" who "say" these things of her, is expressive of the fear and hostility with which a male-centred society encounters a powerful woman. The displacement of the narrative voice here is multi-layered: the poet-narrator places the voice in the Squire of Dames, and the Squire himself only reiterates what he has heard "men say." Spenser distances himself from the articulation by at least three steps. This caution may be a reflection of the danger of the utterance—if Elizabeth were to see herself in this particular mirror, she would certainly find the image less than flattering, and Spenser may end up like Malfont in the court of Mercilla, violently silenced for his "foule blaspheme [of] that Queene" (5.9.25). But the gesture of displacement might also have something to do with the tremendous quantity of gossip generated around the royal body.

Levin suggests that hostility to Elizabeth's rule often manifested itself in rumors and gossip about her sexual activity and productivity. She cites Edmund Baxter, who "openly expressed the not uncommon view that Elizabeth's reputed unchastity disqualified her as a monarch."[45] She was also rumored to have had a number of illegitimate children, some of whom she was reputed to have destroyed.[46] Her frequent royal progresses were said to be a direct result of her sexual liaisons; that is, she went on progress when she needed to deliver. That the royal progresses, ostensibly the monarch's spectacular display of authority and national possession, were undermined in this way suggests the problematic nature for this society of the investment of political power in the female body. Argante, then, might be understood to encompass all aspects of the Elizabethan "problem": the product of incest, she withholds herself from relationships constructed as socially productive, and this form of female autonomy is contested in what "men say" of her.

In the Jones pamphlet, the monstrous body is made exemplary; it is taken as one sign of one woman's involvement in a society of corresponding moral deformity. This body is also made the occasion of speech and writing: the author is "importuned" (Sig.A3^r) by friends to write his brief treatise; these friends assure him "that the report thereof was deliuered them in writing, by a gentleman of good credite & worship" (Sig.A3^r); and Richard Jones assures further publicity by publishing the author's version of this gentleman's narrative. Beyond this network, the author suggests that occurrences like the monstrous birth and the incestuous coupling license "others" (Sig.A4^r) to create narratives critical of the English government and its leader, Elizabeth. The Jones pamphlet, then, draws attention to the ways in which the body becomes the origin and focus of ideological and political fashionings in narrative. Spenser, too, represents a monstrous birth as the occasion of narrative, and that the narrative he constructs, posited as a reiteration of what "men say," implicates his sovereign to such an extent is indicative of the social tensions experienced with a virgin queen who exploited the relationship between court and courtship, yet refused to participate in an exogamous union that would in some way contain her. Argante is a fashioning of the physical body of the monarch, and though Britomart chases her, Argante remains free, a body at large, to critique the queen. In the guise of a celebrant, Spenser becomes one of the Jones pamphlet's "others," writing the queen's body against itself.

University of Western Ontario

Notes

¹ Ambroise Paré, *On Monsters and Marvels* trans. Janis Pallister (Chicago and London: Univ. of Chicago Press, 1982) 54.

² Ibid., 5. Paré itemizes 13 causes of a monster before admitting that some monstrous productions cannot be answered by "human reasons" that are "sufficient or probable" (4).

³ Philip Sidney, *A Defence of Poetry* ed. J. Van Dorsten (Oxford: Oxford Univ. Press 1993) 24–25.

⁴ Peter Stallybrass and Allon White, *The Politics and Poetics of Transgression* (Ithaca, N.Y.: Cornell Univ. Press, 1986) 5.

⁵ I. R., "A Most Straunge, and true discourse, of the wonderfull *iudgement of God*. OF A MONSTROVS, DEFORmed Infant, begotten by incestuous *copulation. between the brothers sonne and the* sisters daughter, being both vnmarried *persons*" (London, 1600) STC # 20575. p. 7. All subsequent citations of this pamphlet are indicated in parentheses within the body of the essay. The pagination in the pamphlet is inconsistent. It begins with a section designated only with signature marks, but then moves into numeral pagination—page 1 seems to begin at what would normally be sig.Bl^r, yet in fact Bl^r is signed elsewhere. My experience with this pamphlet is with its microfilm reproduction; the actual book may contain clues that would account for such bibliographic inconsistency. For the purposes of clarity, I use the numeral pagination where available; in other instances I refer to signature designations.

⁶ Edmund Spenser, *The Faerie Queene* ed. A. C. Hamilton (London and New York: Longman Group, 1977; reprint 1980) 3.7.39 All subsequent citations of *The Faerie Queene* are taken from this edition and references are indicated in parentheses in the body of the essay.

⁷ This is the first instance where I use the pronoun designating the author as male. Though the initials I. R. could be those of a woman, a number of the comments about women in the pamphlet suggest to me a male perspective. The author alludes to "the lightnesse and inconstancy of a great number of this sexe [women]" (2), and, when the pamphlet is critical of men, there is a confessional quality that suggests a shared guilt in the abuses of his sex. I understand the pitfalls in this kind of extrapolation, and am aware that it is certainly not outside the realm of possibility that a woman could assert such things about her own sex, particularly in a society such as Renaissance England where the patriarchal pressures were so strong as to be formative.

⁸ Michel Foucault, *Discipline and Punish: The Birth of the Prison*, trans. Alan Sheridan (New York: Vintage Books, 1979) 24.

⁹ In a later pamphlet, "God's Handy-worke in Wonders Miraculously shewen upon two Women, lately deliuered of two Monsters" (1615), monstrous births are again constructed as punishment for certain sexual behaviours:

to punish the sinnes of some particular parents, God from time to time striketh the womb of the mother, and doubleth his curse, not onely in making her to bring forth with paine and dolour, but to bee deliuered with fearefull and horrid shapes, to astonish the beholders, and affright the sinfull breeders. (sigA3ᵛ)

[10] The narrator, I. R., displaces himself from the narrative of the physical deformities in a gesture that may be intended to lend the description more authority. I. R. defers to a "Gentleman of good credite and worship" (4) and, although no change in style is perceptible, the narrative begins over again discussing both the avoidance of marriage and the incestuous coupling (although this particular telling suggests the possibility that she was having sexual relations with two of her cousins). So her tale is twice told (by men outside its events) before the anatomy of what they argue is its consequence. This doubling of narrative is a frequent occurrence in many of the gallows pamphlets of the period, and, in relation to the notion of the transgressive female, it occurs in Book 6 of *The Faerie Queene,* when Mirabella's story of her "proud" refusal of allegedly suitable marriage partners is told once by the narrator and once again in 'her own voice.'

[11] There is another spectacularly monstrous body that haunts this pamphlet. The author suggests that those men who wish a cure for their incontinent desires should "behould one of these wanton dames [prostitutes], when she is layed and lyeth rotting of the French disease, . . . when one piece is ready to fall from another, and her guts ready to fall out of her belly" (11). The dying body of a prostitute becomes for this author the scene of a pedagogical voyeurism, a public and supposedly self-producing anatomy of the corruption and contagion of monstrous female sexuality. Yet it is the author who provides this anatomy and situates it in a context that directs its meaning.

[12] John Knox. *The First Blast of the Trumpet Against the Monstrous Regiment of Women* 1558 in *The Works of John Knox* ed. David Laing (New York: AMS Press, 1966).

[13] Ibid., 4:401 emphasis mine

[14] Ibid., 4:391 emphasis mine

[15] Ibid., 4:404

[16] Another Protestant critic, Christopher Goodman, is less subtle in his attack. He berates the male power-elite of England for making themselves "bondemen to the lustes of a most impotent and vnbrydled woman: a woman begotten in adulterie . . . contrarie to the word of God" (97). Goodman asserts that

Henry the eight, in marying with his brother's wife, did vtterly contemne the free grace of our Sauiour . . . and also committed adulterous incest contrary to the word of God, when he begat this vngodlie serpent Marie, the chief instrument of all this present miserie. (98)

This orthographical pun has Henry and Catherine producing a Mary (marying) in the act of marrying. Goodman's misogynous, political, and religious objections to Mary become fixated on the moment of her conception as he contemplates the alleged ungodly coupling that results in this "vngodlie" offspring.

[17] Knox, 4:420

[18] Ibid., 4:365

[19] Bruce Boehrer, *Monarchy and Incest in Renaissance England: Literature, Culture, Kinship, and Kingship* (Philadelphia: Univ. of Pennsylvania Press, 1992), 29–30

[20] Ibid., 29

[21] Knox, 4:420 n.1

[22] Knox, 6:48

[23] Henry Kelly, *The Matrimonial Trials of Henry VIII* (Stanford: Stanford Univ. Press, 1976) 242

[24] *The Statutes at Large from the Magna charta, to the end of the eleventh Parliament of Great Britain, anno 1761 [continued to 1806]* ed. Danby Pickering (Cambridge: Cambridge Univ. Press, 1762–1807) Vol. 6, p.123. Boehrer cites this passage, and Kelly gestures to it, yet they both refer to 1 Elizabeth I c.1. rather than c.3. The first "Private Act," however, of the Elizabethan Parliament "restored [Elizabeth] in blood to the late Queen *Anne*, her Highness's mother" (6:Sig.A3ʳ).

[25] Boehrer, 47

[26] Spenser, Edmund, "A Letter of the Authors" in *The Faerie Queene*. ed. A. C. Hamilton (London and New York, 1977) 737.

[27] Ibid., 737

[28] Ibid., 737

[29] Ibid., 737

[30] Judith Anderson, "Arthur, Argante, and the Ideal Vision: An Exercise in Speculation and Parody," *The Passing of Arthur: New Essays in Arthurian Tradition*, ed. C. Baswell and W. Sharpe (New York and London: Garland, 1988) 193–206.

[31] Lawman, *Lawman's Brut* (13th C) trans. Rosamund Allen (New York: St. Martin's Press, 1992) line 14291.

[32] Anderson reminds her reader that in Chaucer's *Sir Thopas* there is a giant, Ollifant, and a dream vision of the fairy queen very much like Arthur's in Spenser's poem.

[33] William Camden, *The History of the Most Renowned and Victorious Princess Elizabeth Late Queen of England* (Chicago and London: Univ. of Chicago Press, 1970) 14

[34] Louis Montrose, " 'Reshaping Fantasies': Figurations of Gender and Power in Elizabethan Culture." *Representations* 25 (1983) 80.

[35] Levin, Carole. *The Heart and Stomach of a King: Elizabeth I and the Politics of Sex and Power* (Philadelphia: Univ. of Pennsylvania Press, 1994) 67.

[36] Lois Bueler, "The Structural Uses of Incest in English Renaissance Drama," *Renaissance Drama* n.s. 15, 1984: 116.

[37] Bueler, 144.

[38] One thinks of Milton's incestuous demonic trinity of Satan, Sin and Death, and Sin's complaint that her son's sexual violation of her has resulted in monsters, which, "when they list into the womb / That bred them they return, and howl and gnaw / My bowels" *(Paradise Lost* 2:798–800).

[39] Carole Levin treats quite thoroughly the varied expressions of this anxiety in her chapter "Wanton and Whore" in *The Heart and Stomach of A King.*

[40] Shakespeare, William. *Shakespeare's Sonnets.* ed. Stephen Booth (New Haven and London: Yale Univ. Press, 1977), 5.

[41] This monster, initially only described with the neutral pronoun "it," is depicted as uttering blasphemies in a male voice that originates in the "poysnous entrails" (5.11.20). After this description, the monster is then gendered female instead of, in accordance with the voice, male. This movement from neutral to female occurs again two stanzas later as the beast is described emerging from its cave, and once again the gendering of the monster as female takes place as the narrator describes the lower regions of its body.

[42] Boehrer, 46.

[43] Ibid., 83.

[44] Ibid., 80–81.

[45] Levin, 76.

[46] Ibid., 81–84.

WILLIAM O. SCOTT

Reading History, Reading Power, Reading Plays: Graham Holderness on Shakespeare's History Plays

SOME SURVEYS OF RECENT CRITICISM of Renaissance or early modern literature distinguish between American new historicism, which concentrates on rethinking the historical past, and cultural materialism, which is said to dominate British thought and to put an emphasis on the uses of the past in contemporary institutions and social practices.[1] One does not expect such dichotomies to be absolute. An interesting exception to any schism would be Graham Holderness, whose volume *Shakespeare's History* encompasses both. Part One, "Shakespeare's History," surveys Tudor historiography and argues that its new awareness and nascent analysis of feudalism enter into the portrayals of events in Shakespeare's second tetralogy; Part Two, "Shakespeare in History," discusses Shakespeare's current status in society as evidenced in criticism, educational institutions, and stage and film performance.[2] Each inquiry puts emphasis on the social uses of history in the time which it concerns, so that history as subject matter of these plays connects well with social motivations for its treatment in the play text and in production. Both inquiries find a variety of possibilities for interpreting the plays in either period.[3]

John Turner, one of Holderness's collaborators in another volume, even conflates the names of the two postulated critical schools by speaking of "the 'new historicism' of cultural materialism."[4] Since historicism is deeply involved in the very texts of literature being studied, the reflexive nature of this criticism of the history plays allows an especially relevant test of critical methods in relation to both the texts and their social context. Though this essay will concentrate on the first of Holderness's two inquiries, the political motivations underlying his work are essential in assessment of it as a direction for criticism.

If the concepts of history in Shakespeare's plays are at issue, one should naturally put detailed questions to those plays, and to do so in this context is not merely to return to the procedures of New Criticism (against which Stephen Greenblatt, for instance, reacted as he worked toward development of new-historicist procedures, from "verbal icons" to "cultural artifacts").[5] Questions of dramaturgy and verbal meaning can have a social pertinence as they guide practices of reading (and presumably of performance too). And since the plays may have various possibilities of meaning in both Shakespeare's time and ours, there is an occasion to consider, specifically within the text, the relationships between subversive meanings and the possibility of their containment; such a dialectic may relate to the social conditions of either era.[6]

As Holderness reviews the concepts of history latent in Shakespeare's dramatizations, he finds that the events of the fourteenth and fifteenth centuries chronicle the decline of feudalism before a new royal absolutism,[7] and that view of feudalism and royalism, as here attributed to Shakespeare, was also later to figure in radical Commonwealth challenges to Stuart absolutism (hence its political appeal to Holderness). Thus, it is implied, Shakespeare's reading of history anticipated developments in empiricist historiography that were made by social reformers a half-century later. With this role established, Shakespeare would provide a literary model for socially progressive attitudes: reflexively, historical inquiry into his treatment of history would reveal the same political tendencies in both Shakespeare's and the present historical studies. However, one must check this conclusion against the range of possibilities encouraged by the dramatic text.

One effect of finding such attitudes toward history in Shakespeare's plays, most notably *Richard II*, would be to qualify the status of such portraits as the one that John of Gaunt gives of England as "royal throne of kings" and "sceptered isle" (2.1.40),[8] so that they express not only a generic patriotism but specifically the ideology of the feudal barons. The actions by Richard against which Gaunt is warning are not merely personal transgressions against patriotism—manifestations of a personal tragedy in the making—but also embodiments of historical transformation from a claimed feudal consensus.

Gaunt resists the change by appealing not to royal absolutism but, quite the contrary, to the position of royalty in the traditions of chivalric law; though he accepts the principle of the divine right of kings, he does not endorse royal arbitrariness. In seeking textual support in the play for such a reading, Holderness relies heavily on the ceremonial and chivalric language of the early scenes (*History*, 46–50) and even offers an interpretation based on concepts in feudal law (*Play*, 26–32).[9] Yet chivalric behavior, at least, seems to be underdetermined: it may not necessarily imply endorsement of a feudal code, but may have other dramatic functions, such as to show Richard's insistence on pageantry and the barons' manipulation of it. Thus personal error, in Richard's misguided attitude toward courtly pomp, would still be relevant. So would his political errors of overriding law and custom. Holderness has provided a corrective to readings of Gaunt's position that might either focus too narrowly on personal failings or give too broad a warrant to royalty based on divine right; his contribution, which should perhaps add and modify rather than supplant, displays the complex interchange of views in the early scenes of the drama.

Another issue which requires close testing against theatrical events is the status of the king vis-à-vis the law. Holderness shows Gaunt to be torn by a dilemma: He is committed to a belief that subjects may not judge a king, but that "God's is the quarrel" against royal misdeeds. Yet he feels impelled to lecture Richard about them. Likewise, York recognizes that Richard's overriding of the principle of inheritance in depriving Bolingbroke of Gaunt's land and title strikes at the principle by which Richard holds his own title. Still he would resist, if he could, Bolingbroke's making the claim at the head of an army. What actually counts in the play is that Bolingbroke in fact does justify his claim by the analogy with Richard's position—"If that my cousin king be King in England,/It must be granted I am Duke of Lancaster" (2.3.123–24)—and musters supporters who in effect underwrite not only that assertion but eventually a much greater and more dubious extension of power. Questions of right, whether or not they imply opposing concepts of royal authority, are made moot by the actualities of power, and dramatically this is the process that Shakespeare shows us.

Thus the historically specific legal contests that Holderness emphasizes turn out to matter less than more enduring relationships of power. Moreover, an important component of power in those days was indeed the argument of divine sanction, made on both sides of the struggles. Though Holderness is probably right in not giving absolute authority to Gaunt's version of the claim, not only the prophecies later in the play but developments in sequel plays suggest the role that fear or hope of divine intervention could actually have in the political contests themselves. And the prophecies about the ill effects of deposing Richard do certainly come true politically, regardless of whether one accepts the divine agency that the prophecies sometimes invoke, and regardless whether there are arguments on the other side against not deposing him. Whatever the temptation to dismiss rhetoric as ideological mystification, its actual effects within a power struggle must be fully reckoned with.

Holderness wants to insist on historical specificity in Shakespeare's portrayal of fourteenth- and fifteenth-century events partly in order to soften the implications for Tudor politics, which would in turn arouse the familiar debates (decried in some other of these essays) whether the plays attempted to subvert the dominant ideology or ended up neutralizing such subversion and reinforcing orthodoxy. Thus he argues:

> As long as the plays are conceived as expositions or articulations of an ideology they remain *instruments* of that ideology: power-struggles are seen either as the operations of divine providence [as in traditionalist readings] or as internally dissonant elements in a strategy of idealization [as in cultural-materialist readings]. But if we locate those power-struggles within a specifically realized vision of a unique historical moment, in which historically constituted social groups and historically determined ideologies are shown contesting the grounds of political power, then they become objectively visible *as* power-struggles, and cease to function merely as strategies of legitimation for the Tudor regime. (*Play*, 57)

This is to give history the role of detachment, in effect to secure Shakespeare the same freedom in treating English material that he later had in dramatizing Roman history. In a slightly different formulation soon afterward, though, Holderness clarifies that to operate outside Tudor ideology is not to ignore it: "We argue that the plays do indeed articulate contemporary Elizabethan-Jacobean ideology; but in such a way as to render the operations of that ideology visible" (*Play*, 58).[10] Given that possibility, which he seconds with a quotation from Macherey, the claim of historic specificity does not seem necessary after all, if dramatic interplay carries out a critique. It should be possible to be critical of ideology while talking about power either in the abstract, or else in an historical example with more or less vague contemporary resonances. It is welcome, though, to be relieved of disputes between containment and subversion (valid though the concepts themselves may be when left suspended in dialectic), or of the gloomy vision of a Shakespeare whose every effort at subversion is doomed to be thwarted. And it is salutary to consider that other motives enter into claims by the contestants of divine warrant for their positions, if one does not ignore that such claims could themselves be strategically powerful.

Holderness's notion of the heterogeneity of history plays as a genre, which would be an aesthetic counterpart to the political/historical exchanges considered so far, can have implications for politically-aware interpretive practices. One feature of the genre is its capacity to incorporate elements of the pastoral. Holderness does not define pastoral, but he cites the Arden editor's designation of it in the garden scene (3.4) of *Richard II*, where gardeners propound the art of good government in horticultural terms, and he observes that pastoral is always really urban and courtly, a vehicle of a nostalgia for simplicity and of a political commentary that focuses on justice and injustice (*Play*, 20–23). His actual examples of pastoral from other parts of *Richard II* (*Play*, 33f.) describe Richard's professions of concern for the physical condition of England's earth and Bolingbroke's allusion to sun and earth in consoling himself for his banishment, as well as Bolingbroke's anger about the damaged parks and forests of his seized estates. If these examples really do count as pastoral, they show how thoroughly aristocratic it is.

Perhaps more revealing of the emotive and social orientation of this play is the oddity that aristocratic nostalgia and escapism do not actually seek pastoral innocence as an outlet in crisis. Even Richard's longings are religious, for beads and an almsman's gown, and ultimately "an obscure grave" (3.3.147–54); confronted more immediately with misfortune in prison, he muses about being a beggar, but again knows that his honest goal is nothingness (5.5.32–41). Somehow he walks an edge between self-indulgent pathos and realistic self-assessment, personal qualities that express well some political potentials of monarchy. Though Holderness does well in shifting assessment of Richard from the *purely* personal, here is an instance where the personal has wider implications. What is dramatized (whether or not one calls it pastoral, and whether or not it seems escapist) concerns politics, and it also evokes a range of widely-felt and, to some degree at least, honest emotions.

Another generic property of the history play that has varied overtones which bear in practice on the issue of escapism, and that again can relate to politics, reading, and performance, may be defined through Bakhtin's concept of carnival. Holderness describes carnival as a popular expression of opposition to authority (a subversion that coexists with, but importantly is not canceled by, its containment); he thinks of it as a good context for understanding Falstaff, though in turn he finds in the character a moralistic counter-element along with carnival itself (*History*, 83–96). He sees the same contradictions coexistent in Prince Hal, for instance in his crucial first soliloquy, for when the Prince contemplates his present and his future, he resolves,

> If all the year were playing holidays,
> To sport would be as tedious as to work;
> But when they seldom come, they wished-for come,
> And nothing pleaseth but rare accidents.
> So when this loose behavior I throw off
> And pay the debt I never promisèd, ...
> My reformation, glittering o'er my fault,
> Shall show more goodly and attract more eyes
> Than that which hath no foil to set it off.
> (*1 Henry IV*, 1.2.198–203, 207–9)

Holderness says of this,

> The relation between 'work' and 'holiday' articulated here is very much a dominant/subordinate antithesis: 'holiday' is a temporary release from the permanent responsibilities of 'work', a transient suspension of quotidien duties and obliga-

tions. The Prince expresses the 'official' attitude towards saturnalian licence: its strictly limited function is that of confirming ... statutory authority and constituted order.... what Falstaff has inverted, the Prince sets upright again; light and the sun are re-established in their dominant relation to darkness and clouds. (*History*, 100–101)

This is subtle, and it catches well the social implications of witty verbal inversions in the dialogue between the two. It misses, however, the final inversion of values in "holiday" and "work" that the Prince attempts: he wants to convince the world that his *reform* is what is the true holiday. Operating as it does against the comedy of the carnivalesque grotesque body and much else (including the popular legend of the wild young prince) that gives this play its life, this inversion is audacious of the Prince, and of Shakespeare too. Its audacity is yet another carnivalistic move, an attempted inversion of an inversion, representative both of contending characters in the play and warring impulses within the Prince. In any case, the only future for escapism for a prince is indeed to incorporate it into his work.

Political attitudes toward escapism are implicated in reader or audience reaction to a sequel dramatic situation that does try to encompass play in the grimmest work, the motif of the disguised king that figures on the eve of battle in *Henry V*. Building on an essay by Anne Barton,[11] Holderness associates that detail of plot with folk legend and a popular egalitarian spirit; unlike her, he considers that these latter features continue to live in Shakespeare's history plays (*History*, 34–37). In his reading, the egalitarianism that the disguised king professes to the soldiers in 4.1 is an ideology whose unreality is displayed in the soliloquy that follows the episode (*Play*, 77–79). Again, Holderness makes useful commentary on social implications of a dramatic device. One might consider further, though, that once again the impossibility of royal escape is at issue—not in order to indulge in pathos over the burdens of kingship, but rather to recognize its political constraints as limits on the institution.[12] One must give the king some credit (however grudgingly Henry V is given credit for anything now) for raising the issue of equality, even if deviously, in both this quiet conversation and his battle rhetoric. Perhaps his egalitarian professions, like the disguise through which he partly tries to enact them, are a fantasy whose full consequences he finally cannot, and would not want to, acknowledge.

But with a no-nonsense realism that puts hard challenges to the king's egalitarian and patriotic language, the soldiers speak then, both to him and to the audience, for the marginalized, often unnamed, figures of history. Among other functions, their suspicions about the morality of the war, a matter which is beyond their own knowing, invite the audience to fill in the motives of the churchmen who helped to instigate it. This is probably the closest we get in Shakespeare's history plays to the Brechtian dramaturgy that Holderness likes to invoke. Themselves not tied to specific historical roles and deeds, the soldiers give the king the occasion (in an escape that is no escape) to think more broadly about events, his role, and the general conditions of life. And the audience can contemplate these matters at a distance from (though partially with the aid of) the royal consciousness that often dominates thinking about history.

Thus the broader sense of life in the plays, beyond what is given by official historiography, owes great vividness to characters who are flatly unhistorical or not themselves in the line of power. As they may be living examples to the monarch of what is forever beyond his reach (though actually important for him to understand), they serve the audience as a corrective filling-in of values, a poetic supplement to history. Such are Falstaff and the other tavern characters, the women who are victims or at most contenders for power through men, and the Bastard in *King John* (whose sudden patriotic fervor follows hard after his perception of popular unrest in England).[13] Even marginalization or virtual absence can be an effective force, as Holderness shows in reading the minimal place of women in *Richard II* (*Shakespeare Recycled*, 73–88).

Through his reading strategies that emphasize the political implications of generic variety, Holderness displays the richness of representation in Shakespeare's history plays. Perhaps, in assessing the result, one should make a reversal of figure and ground: The plays are a context for history (or at least for the doings of the powerful). In this transaction between history in a narrow sense and the play that tries to express it better by embroidering and falsifying, Shakespeare's own position may be ambiguous or duplicitous, as expressed by Phyllis Rackin (making use of words of Sir Philip Sidney): "As a poet, the dramatist works in imitation of divine providence to teach the ways of righteousness and draw his audience 'to as high a perfection as our degenerate souls, made worse by their clay lodgings, can be capable of.' As a commercial playwright, he deceives and manipulates for his own profit like a Machiavel."[14] Although Holderness might well refuse these last turnings, he is a proper model for a reading practice that engages both politics and the specifics of the dramatic text. As he asks what history represents for Shakespeare and how it is variously embodied in the plays, he enables questions about political forces and about the dramatic, and therefore social, context of history.

University of Kansas

Notes

[1] An influential example is Louis Montrose, "Renaissance Literary Studies and the Subject of History," *English Literary Renaissance*, 16:1 (Winter 1986), 6–7. Suitably, he qualifies the distinction carefully.

[2] *Shakespeare's History* (Dublin: Gill and Macmillan, 1985).

[3] The connections between the two topics, and the possibilities of variation within each, are described in the concluding "Politics of Culture" in *Shakespeare Recycled* (Hemel Hempstead: Harvester Wheatsheaf, 1992), 228–32. Much of this book is a reworking of *Shakespeare's History*, with added theorizing and other material. The plays "enact a radical shift from the monarchist framework of the Tudor myth to a problematic of secular and positivist historiography [i.e., a concept of history that was yet to develop]" (229), and they can be read or performed now either conservatively or radically.

[4] Graham Holderness, Nick Potter, and John Turner, *Shakespeare: The Play of History* (Iowa City: Univ. of Iowa Press, 1987), 4. He uses this phrase in the process of saying that the authors want to distance themselves "to some degree" from that school and to hold out for the partial autonomy of cultural artifacts. That the distinction is, as claimed, one of degree only will appear from the results.

[5] *Learning to Curse* (New York: Routledge, 1990), 3.

[6] General issues of subversion and containment in the Renaissance are described acutely, with reference mainly to Louis Montrose and Stephen Greenblatt, by Jean E. Howard, "The New Historicism in Renaissance Studies," *English Literary Renaissance*, 16:1 (Winter 1986), 30–41. Insofar as such matters

can be anchored in a textual dialectic, I think it would be a great advantage, though it is true that institutions within which the text functions might have the last word on its use.

[7] *Shakespeare's History*, 27-39; *Shakespeare: The Play of History*, 17-19. Henceforth these are referred to as *History* and *Play*, respectively. These books cite J. G. A. Pocock, *The Ancient Constitution and the Feudal Law* (Cambridge: Cambridge Univ. Press, 1957).

[8] Quotations are from *Complete Works*, ed. David Bevington, 4th ed. (New York: Harper Collins, 1992).

[9] However, since baronial limitations on royal power depended greatly on Magna Carta, one would have thought that—if that was Shakespeare's point— he would have made something of Magna Carta in *King John*. In a review article (*Studies in English Literature*, 29 [1989], 364), J. L. Simmons argues that Holderness's description of strife between king and barons really applies better to Marlowe's *Edward II* than Shakespeare's *Richard II*.

[10] A more recent formulation is this from *Shakespeare Recycled*: "It is via the strategic interrelating of different discourses that the plays speak of their own time, the later sixteenth century. They do not address the present directly, by universalist historical generalization or contemporary political allegory: but implicitly, by their structural organization of ideologies and by the peculiar character of a historiography embodied in dramatic form" (230).

[11] "The King Disguised: Shakespeare's *Henry V* and the Comical History," in *The Triple Bond*, ed. Joseph G. Price (University Park: The Pennsylvania State Univ. Press, 1975), 92-117.

[12] If there is a place (perhaps unspoken) for such considerations within sixteenth-century thought, it might take the form of the descriptions of various forms of government and their perversions in Book III, Chapter 7 of Aristotle's *Politics*—even though Renaissance writers living in monarchies generally concluded by settling on the superiority of that form. An example would be the first few chapters of Sir Thomas Smith's *De Republica Anglorum* (1583), ed. Mary Dewar (Cambridge: Cambridge Univ. Press, 1982).

[13] I emphasized this development in my paper "The Genesis of Agency: the Bastard in *King John*" for the Shakespeare Association of America conference in April 1994.

[14] Phyllis Rackin, *Stages of History* (Ithaca: Cornell Univ. Press, 1990), 80-81. Other parts of the book relate to the roles of women and other marginal figures, and to the processes of history and fiction.